B

BURYING MUSSOLINI

ORDINARY LIFE IN THE
SHADOWS OF FASCISM

PAOLO HEYWOOD

CORNELL UNIVERSITY PRESS
Ithaca and London

First published 2024 by Cornell University Press

Library of Congress Cataloging-in-Publication Data
Names: Heywood, Paolo, author.
Title: Burying Mussolini : ordinary life in the shadows of
    fascism / Paolo Heywood.
Description: Ithaca [New York] : Cornell University Press,
    2024. | Includes bibliographical references and index.
Identifiers: LCCN 2024004818 (print) | LCCN 2024004819
    (ebook) | ISBN 9781501778278 (hardcover) |
    ISBN 9781501778285 (paperback) |
    ISBN 9781501778292 (epub) | ISBN 9781501778308 (pdf)
Subjects: LCSH: Mussolini, Benito, 1883–1945—Influence. |
    Fascism—Social aspects—Italy—Predappio. |
    Ethics—Anthropological aspects—Italy—Predappio. |
    Fascism and culture—Italy—Predappio—History—
    20th century. | Fascism and culture—Italy—
    Predappio—History—21st century. | Fascism—Italy—
    Predappio—Historiography.
Classification: LCC DG571 .H49 2024 (print) | LCC
    DG571 (ebook) | DDC 945.091—dc23/eng/20240220
LC record available at https://lccn.loc.gov/2024004818
LC ebook record available at https://lccn.loc.gov/
2024004819

I reflected, not for the first time, how mistaken it is to suppose there exists some "ordinary" world into which it is possible at will to wander. All human beings, driven as they are at different speeds by the same Furies, are at close range equally extraordinary.

—Anthony Powell, *A Dance to the Music of Time*

CONTENTS

Illustrations

Acknowledgments

This book is the product of my good fortune in friends, colleagues, teachers, students, and family, in Italy and abroad.

In Predappio and its environs, a great many people made me feel welcome, put up patiently with my endless questions, and in some cases took me into their families. I owe my own family a debt of gratitude for introducing me to Predappio and its history when I was a child, in particular my Predappiesi aunt, Marisa Valbonetti, her sister Marina and family, and my cousin Massimo Gardini. My mother, Paola; my uncle Giorgio Gardini; and Federica, Gianni, Francesca, Gabriele, Marianna, and Anita have all been there from the beginning, too. In Predappio itself I found further family: Carlo Giunchi, Liliana Villatora, and their children, Eleanora and Emanuele. To Carlo, especially, this book owes an incalculable amount, as do I for his friendship. I am extremely grateful to all the many others in Predappio who gave me their time and let me into their lives, not least to Virna Giunchi for her help in securing artwork permission, and to former mayor Giorgio Frassineti.

Outside Predappio itself but deeply involved in and knowledgeable of its history, several people helped shape my thinking in this book, including Roberto Balzani, Roberto Bui, Claudia Castellucci, Miro Gori, Mario Proli, and Gianni Saporetti. I am especially grateful to Patrick Leech and his family; Patrick has not only been an invaluable intellectual interlocutor but also a patient reader and a kind and generous friend.

I am very lucky to have conducted most of the research for this book as a junior research fellow at Homerton College and in the Department of Social Anthropology at Cambridge University and to have had the additional backing of a European Research Council grant on "European Parrhesias in Comparative Perspective" while doing so. My fellow researchers on that grant, Fiona Wright and Taras Fedirko, are friends and colleagues whom I am grateful to have had with me in this endeavor.

In Cambridge, Durham, and beyond, I am fortunate to have had other wonderful friends and colleagues with whom to exchange thoughts and ideas, especially Catherine Alexander, Barbara Bodenhorn, Yulia Egorova, Joe Ellis,

Nicholas Evans, David Ginsborg, Robert Gordon, Sarah Green, Stephen Gundle, Leo Hopkinson, Sophia Hornbacher-Schönleber, Carrie Humphrey, Tim Jenkins, Annastiina Kallius, Webb Keane, Elisabeth Kirtsoglou, Michael Lambek, Michael Lempert, Tommaso Leonardi, Hallvard Lillehammer, Nick Long, Marta de Maghalães, Jonathan Mair, Elena Miltiadis, Natalie Morningstar, Irene Peano, Anthony Pickles, Felix Ringel, Andrew Sanchez, Bob Simpson, Rupert Stasch, Alice Stefanelli, Felix Stein, Simona Storchi, Soumyha Venkatesan, and Tom Widger. I am also very grateful to Jim Lance and the staff at Cornell University Press for shepherding this manuscript though to publication.

Some portions of this book have been published in articles in *American Anthropologist and Comparative Studies in Society and History*, and in chapters in the following volumes I have edited or coedited: *Beyond Description: Anthropologies of Explanation* (2023); *New Anthropologies of Italy: Politics, History, and Culture* (2024); and *Freedoms of Speech: Anthropological Perspectives on Language, Ethics, and Power* (2024). I am grateful for permission to reuse this material.

I owe a very particular debt of gratitude to those who have read parts or all of the manuscript and given their feedback: Hannah Brown, Matei Candea, Joanna Cook, Harri Englund, Michael Herzfeld, James Laidlaw, Patrick Leech, Hannah Malone, Adam Reed, Joel Robbins, Charles Stewart, and Tom Yarrow. To all of these I feel a very deep sense of gratitude for their ongoing friendship and intellectual companionship, and I cannot thank them enough for all they have done in making this book better than it would have been otherwise.

My parents, Peter and Jennifer Heywood; my daughter, Beatrice, who arrived in the world at the same time as this book; and Bertie the dog have all been great sources of support, and the person I owe not just this book but also everything else to is my wife, Joanna Cook. If there is merit in this book and in me, I know that it is thanks to her brilliance and devoted care and attention; and every day, in my own very ordinary life, I count myself the luckiest man in the world to share my ideas and that life with her.

BURYING MUSSOLINI

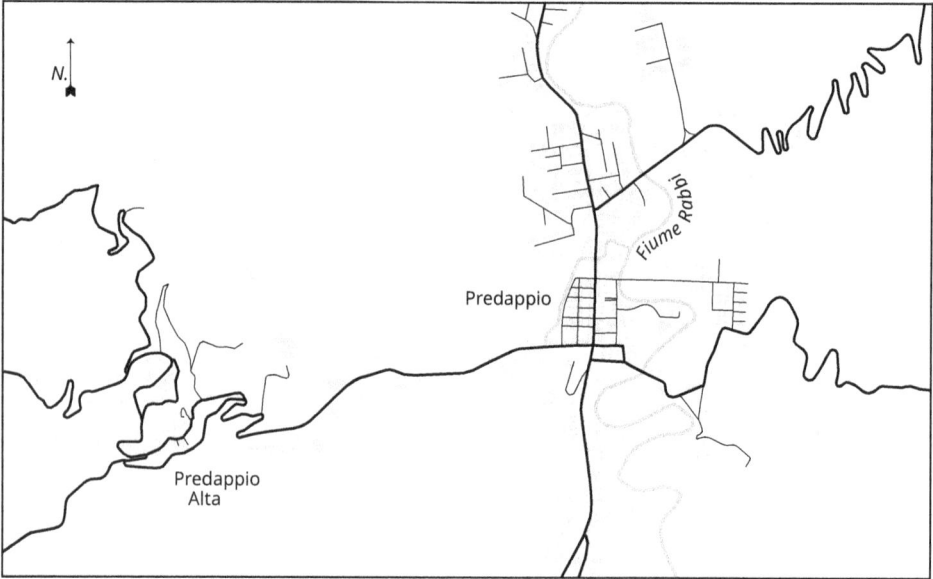

MAP 1. A regional map of the town of Predappio and Predappio Alta.

Introduction
The Fascist Parenthesis

At around 2 p.m. on the afternoon of July 29, 1883, Benito Mussolini was born in the small Italian *comune* of Predappio. On August 31, 1957, almost exactly seventy-four years after his birth, and twelve years after his death at the hands of a firing squad, Mussolini returned home to his final resting place in Predappio, much to the discomfort of many of its inhabitants. Since then, his body—or what was left of it after a series of post-mortem misadventures—has lain in the family crypt, surrounded by those of his wife, children, parents, and other immediate relatives. Over the next six decades, through cultural and political revolutions in his home country and beyond, and despite changes in demographics, mores, language, and fashion that he himself could not have imagined, he has not wanted for visitors, and for them one particular color has remained in style: black.

Mussolini's actions and ideas changed the course of history and the world. This book is about those ideas and partly about how they changed history, but as an ethnography it is also about how they continue to change the small Italian *comune* of Predappio itself. It is about the town that—willingly or otherwise—plays host to those who come from Italy and abroad to visit Mussolini's grave. This is not primarily a history book, because Fascism has emphatically never simply been "history" in Predappio. This book is about the afterlife of an ideology whose adherents believed it to be eternal precisely because they often saw it not as ideology or political theory but as an expression of ordinary, everyday life; because its truth was action and deeds, not words and theories. This book is about the connection of such beliefs to contemporary political life and about the nature of their existence, in Predappio and beyond, over the intervening years: about whether or not such beliefs have lain, dank and moldering, in Mussolini's grave, or whether they have escaped his fate.

Imagine yourself set down on an island. The borders of this island are not seas but time (Sahlins 1976), and this island is a living museum to one of the darkest periods in recent human history. It is an island because, although it is surrounded by other towns and villages of a similar size, it is unlike them in certain notable respects, and it exists, like any island, in stark contrast to its surroundings.

Some of these contrasts are strikingly obvious, even to a casual observer. For instance, many of its neighboring villages are divided up by windy, cobbled lanes, which can make them hard to navigate for an outsider and means that driving around on them is often a rather bumpy experience. This town, instead, has a paved main street that runs straight, wide, and true through its center, with other, equally driver-friendly side streets leading off the main street at perpendicular angles.

The buildings of other nearby villages, particularly older buildings such as churches or small hilltop forts and castles, are often constructed of stone (sandstone or limestone), while many of the principal buildings of this town are made of marble or concrete blocks. Residential buildings of other villages are usually houses or apartments formed by subdividing older, large hive-like structures, whereas this town is populated by multilevel residential complexes with space for large numbers of families.

Like its neighbors, this town has a history. Unlike its neighbors, that history does not stretch back to the Roman or medieval eras, but less than one hundred years. In one of the town's bars, you can see sepia photographs on the wall that chart some of the early construction work. This town is a monumentalist's dream, a modernist cathedral in a desert of medieval castles and stone walls.

If you were to stand in the main square of this town on any given morning, you might well notice an elderly woman step gingerly from a doorway. This is Valentina, and her town is Predappio, the center of a *comune* of around six thousand people in the inland southwestern area of the Italian region of Emilia-Romagna.

Valentina does her shopping twice a week.[1] To get to the Conad supermarket on Via Matteotti, she must take the stairs down to the ground floor of her apartment block, a descent that can take some time as she is nearly ninety years old. She has lived in Predappio since she was born in the old medieval village

FIGURE I.1. Facade of the Church of Saint Anthony. Photo courtesy of Hannah Malone.

of Predappio Alta, and so she takes pleasure in referring to herself as "DOC" (*Denominazione di Origine Controllata*—used to signify the authenticity of regional wine in Italy). At home she keeps a photocopy of a parchment with civil statutes of Predappio dating back to 1383. She can remember the construction of New Predappio in the 1930s, a visit by the king of Italy, the large public funeral of Mussolini's son Bruno, and the hunger and pain of the Second World War, which left her with lasting injuries that make it even more difficult to climb down her staircase.

As she leaves her apartment block, Valentina will pass the grandiose church of Saint Anthony in the eponymous piazza, whose foundation ceremony she watched as a child. Its date of completion in the Christian calendar is marked in large letters on its facade. Next to this, however, the year is also given in the "E.F.," or *era Fascista*, as Year 13 (figure I.1). Valentina will pay no attention to this, having seen the same inscription every day of her life since 1934.

FIGURE I.2.   The former Casa del Fascio, Predappio. Photo courtesy of Hannah Malone.

She will cross the square to the opposite side of the church, where she will step onto the pavement in front of the largest building in Predappio. It is shaped like a huge arrow pointing into the square and topped with a bell tower that rises higher than the spire of the church. It is the former headquarters building of the Italian Fascist Party (PNF), the Casa del Fascio, or "House of the Fasces" (figure I.2). Now the panes of glass in its large doors are broken, and pigeons roost in the bell tower. The building has been largely empty since the war ended, and Valentina will pay it as little attention as she paid the inscription on the church.

She will walk past the post office and the carabinieri barracks, whose construction in the 1930s she can remember, too, along with that of the large apartment blocks next to them.[2] On her way down Via Matteotti—she can remember when this street was named after Mussolini, instead of his regime's most famous victim—she may well be stopped by a lone tourist or a family of visitors. They will ask (usually politely) for directions to the cemetery, which she will be able to provide, as she goes there to tend the graves of her own relatives as often as she can. She will not ask why they want to go to the cemetery, nor make any further comment. Neither will she have any particular reaction if they are wearing black, as such visitors often do, though if they are dressed in some sort of uniform, she confesses she may feel "annoyed" at the obligation to remember a war that left her with lasting scars. Otherwise, she thinks, they can come and be gone in an hour or so without bothering people. "They're only coming to visit a dead person, just as I do when I go to the cemetery," she says.

Further down the street, she will pass a shop; there will likely be a few more tourists outside looking in the window and more still inside talking to the proprietor. Italian flags fly outside the shop, and a large stone eagle sits on the pavement by the door (figure I.3). In the window are more eagles, more flags, busts of Mussolini in various sizes, wartime medals, and key rings with Fascist or Nazi symbols attached to them. Sometimes there are stickers with antisemitic slogans attached to the glass pane of the door. Unless the owner is outside tending to his displays and the two of them exchange a hello, she will walk on past the shop with no further thought. "The shops annoy me a little because they have those eagles, the statues. . . . I don't really pay any attention to them though, even it would be better if they weren't there. It's all rubbish anyway, nothing special, just something they do to make money."

After this shop she will pass another public square, though this one is shaped as a semicircle. If she looks to her left at this point—which she will not do

FIGURE I.3.   A "souvenir" shop in Predappio. Photo courtesy of Hannah Malone.

FIGURE I.4.   The *casa natale* (birth house) of Mussolini. Photo courtesy of Hannah Malone.

unless she has a particular reason—she will see, at the precise midpoint of the semicircle, the nondescript, ordinary-looking, nineteenth-century house in which Mussolini was born (figure I.4).

A few more tourists might be climbing the small hill toward it, but it is off her route, and she will carry on toward the supermarket. She will do her shopping at the Conad, a hundred yards or so further on, chatting to the cashier as she pays, and return home via the same route. She will do the same thing a few days later, just as she always has, every few days, throughout her life.

To spend time with Valentina, and to hear her and her sister talk of their daily routines, is to get a glimpse into what anthropologists and other social scientists often call "ordinary" or "everyday life," at least as it is lived in Predappio. Valentina is an elderly Italian lady who has lived in the same place for her entire existence. She does the shopping, cleans her apartment, cooks food for herself and her sister, and delights in visits from her extended family. People in the town speak of her with respect, because of her age and because she and her sister are kind and pleasant people with whom to interact.

So far, so ordinary. Yet there is something surreal about this particular vision of ordinary life, lived as it is in a context many would see as (and Valentina would admit to being) quite extraordinary, suffused as it is by the history and symbolism of one of the most odious political movements to have emerged from western Europe.

Until the early 1920s, there was nothing particularly notable about Predappio. It consisted of an old medieval village centered on a hill fort, with little or nothing to distinguish it from its neighbors. A little way down the hill from this medieval village was the *frazione*—an administrative designation even smaller than a village—of Dovia, a tiny hamlet of a few houses and an osteria for travelers on the road to and from neighboring Tuscany.

All of this changed dramatically with the ascent of Predappio's most famous native son to the premiership of Italy. As I describe later, Dovia was rebuilt from the ground up as "New Predappio," a model Fascist town and an open-air exhibition of the early life of Italy's Duce. An airplane factory was built into the hills around the town, thousands of migrant workers moved into newly built apartments, and tourists arrived in throngs to ogle at the straw bed on which the young Mussolini was supposed to have slept.

The fall of the Fascist regime in 1945 brought a concurrent fall in the fortunes of its leader's hometown. Unemployment rose, the population fell, and the town was described by one Fascist sympathizer in 1953 as "the poorest and most abandoned, the saddest and most wretched town in all Italy" (Bosworth 2002, 338; Luzzatto 2014, 174). The return of Mussolini's remains to the family tomb in 1957, however, brought the return of something else to Predappio: Fascist tourism. Since then, the town has played host to around a hundred thousand such visitors a year. They come to genuflect at Mussolini's tomb or to participate in one of three annual ritual marches honoring special dates in the Fascist calendar.[3] Now, for most Italians who have heard of Predappio, the town is synonymous with the man it gave birth to back in 1883 and the movement he led. The town is, in a way, the geographical embodiment of the famous historical judgment Italian philosopher Benedetto Croce passed on the period of Mussolini's rule: a Fascist parenthesis.

In these and other respects, all well known to its inhabitants, Predappio is a rather extraordinary place, an island of a very particular sort. What effect, then, does this have on how ordinary life is lived there? In an aside in a lecture titled "On Doing Being Ordinary," American sociologist Harvey Sacks pointed out the work often involved in making things appear "ordinary": "Whatever you may think about what it is to be an ordinary person in the world, an initial shift is not [to] think of 'an ordinary person' as some person, but as somebody having as one's job, one's constant preoccupation, doing 'being ordinary.' It is not that somebody *is* ordinary; it is perhaps that that is what one's business is, and it takes work, as any other business does" (1985, 414). Sacks's point is the communicative labor we engage in to render things "normal," "usual," and "ordinary," and ourselves as "ordinary people" (see Herzfeld 1988 for a similar point).

For some people, though, Sacks adds, that task is complicated: "If, for example, you are in prison, in a room with no facilities at all; say, it has a bench and a hole in the floor and a spigot; then you find yourself doing things like systematically exploring the cracks in the wall from floor to ceiling, over the years, and you come to have information about the wall in that room which ordinary people do not have about their bedroom wall. . . . But it is not a usual thing to say, well, this evening I am going to examine that corner of the ceiling" (1985, 415).

The sense in which I want to suggest Valentina and other Predappiesi are similarly restricted in their capacity to "do being ordinary" is not quite analogous to Sacks's prisoner. The townspeople have things to do that are ordinary that other people in other places do, too. Predappiesi go shopping, cook, clean, go to work, have an ice cream or a coffee at the local bar—and in these respects, they are just like Italians all over the country and people all over the world.

But they do these things in a context that seems rather extraordinary to most people who have heard of it or visited. Valentina lives in an apartment building that was built by the Fascist regime to be the local hospital. Signs of these origins are all over it, and she knows them well. To do her shopping, she walks through her small town, a town she watched being built from the ground up from nothing, in celebration of its most famous son. She interacts with tourists whose purpose she knows is to visit his grave, in the same cemetery in which her parents and brothers lie. She passes a shop that sells busts of him, as well as the same uniforms that make her marginally annoyed when tourists wear them in the streets. Her local supermarket is about one hundred yards from the house in which Mussolini was born.

Valentina knows all these things. She knows that cooking is ordinary, but that the apartment in which she does so is not, as far as others are concerned. She knows that going shopping is ordinary, but she knows that most people do not shop in a supermarket next door to Mussolini's house. She knows that giving directions is an everyday activity—indeed, she has to do so almost every day—but that most people are not giving directions to the tomb of a Fascist dictator. She knows that tending to the graves of her relatives is an ordinary thing to do but that it is unusual to do so surrounded by men in black, marching around with their arms raised in the Roman salute.

Perhaps if she were talking on the telephone about her daily life to an alien or to a foreigner who knew absolutely nothing about Predappio, she could successfully "do being ordinary" in Sacks's sense, by cutting away all this context. In a way, that is what she and other Predappiesi have often done, by lying to outsiders about where they come from, deflecting questions about their origins or hometown whenever they are able. This is also, in a sense, what Valentina does when she simply ignores contextual cues that would leave many outsiders open-mouthed, like the fasces outside her building, the *E.F.* on the church facade, or the monumental ruins of the Casa del Fascio. But as soon as this context encroaches (and, as we will see, all kinds of things cause that to happen), then ordinariness becomes a lot more difficult to do, though she attempts it in her descriptions of parts of the context that she knows will surprise others: tourists, black-shirted or not, are "visiting a dead person, just as I do"; she avoids paying attention to what are often euphemistically referred to as Predappio's "souvenir shops" but insists they are "nothing special," just another way in which people try to make money. So, when Valentina climbs down her stairs every week, is she descending into the ordinary (Das 2012), though her shopping trip involves things that even someone from a neighboring village would find strange and unusual? If so, what kind of ordinary life is it? How do we describe the attempts Valentina and other Predappiesi make to perform what Sacks called "doing being ordinary" in the surroundings of their extraordinary home? What does it mean to have to work at producing "the everyday" in a town suffused with the heritage, signs, and symbols of a political ideology that in Italy and abroad is seen as anything but ordinary?

This book is the story of what such work looks like. Like many ethnographies, the book is an account of ordinary life in a particular place. What is distinctive about it is that in this particular place, the notion of "ordinary life" has itself come to take on a marked and salient status. That is in part, as I will describe, because ordinary life took on a marked and salient status for Fascism, and the fates of Predappio and Fascism have always been intertwined. But, paradoxically, it is also because the sustained pursuit of ordinary life has become the primary way in which Predappiesi seek to escape that intertwined fate and the shadow of Mussolini's grave. Examining how that state of affairs has come to be the case and what this pursuit of ordinary life looks like is this book's primary object, and examining it will, I hope, open up new ways of thinking about the meaning of ordinariness and about the specter of Fascism.

Ordinary Life and "Ordinary Life"

Ordinariness is everywhere. Indeed, its ubiquity is part of what makes ordinariness so hard to bring into focus as an analytic term, as noted by a number of those who have tried (e.g., Highmore 2002; Sayeau 2016; Sheringham 2006). Seemingly by definition, it is simply the unremarkable backdrop to our existence, worthy of note only when it is disrupted and we are forced, as many people were by the COVID-19 pandemic, to search for a so-called new normal.

As well as being ubiquitous in, as it were, ordinary language, ordinariness and everydayness are also not hard to find in social scientific scholarship. Sociologists, geographers, historians, and political scientists, among others, have discovered an inordinate number of things that can be said to be ordinary or everyday: Stalinism, resistance, utopias, shame, ethics, politics, religion, and violence, to name but a few examples, have been prefaced with one or other qualifier.

In my own discipline of anthropology, *ordinary* and *everyday* can probably lay claim to being two of our favorite adjectives (perhaps trumped only by *cultural* and *social*, both the subject of recent and extended reflexive critique). *Argonauts of the Western Pacific*, one of our discipline's foundational monographs, famously includes Bronislaw Malinowski's injunction to anthropologists to examine the "imponderabilia of actual life," "the even flow of everyday events, the occasional ripples of excitement over a feast or a ceremony, or some singular occurrence" (1922, 17). Interestingly, and despite the enduring fame of this remark about the "imponderabilia of actual life" (and the fact that it is frequently misquoted to refer to "everyday life"), Malinowski uses the words *everyday* or *ordinary* on only five occasions each throughout the entire six hundred or so pages of *Argonauts*. The majority of these occurrences are fairly straightforwardly adjectival: a certain ornament is everyday, particular occupations are ordinary, as indeed are some forms of sorcery and magic.

Fast-forward half a century, though, to another great canonical anthropological text, Clifford Geertz's *The Interpretation of Cultures*, and things are different. Not only do both words appear with a great deal more frequency (twenty-nine instances of *everyday* and thirty-three of *ordinary*), but the grammar of their usage has also changed. They are no longer exclusively adjectival. In the most famous essay of the book, "Thick Description," Geertz describes the task of anthropology as "looking at the ordinary" (1973, 14). The rest of the book is similarly filled with references to everyday life and ordinary experience not as descriptions of a particular kind of life in a specific place—the wearing of a certain ornament or the preparation of particular foods, say, as in Malinowski—but as abstract nouns. This is despite the fact that they are often invoked to point precisely at the concrete, situated nature of this life, as for instance, here: "The everyday world of common-sense objects and practical acts is, as Schutz says, the paramount reality in human experience—paramount in the sense that it is the world in which we are most solidly rooted, whose inherent actuality we can hardly question (however much we

may question certain portions of it), and from whose pressures and requirements we can least escape" (Geertz 1973, 119).

Something changed, in other words, in the conceptual landscape of
anthropology—and, perhaps, more broadly of the social sciences—in the space
of that half-century between Malinowski and Geertz. In truth, many things
changed, but one important such change was that *ordinary* and *everyday* went
from qualifying certain phenomena to becoming phenomena in their own
right; they earned definite articles ("the ordinary"), becoming, as Geertz puts
it several times, a "world" or a "context," instead of simply marking a specific
activity or object as a matter of routine or normality. "The ordinary" as a cat-
egorical form came alive in our analyses, detaching from the various particular things in the world it was supposed to mark out. "Everyday life" became a
privileged object of social scientific analysis (see Sheringham 2006).

A persuasive case can be made for locating some of the origins of this
change in the thought and influence of Ludwig Wittgenstein. In anthropology, Geertz, for instance, famously drew on Wittgenstein and his disciple, Gilbert Ryle, in making the arguments of "Thick Description," and a number of
Geertz scholars have pointed to the substantial influence Wittgenstein had on
him in this regard, with one suggesting that Geertz's central ambition was to
become the "Wittgenstein of anthropology" (Rosaldo 1997; Springs 2008;
Shweder 2007). Wittgenstein was also influencing scholars across the Atlantic
in the United Kingdom: Rodney Needham drew on Wittgenstein around the
same time as Geertz in his critique of structural-functionalist categories (1975),
and Edmund Leach acknowledged Wittgenstein's influence on a very similar
and equally powerful argument (Leach 1961; 1984). Like Malinowski when he
invoked "the imponderabilia of actual life," these arguments objected to "bare-
bones" or "skeletal" accounts of social life, but unlike Malinowski, they now
had a philosophical idiom in which to articulate an alternative. "The ordinary"
was no longer imponderable.

The central purpose of Wittgenstein's later philosophy—if not also his
earlier work (see, e.g., Crary and Read 2000)—was to take us away from the
search for general laws, abstraction, explanations, and definitions. Instead, he
famously enjoined philosophers to "look and see" at the actual usage of concepts in ordinary life. Traditional epistemologists distorted language when they
tried to make it ask questions such as "Is this my hand?," "Does that tree exist?," and "Do I know this is a bit of wax?," and attention to ordinary language
was the therapy for such distortions. The task of philosophy should not be to
explain concepts by abstracting them from their everyday use—asking how
we can know a thing, for example, by posing skeptical objections to knowledge in general—but to describe that use and thus understand the ways in

which concepts' meanings and place in the world are inextricably interlinked. Wittgenstein himself gives us an anthropological example of this point in action in his *Remarks on Frazer's "Golden Bough"* (2018), in which he criticizes Frazer's evolutionist explanations of religious ritual and argues instead that what is needed to understand a specific ritual as a practice is "grouping the facts alone" that allow us to see "just the connections" among its elements (46).

Take, for another example, a well-known paper, "Other Minds" by J. L. Austin (1946), who was a doyen of what is often called "ordinary language philosophy," a movement that drew extensively on Wittgenstein's ideas. In this paper, Austin points to how silly philosophical skepticism sounds when applied to the sorts of specific knowledge claims we usually make: if I claim to know that a bird in my garden is a goldfinch, my claim stands or falls on criteria related to its identity as a goldfinch (or not)—for example, does it have the correct plumage or eye markings, can I see it properly, do I possess the right information about goldfinches? So, if I am wrong in thinking it a goldfinch, there is no further implication about my capacity to know anything per se—the problem is one of specific identification, not of general existence. The bird not being a goldfinch does not cause me to doubt its reality. Part of the point here is that "ordinarily" we do not pose the sort of general questions traditional epistemology does ("Does the bird exist?") but rather specific and particular questions ("Is the bird a goldfinch or a sparrowhawk?"). Similarly, the claim to knowledge here is a particular claim to knowledge and could be satisfactorily upheld or rejected long before arriving at worries about whether one were in fact dreaming the goldfinch or living in a matrix controlled by computers with a fondness for garden-variety birds.

In anthropology, the influence of Wittgenstein on conceptions of ordinariness and everydayness is today at its clearest in a recent turn to what is called "ordinary ethics" in the discipline, in which Wittgenstein is often explicitly invoked. In his introduction to a groundbreaking volume called *Ordinary Ethics*, Michael Lambek notes that the book's title "echoes arguments of Wittgenstein and Austin with respect to 'ordinary language'" (2010: 2), and he goes on to posit anthropology as a response to Austin's call for "fieldwork in philosophy": "Ethnography supplies case material that speaks to the urgency and immediacy yet ordinariness of the ethical rather than reverting to hypothetical instances and ultimately to reified abstractions. . . . The individual incident is located within a stream of particular lives and the narratives that are constituted from them, changing its valence in relation to the further unfolding of those lives and narratives and never fully determined or predictable" (2010, 4).

Veena Das's work is still more explicit in its acknowledgment of a debt to Wittgenstein and especially to Stanley Cavell's interpretation of him, and her

2020 book, *Textures of the Ordinary*, is subtitled "Doing Anthropology after Wittgenstein." In its introduction, she declares she is interested in

> the everyday . . . as the site on which the life of the other is engaged but this Other is not the radical Other of either philosophy or anthropology. As an anthropologist I am attuned to concrete others, even daring to suggest that it is in following concrete relations, quotidian turns of events, the waxing and waning of intensities, that we learn to be in the world. I have taken inspiration from Wittgenstein's idea that the task is to lead words back from the metaphysical to the ordinary and to make do with what words we have in hand. (2020, 10)

Though use of concepts such as the ordinary and everyday life in the social sciences extends far beyond this specific stream of literature, this quote neatly encapsulates the paradox of ordinariness as we think of it, as well as its affectively seductive qualities. "The ordinary" in this quote refers on the one hand to "concreteness," in the sense that what is ordinary is simply what we find around ourselves (or "in hand"), such as certain ornaments in the Trobriands; on the other hand, while the subjects of such ordinariness are concrete and quotidian, they exist in an ordinary metaphorized as "the site," singular, spatiotemporal, and specific. Ordinariness comes thus to seem both quintessentially particular—it is whatever happens to be at hand—and at the same time abstract: as a scale, prefixed with a definite article ("the ordinary") it encompasses all such particularity (cf. Lempert 2013; Fadil and Fernando 2015); wherever we may find it and whatever concreteness it contains, it will always be "the ordinary," and we should always wish to find ourselves led "back" to it, away from "the metaphysical."

Regardless of exactly how far Wittgenstein was individually responsible for the emergence of the ordinary as a distinct area of concern in the social sciences, my interest here is in a particular set of grammatical consequences (as Wittgenstein might have put it) of this shift from Malinowski's "an everyday ornament" to Das's "*the* ordinary" and "ordinary life" as an abstract noun. The differences between the two forms of use point to two senses in which we—and Predappiesi such as Valentina—might go "in quest of the ordinary," as Cavell puts it (Cavell 1988). Put most simply, the difference I want to point to is that between "the ordinary" conceived as a formal category or domain, on the one hand, and on the other hand the stuff in the world this category is supposed to pick out.

Much usage of *ordinary* and *everyday* in anthropology and the social sciences is intended to point to particularity and specificity, as in the quotes from Lambek and Das above. This is obviously part of what makes these terms so well suited to anthropological use, given our historical preference for the "small-scale" and for description over explanation (see Heywood and Candea 2023). To understand a phenomenon in this sense of ordinariness is to find it emplaced, to grasp its meaning in a given context, to understand its grammar or the criteria for its use. It is, in other words, to understand it in its concreteness—to be able to point to it within a "web of signification" as Geertz would put it, not to isolate it from that web in order to provide it with a bare-bones universal definition. This is what Cavell means when he describes the ordinary as necessarily conventionalized, contingent, and arbitrary; it is precisely this sense of conventionality, of the ordinary's rootedness in the arbitrariness and particularity of grammar and language, that he sees as giving rise to the fears of skepticism. This is what anthropologist Cheryl Mattingly intends when she describes "the doing of ordinary life" as "a messier affair" than simple routine or training (2013, 308). This is what Jack Sidnell, Marie Meudec, and Michael Lambek mean when they argue for locating ethics in the "immanent" or "ordinary" by suggesting that "conduct and judgment emerge in specific situations," or when they say that to speak of immanence "is to acknowledge the temporal and experiential dimensions of the ethical, and the contingent, underdetermined, unfinalized and unpredictable aspects of action and judgment" (2019, 313).

All of the above, with its emphasis on specificity, immediacy, and particularity, is roughly what I meant when I referred earlier to the stuff in the world that we seek to pick out when we call it ordinary or refer to its place in ordinary or everyday life: Malinowski's Trobriand ornament, say, and its place and meaning in context. So that is one side of the distinction I want to draw: what social scientists want to point to when we call something ordinary. In doing so we draw phenomena out of the realm of the general, the abstract, and the formal, and "down" into the world of everyday life, in all its messy, contingent, arbitrary particularity.

Valentina's life is eminently ordinary in this sense. She does all the sorts of things that social scientists often characterize as ordinary or everyday: she goes shopping, cooks, cleans, sees her family and her friends, has arguments with them sometimes, and does them small acts of kindness at others. She does these things in her own particular, specific, and concrete fashion. The context in which she does these things is in many ways remarkable, but in that sense every context is remarkable, insofar as it generates ordinary life in all of its specific particularity.

That is one sense in which we might use the words *ordinary* and *everyday*. The other sense, which emerged, at least in anthropology, at some point in the fifty years between Malinowski and Geertz, is somewhat paradoxically different. In this latter sense, ordinary life has become a formal category—indeed, in some branches of the social sciences *the* category—of analysis. It has grown, in some cases, a definite article, as "the ordinary." In other words, it is itself rather far from being ordinary.

The point of invocations of ordinariness in the social sciences is often to take us "down," as Das and others have it, into the granular specificities of life in all of its particularity. Yet in labeling such specificity as everyday life, ordinary life, or the ordinary, we pull it back "up" again into the realm of formal categories and abstractions. This is why we might be perfectly able to understand what social scientists mean when they tell us that some phenomenon is or is not a part of everyday life in some context, while also remaining unconvinced if these social scientists were to try to tell us that ethics or values inhere in the realm of everyday life or that we should examine everyday life instead of something else, such as social structure or events. In the first case, "everyday life" is being used to qualify another phenomenon, while in the second case, it has become a phenomenon in and of itself. In the first case it is almost synonymous with context, whereas in the second cases it has become a particular *kind* of context.

We could think of the twin meaning of the everyday by returning to our garden goldfinch and thinking in terms of the distinction Cavell draws in his reading of Austin's "Other Minds" paper between "specific" and "generic" objects. Cavell's point is that it is uncharitable for Austin and others to deploy the goldfinch sort of case as an example of the nonsensicality of skeptical questioning, because skeptics themselves do not choose examples in which correct description or identification is at issue. Bits of wax, tables, tomatoes, and so on are chosen instead, because, Cavell argues, the point is that they should be invulnerable to objections of the sort one can make to claims of identification. There should be nothing else to doubt about them but the claim to existence. Cavell calls these "generic objects," as opposed to "specific objects." The distinction is not about the nature of the object, but the kind of knowledge of it we can have (Cavell 1979, 76–77).

My point here is that we have, in general, used the categories of "the ordinary" or ordinary life as if they were what Cavell calls generic objects, even though our point in using them is very often to turn something else—some particular thing or practice—into a specific object. We have become very good at distinguishing the equivalents of goldfinches from sparrowhawks: at showing how context affects how we understand and experience phenomena. But in the process, we have invested one particular kind of context with enormous levels of metaphysical significance. Part of what I want to do in this book is to bring the formal category of "ordinary life" back down to earth: to examine a context in which ordinary life as a form has become an object of interest, work, and desire.

In some ways this doubleness of the ordinary is unsurprising. Geertz himself (1973), alongside Marilyn Strathern (1995, 159) and others, made the same point about culture, and one might wonder whether ordinary life has in some ways come to take over the function of culture in anthropology in the wake of some disillusion with that concept. Yet there is something particular to notions of everyday or ordinary life not quite captured in the notion of culture, though some, such as Raymond Williams, equate the two ([1958] 2001). There is nothing inherently oxymoronic in the idea that culture can be both form and content, specific variation and general category of such variation, whereas there is something more of a performative contradiction in the invocation of "the ordinary" as a general category, for the purpose of insisting that we examine it, instead of general categories. In other words, in this sense we are still like the skeptical philosophers in Wittgenstein's garden, asserting their knowledge of a tree: when we speak of "the ordinary," we often do not sound very ordinary at all.

In this respect, we have something in common with Valentina and other Predappiesi, whose quest for ordinariness is also precarious, if for different reasons. Indeed, I raise this distinction between the form and content of the ordinary not to point out a paradox, but because I argue in this book that the same thing that happened to anthropology (and other social sciences) between Malinowski and Geertz happened to Predappio, too, in a process that began, in fact, in the same year in which *Argonauts of the Western Pacific* was published (see chapter 1). Just as in anthropology the idea or form of "the ordinary" came to take on significance beyond any particular context in which it might be used—came, as it were, to have a life of its own—so, too, in Predappio, over the past century, the form or idea of ordinary life has come to have an existence apart from the actual practice of living.

What I want to suggest is that the *form* of ordinariness or everydayness—the presence of a particular kind of scale of existence (Lempert and Silverstein 2012; Summerson Carr and Lempert 2016) that we can label with those words—can have an ordinary, everyday life of its own. As forms and categories, in other words, "the ordinary" and ordinary life are themselves not context-free: they have their own specificities and particularities depending on how, where, when, and why they appear. As I will describe here and throughout this book, "the ordinary" as a form has a history (or histories); it is, like any other phenomenon, specifically located when it is invoked; and it has its own social life. Indeed, pursued in this way, one might better speak of "ordinaries," rather than "the ordinary," in much the same way as Austin's ordinary ornithologist would speak of varieties of bird, instead of asking whether or not "the" bird exists.

This sense of a specific, plural, contingent, and ethnographic category of ordinary life also chimes with insights from scholarship on the roots and history of interest in "the ordinary," as well as some philosophical inquiries into ordinariness. Charles Taylor, for instance, has famously described the "transvaluation of values" by means of which "the locus of the good life" shifted "from some special range of higher activities" and became placed "within 'life' itself." "Under the impact of the scientific revolution," Taylor tells us, "the ideal of *theōria*, of grasping the order of the cosmos through contemplation, came to be seen as vain and misguided" (1989, 213). Taylor locates the origins of what he calls "the affirmation of ordinary life" in the Reformation and its opposition to any form of mediation between God and worshipper. The monastic life is repudiated, and the personal commitment of the ordinary Christian becomes the yardstick of religious value. We will see in chapter 1 some of the genealogical links between these developments and the thought of early Fascism.

In that first chapter and the next, I will show how the categories of ordinariness or everydayness themselves—not just the things that might fall within them—came to take on a special and particular salience through Predappio's remarkable history and relationship to Fascism, just as they have in the history of anthropology. Predappio, in many ways, owes its existence to the pursuit of a very particularly Fascist vision of what ordinary life should look like. Moreover, in the remainder of this book, I will aim to show that today, Predappiesi work to shape, create, and pursue a different but equally particular vision, or set of visions, of the form of ordinary life.

My claim is not that Predappio is unique in this regard but that it is an especially acute case of the more general fact that the form of ordinary life—like its contents—is not a metaphysical reality deserving of a definite article, a privileged locus of truth and virtue, but an always precarious and contingent effect of work and effort, and an effect that will differ depending on what kind of work goes into it and to what end. Valentina and others like her are not seeking to descend into an ordinary life that is already present at some fundamental level of reality. They are trying to produce a sense of ordinariness with its own specific formal attributes. The threat to that attempt does not come from another general or fundamental phenomenon such as skepticism, or violence, or rupture, as it does in accounts that take the status of ordinariness for granted. It comes, like the townspeople's sense of ordinariness, from the specifics of their history and indeed precisely from their actual ordinary lives insofar as they are suffused with what they seek to escape from (Das 2020, 66).

As I noted earlier, this book, in other words, is partly—like the majority of work in anthropology—an ethnography of everyday life in a particular context, the unmarked, habitual, routine existence of normal people. But it is also an ethnography of "everyday life": the intensely marked efforts in life (and sometimes scholarship) that go into creating a certain scale at which things can be classified as "routine" and "normal."

On Certainty and Damned Fascists

I lived and carried out fieldwork in Predappio intermittently over the course of four years between 2016 and 2020. However, I have also known the town for most of my life. An aunt of mine by marriage was born in Predappio, and my maternal family have a summer house in a village about a twenty-minute drive further into the Apennine mountains toward Tuscany, which I have been visiting most summers since I was born. To get to this village you have to drive through Predappio. I can remember being struck even as a child by how different Predappio was from its neighbors. I can also remember, once I had reached an age of political consciousness, the shock I felt looking out of the car window at the architecture, the tourists in black, and the busts of Mussolini outside the souvenir shops. While such buildings, people, and objects may be found scattered throughout Italy, nowhere are they so thoroughly concentrated in such a small space, and nowhere else are they freighted with the weight of Predappio's particular history as Mussolini's birthplace.

However, after four years of sustained fieldwork there, what most struck me was that life in Predappio passes largely without discussion of Fascism. The features of the town that leave outsiders open-mouthed in horror and others in wonder pass largely without comment from Predappiesi themselves, as we have seen in Valentina's shopping trip. Like the characters in China Miéville's wonderful 2009 novel *The City and The City*, who inhabit one of two warring cities that occupy the same physical space and have to learn to "unsee" what belongs to the enemy, it is as if Predappiesi such as Valentina have developed a blind spot for exactly what appalls (or, in the case of certain sorts of tourists, delights) outsiders about their home. This is the puzzle I want to explore here and to a large extent throughout this book, as it connects to the ways in which ordinariness matters in Predappio.

It would make perfect sense to find strong sentiments and attitudes toward Fascism in Predappio, which is more suffused and saturated with the symbolism, history, and politics of Fascism than possibly any other place in the world, as I will describe. To many other Italians, and to those abroad who have heard of it, it is simply impossible to think of Predappio without thinking of Fascism. Because Mussolini was born there, because he is buried there, because it was built by the regime in its favored architectural style, because it was mythologized by the regime and tourists were brought there to wonder at Il Duce's humble origins, because neo-Fascists have come on pilgrimage to it ever since Mussolini's body was returned, because a Google image search for Predappio returns shop windows with busts of Hitler in them among its first results—for all these reasons and others, many Predappiesi have spent most of their lives lying about their origins to outsiders. As people often told me, as soon as you said you were from Predappio, other people would make assumptions about you: sometimes this would produce a positive reaction, and people would extol the virtues of your erstwhile fellow citizen; more often it would produce a negative reaction, and you might find yourself the object of frowns and whispers (see chapter 5). In either case you could not avoid your conflation with whatever people took Fascism to be. As Roberto Bui, a prominent Italian intellectual and member of the Bolognese Wu Ming collective, put it in a series of blog posts about Predappio (see chapter 6), "it is not just a question of 'one tomb in a cemetery': *the whole town* is a projection of Il Duce's body, and is seen as his extended sepulchre, the place of veneration for his remains. Throughout Italy, that is what 'Predappio' means" (2017; my translation, italics in original). This neatly encapsulates very widely held attitudes to Predappio on the part of outsiders who know of its existence: it is impossible to divorce it from Mussolini and his politics.

So, had I arrived in Predappio to find a town full of more or less convinced partisans of Mussolini and Fascism, I would not have been surprised. Mussolini is Predappio's most famous son, and he built the town itself, together with the economic and tourism infrastructure that brought it wealth and fame throughout the years of his regime. Some elderly people there knew his family well and tell stories of his infancy that they heard from their parents and grandparents. Moreover, although most of its wealth, prestige, and prosperity disappeared after the war, those who kept coming to Predappio, those who continue to bring money and commerce to its businesses, are all of one particular political color. There are plenty of reasons why people in Predappio might be, or call themselves, Fascist.

But neither would I have been terribly surprised to find a town full of convinced anti-Fascists, possessing absolute moral certainty in regard to Fascism. The region in which it is situated, Emilia-Romagna, has one of the most famous and vibrant traditions of republicanism, socialism, and anticlericalism in Italy, and Predappio is no exception: before 2019 it had never elected a mayor from any party but the Italian Communist Party and its descendants. In fact, as

I will describe in the next chapter, Mussolini himself was a fervent and convinced socialist when he lived in Predappio, just as his father, a local councillor, was. Given this heritage, one perfectly plausible reaction to socialist-turned-Fascist Mussolini would be to disown him vociferously. So there are also plenty of reasons why a morally certain anti-Fascism in Predappio would make sense.

Indeed, in a great many places in the world one might reasonably expect to find at least one of these attitudes about Fascism. It is a subject on which people often, certainly in Europe and the United States, tend to feel quite strong moral sentiments, rather than apparent neutrality or ambiguity. As far back as 1940, the US Supreme Court upheld the conviction of a New Hampshire man jailed for calling a local official "a damned Fascist," on the basis that these were not words protected by the First Amendment because they were "fighting words," which "by their very utterance inflict injury or tend to incite an immediate breach of the peace." Even in 1940, the man did not need to specify what in particular about being a Fascist required damnation for the Court to reach such a verdict. Today, knowing all we do about the events of the five years that would follow this case, such specification is, for many people, even more redundant.

Despite the fact that a recent resurgence of interest in Fascism has led people (back) to debates about exactly what it is and how to define it (see chapter 5), rarely if ever have such debates led people to question its moral valence. Many people use the word as the Supreme Court interpreted the man to be doing, as insulting and offensive in itself, akin to accusing someone of a crime (and being a Fascist *is* a crime in several legal jurisdictions). I suspect, in other words, that for many readers of this book, the negative moral judgment implied in describing someone or something as "Fascist" is a form of basic moral certainty (see, e.g., Lichtenberg 1994; Markie 1986; Pleasants 2007, 2009). One need not explain what it is about being a Fascist that produces such negative moral judgment, and indeed if one did, it would sound rather peculiar in many cases. As the man from New Hampshire implied, a Fascist is damned for being a Fascist, and nothing more need be said.

Often much more is said about Fascism, depending on the way that language is being used. Many historians take considerable pains to describe all the reasons that Fascism or, more precisely, Fascist regimes or individuals deserve the negative moral judgment that usually comes with the word. Writing the history of Fascism, though, is a very specific way of using the word, and even in this sort of case most historians do not write as if they understand their duty to be persuading the reader of the evils of Fascism, Indeed, it is hard to imagine a mainstream historian writing as if people *require* persuading of such a claim. Rather, the point is to document in ever more accurate detail why we believe this claim and to remind us why we do so.

Things are more complicated in Italy, despite the existence of laws puta-tively designed to punish the expression of positive sentiments or intentions regarding Fascism (Heywood 2019). As well as morally ambiguous attitudes to Fascism—encapsulated in the stereotypical assertion that, though he made some mistakes, "at least Mussolini made the trains run on time"—there are also many people who believe Fascism to have been a largely or wholly posi-tive force. A great many such people visit Predappio on a regular basis, whether for one of the three annual anniversary marches or as a day's excursion to visit Mussolini's tomb and buy a replica *manganello* (a club that Fascist thugs used to beat their opponents) from one of the souvenir shops that line the main road. These people are often perfectly open about their opinions on the matter, and on the anniversary days many of them appear in black Fascist uniforms or in T-shirts bearing pro-Fascist slogans, and they are not arrested or other-wise sanctioned for it (see also Gretel Cammelli 2015, 2017; LoPerfido 2018).

One might, as I've suggested, imagine that among people who actually live in Predappio, one would find such strongly held convictions, or forms of moral certainty, about Fascism, whether for or against. Predappio is, as the quote above from Roberto Bui suggests and as I will illustrate throughout this book, a metonym for Mussolini as far as most of Italy is concerned, so having an opinion about the one is usually the same as having an opinion about the other. The history of Fascism and the history of Predappio have always been inter-twined, so its inhabitants have had quite some time to make up their minds on the subject in either direction. They have also had one hundred years of practice in answering the questions of outsiders, for whom their home is en-tirely defined by its relation to Fascism. Yet people in Predappio largely do not place themselves in either camp in relation to historical Fascism or their con-temporary visitors in black and indeed, as I will describe, go to some effort to avoid discussion of the subject.

A number of possible and plausible explanations for this lack of open moral certainty regarding Fascism spring to mind. For instance, one might point to more general facets of the broader national and international political climate: the gradual decay of the strong anti-Fascist sentiment that animated the postwar Italian constitution, the collapse of Communism and of the Italian Communist Party (PCI), the failure of the Italian state to enforce anti-Fascist legislation, and the recent rise of nationalism and anti-immigrant feeling in Italy and elsewhere. These factors are all likely to have played a part in shaping Predappiesi's attitudes toward Fascism, especially as those attitudes seem to have varied somewhat alongside such wider geopolitical changes, as I will describe.

In some sense we can see a version of what Michael Herzfeld calls "cultural intimacy" (2016 [1997]) at work in Predappiesi's attitudes to their heritage. As

I describe later, many Predappiesi have stories of personal encounters between Mussolini and their parents or grandparents, and they tell these stories—in private homes or in lowered tones in public among friends—with a degree of pride at their proximity to a man who shaped globally significant events. But there are rarely any nudges or winks here (Herzfeld 2016, 6). Although some few on the extreme right in the town may feel pride in identification with the man himself, any sense most Predappiesi have of being held together by their unique relationship to Mussolini does not usually come with any form of identification with him. For the most part, what is culturally intimate here—that is, what is held back from outsiders—is simply open acknowledgment of their home's history: as I have noted, many Predappiesi have tended simply to lie to outsiders about even the fact of being from Predappio.

The explanation I want to focus on for the way in which Fascism is treated in Predappio today is in some ways as general as those offered above, but it also takes on a specific inflection in Predappio, one that will bring us back to ordinariness. Predappio is a *comune* of approximately six thousand inhabitants, most of whom live dispersed in the countryside surrounding the town itself or in peripheral and even smaller villages such as Predappio Alta, Fiumana, and San Savino. As in small communities everywhere, most people who live in Predappio itself know one another and one another's families very well indeed. They know one another's working and living circumstances, habits and preferences, and histories and frequently the histories of one another's parents and grandparents as well. They interact with one another on a routine basis, at church, in the local bars, at town council meetings, in restaurants, and casually on the street.

They do so regardless of their ideological coloring and what they happen to think about Fascism. Giorgio Frassineti, the mayor of Predappio over the course of much of my fieldwork, was, for instance, from the Democratic Party (PD), the successor to the Italian Communist Party. He is "of the left," as every postwar mayor of Predappio has been before 2019, and he is frequently referred to as such by his constituents, warmly or otherwise. When he passes one of the owners of the shops selling Fascist "souvenirs" in the street—as he does frequently, because it is impossible for him not to do so in a town so small—he might greet them as he would any other constituent and sometimes pass the time of day. Though he told me he avoids entering the souvenir shops if at all possible, this is at least in part because, while mayor, he was afraid of being photographed inside by a passing journalist and getting into even more trouble with the left in the region more broadly than he already is, for reasons I describe in chapter 6. His objection to entering the souvenir shops is largely practical, in other words, rather than principled. I have also known him to make an exception to this rule when prevailed upon to drink a glass of Mussolini-themed wine with one of the proprietors.

The village abounds with examples of this sort of everyday pragmatism. Some people, for example, will explain their lack of objection to the Fascist anniversary marches by pointing to the money they bring to the town in the form of visitors to the souvenir shops and to local restaurants. Those who oppose the marches will often cite the very same thing in support of their own arguments and claim that they bring money only to a small number of families and that to most they bring only inconvenience, closing the roads and swamping the village with rowdy, badly behaved men. Going back further in history, such pragmatism becomes, at least at times, only more pronounced, as I will describe in chapter 2: people's memories are filled with amusing or rancorous descriptions of *voltagabbana,* or turncoats, whose ideological coloring changed depending on what was perceived to be advantageous. The sort of pragmatism involved in these stories is merely an extreme—though prevalent—form of a generalized attitude of pragmatism that many people hold in relation to their home's Fascist heritage (see Herzfeld 2009 for comparable examples of Italian pragmatism).

We have returned, in other words, to the question of the ordinary: of the vagaries of social life, instead of theories and ideologies; of messiness and practicality, instead of coherence; of just "getting by." Predappiesi, like anthropologists, recognize the need to take *la vita quotidiana* and its requirements into account. You cannot live in Predappio without living *with* Fascism. Because this book—like any ethnography—is partly intended to be an account of such quotidian existence, in a small but rather unique context, then it will also be concerned with the practical requirements for this existence. Indeed, it would not be terribly difficult to tell the story of Predappio and its ambiguous moral epistemology of Fascism as one of gradual accommodation to the fact that thousands of neo-Fascists descend on the village every year and that some benefit has been gleaned from this, at least by some; or to the fact that there are few Predappiesi whose parents or grandparents did not wear a Fascist uniform at some point in their lives, as is true in towns and villages across Italy.

This story of pragmatic accommodation to Fascism as both an intrinsic part of Predappio's past and an everyday feature of its present is only half the story, however, just as remarking on the similarity between Predappiesi accommodations to everyday life and ideas about everyday life in anthropology masks some important differences between them. That is because a marked concern for pragmatism, and indeed for the category of ordinariness, was at the heart of the Fascist project and of the creation of Predappio itself, as I show in more detail in chapter 1. In other words, the ordinariness of Fascism in Predappio—its pervasive invasion of so many aspects of existence and the fact that Predappiesi have come to live with that—is not itself ordinary; it is marked and significant and has always been so.

Out of the Ordinary

So, the other half of this story is that the ordinary or everyday accommodations Predappiesi make to their town's extraordinary heritage and politics, their distinct lack of moral certainty in regard to Fascism, is not itself another kind of certainty. It does not "go without saying" that thousands of men in Fascist uniforms marching through your town three times a year deserve no comment. It is not obvious that there being a dictator's tomb next to the graves of your grandparents should pass largely unremarked. You do not naturally take it for granted that your home is famous the world over as a premier site of neo-Fascist pilgrimage.

Predappio is not really an island. Its inhabitants are perfectly well aware of the celebrated or infamous status of their town in Italy and abroad. They know there is nothing ordinary or everyday about that status, even as they often behave as if it were ordinary and everyday. Like social scientists, in some ways (and in a different sense, as I will show in chapter 1, like early Fascists), Predappiesi have come to invest significance not only in everyday or ordinary things but in everydayness and ordinariness itself, as a scale. It has come to matter to act *as if* ordinary life in Predappio really were just plain old ordinary.

My account of this will in some ways resemble other anthropological accounts of ordinary life. In a recent book chapter devoted to "the politics of the ordinary," Veena Das, for example, describes the efforts of a local nongovernmental organization (NGO) worker to bring water and electricity to an "unauthorized colony" in Delhi (2020). "What could ever be of theoretical interest, one might ask, in the trivial details in which the perils of everyday life here are expressed," Das asks rhetorically (59–60), before concluding the chapter with the thought that it is in such attempts to "bring about an everyday that could be better, more attuned to their desires" that the "politics of the ordinary" is expressed (92). Her distinction between the "actual everyday," in which people are entangled and enmeshed in their daily lives, and the "eventual everyday" they wish to create resonates in many ways with my characterization of life in Predappio.

In Das's account, the "eventual everyday" is the object of work and construction, just as I will describe "everyday life" in Predappio. But in Das's account, the "everyday" character of the "eventual everyday" appears given: the politics of the provision of basic infrastructure like water and electricity is taken to be exemplary of "everydayness." The NGO leader she describes strives for something (basic infrastructure) that Das is comfortable describing as everyday, for understandable reasons—whereas throughout this book, I will seek to draw attention to the fact that one of the things Predappiesi strive for is *a sense of "everydayness" itself.* The everyday character of debates over basic infrastructure, as we will see in chapter 6, is precisely a part of the politics of scale at work in these debates, not given in their nature or a result of my classification of them. In other words, it is true that there are certain political questions that we might, with Das, readily scale as "ordinary" or "everyday" and that are important to Predappiesi; but it is also true that those scales themselves are important to Predappiesi, too.

In describing this rather particular "quest for the ordinary," this book combines two key anthropological insights of the past two decades. The first is that a scale—such as "ordinary life"—is, in the words of E. Summerson Carr and Michael Lempert, "a practice and process before it is product" (2016, 8–9). Anthropologists (and other social scientists) have increasingly come to attend to the ways in which certain phenomena are scaled by actors themselves as, say, "local" or "global" (e.g., Latour 2005; Helmreich 2009; Tsing 2000, 2005, 2012; Glück 2013; Lempert 2012); "public" or "private" (e.g., Gal 2002; Benhabib 1998; Özyürek 2006); or "national," "regional," or "civil" (Ben-Yehoyada 2017; Candea 2012; Ferguson 2006; Mitchell 1991). This is true even though, rather than because, anthropological and social scientific analysis is itself replete with its own metaphysics of scale: "we ontologize scalar perspectives, rather than ask how they were forged and focused" (Summerson Carr and Lempert 2016, 8; see also Strathern 2004). That is perhaps especially true, as I have suggested above, of the scale of the ordinary and the everyday: in addition to the standard trope of "everyday life" (e.g., Schielke 2009) and the particular school of "ordinary ethics" we have encountered (e.g., Das 2007; Lambek 2010), we also have "everyday resistance" (e.g., Scott 1985), "everyday utopias" (e.g., Cooper 2014), "everyday religion" (e.g., Ammerman 2007), "everyday politics" (e.g., Boyte 2004), "everyday shame" (e.g., Probyn 2004), and "everyday violence" (e.g., Bourgois 2009), to give just a few examples. This book, in contrast, seeks to put the scale of the everyday in question: to ask what it looks like in a specific context and how it is shaped as such through practice and action.

Because the everyday is shaped, formed, and cultivated in Predappio, the second key set of anthropological insights this book draws on emerges from what is often called the anthropology of ethics (e.g., Laidlaw 2002, 2012; Faubion 2001, 2011; Lambek 2000, 2015a). These insights boil down to the idea that what people do in and with their lives is at least in part shaped by the values and virtues they pursue—that cultivating the virtue of Islamic piety, for example, means engaging in a certain set of practices that are seen to generate and to sustain that virtue (Mahmood 2005; Hirschkind 2006).

Recent literature on ordinary ethics has formed an important set of conversations within the broader anthropology of ethics, and a great deal of recent debate in the discipline has focused on the question of whether ethics resides in the domain of ordinary life, inherent in the everyday interactions we have with others, or whether it is more properly located in reflective projects, focused on the cultivation of ideals and virtues (e.g., Clarke 2014; Heywood 2022, 2023a; Laidlaw and Mair 2019; Lambek 2015b; Lempert 2013; Robbins 2016; Zigon 2014). I will engage with some of these debates throughout the course of this book. What I will seek to show where I do so is that combining the notion of scale as an outcome, not a premise, of human action with an interest in the virtues people strive to cultivate allows us to see ordinary or everyday life as the object, not the site, of ethical work.

Certain scales—both in our own analyses and in the lives of those we study—can come to take on ethical import, can come themselves to seem valuable and worthy of pursuit. This is true, I think, when we instrumentalize notions of "the ordinary" against anthropological arguments in favor of attending to the "transcendent" and vice versa, just as it is when we claim that failure to attend to "neoliberal political economy" ignores "the real, systemic causes of inequality," as Summerson Carr and Lempert note (2016, 8). This ethicizing of scale also takes place, as I will describe, in contemporary Predappio.

As in much of the literature on ordinary ethics, the pursuit of ordinariness in Predappio is not a clearly set out or easily articulable project, as is, say, Saba Mahmood's description of pietist Islam (2005). It is not like a creed or a religion with a list of tenets, and of course not all Predappiesi feel the same way about it or pursue it in the same fashion, though I think my descriptions of generally held attitudes would be easily recognizable to most who know the town.

However, unlike some of the literature on ordinary ethics, I do not think this somewhat nebulous quality of the pursuit of ordinariness as an ethical value comes down to an inherent quality of ethics more generally. Instead, I think it is built in, in some sense, to the nature of the project I describe: as we have seen earlier, once ordinariness is marked out and explicit, once it becomes in and of itself an object of concern, it ceases to be ordinary. So pursuing ordinariness as a value requires one to do so sotto voce, if one is to do it well. Indeed, we will see in chapter 2 the distinction Predappiesi draw between two exemplars of ordinariness precisely in terms of how self-conscious and declamatory their pursuit of ordinariness is. Loudly proclaiming one's ordinariness, as early Fascist propagandists sometimes did of Mussolini, for example, is itself quite far from being ordinary and is liable to make one look as if one doth protest too much.

Though the chapters of this book are thematic in so far as they treat particular topics, they also narrate a broadly chronological story about the way in which ordinary life as an ethicized form or scale has become detached from the reality of ordinary life in Predappio over the past one hundred years and has taken on a life of its own. In chapters 1 and 2, I will set out the historical conditions that led to ordinariness becoming a key concern there, both in the particulars of Predappio's own history and its imbrication in the broader intellectual and political currents of Italian Fascism. Chapter 2 will also commence the story of how Predappiesi relate to this history, a story that will continue throughout the book.

In chapter 3, I describe the ways in which that history continues to live on in contemporary life in the ritual marches that dominate the town on three key anniversary dates every year. I describe the development of these ritual marches over the postwar period and the history of Predappiesi relations with them. I show how Predappiesi react to these rituals—as they do more generally to invocations of Fascism—by conscientiously performing a version of everyday life, despite the "carnival of Mussolini" going on around them. In chapter 4, I discuss Predappio's urban space and material heritage, which is almost entirely dominated by the style of the Fascist regime. I point to the ways in which the use of Predappio's urban space is marked by attempts to empty out its history, in contrast to classic anthropological and sociological accounts of everyday space as the accumulation of memory.

Chapter 5 describes the place of talk about Fascism in ordinary language, noting the ways in which such talk evinces skepticism about ever truly being able to identify a Fascist and the fact that such ambiguity contrasts with the ways in which non-Predappiesi identify the town as practically synonymous with Fascism. Chapter 6 extends chapter 5's discussion of the place of politics in Predappio by juxtaposing two debates: one, an international controversy over a proposal to site a documentation center on Fascism in the ruins of Predappio's old Fascist Party headquarters; and the other, a local set of debates over the management of the town's recycling. I show how the scales of "international" (and "abstract") versus "local" (and "ordinary") are outcomes of the course of such debates, rather than premises for them.

In concluding the book, I return to some of the larger issues I have sought to raise in this introduction: that sometimes, at least, "being ordinary" takes work and that what exactly being ordinary means as an ideal toward which one works will vary depending on historical and social circumstances. That is a descriptive claim about life in Predappio in particular. Being ordinary in Predappio does not, when I describe it here, mean being ordinarily wealthy or ordinarily tall or short, fat or slim; it means—in regard to ethics, to space, to kinship, to ritual, and to politics (for to be ordinary, as I try to show in chapter 6, is not the same as to be apolitical)—having little or nothing to do with the subject that everybody else in Italy associates with Predappio: Fascism.

Anthropology and Populism

Anthropologists writing about the recent rise of populist movements have increasingly begun to worry about the overlap between some of the underlying ideas behind such movements and some of our own preferential disciplinary assumptions (e.g., Holmes 2019; Mazzarella 2019). To take but one recent example, Annastiina Kallius has evocatively described the ways in which the Fidesz regime has dramatically transformed the epistemological landscape of Hungarian politics, ushering in an understanding of truth that is closer to Romantic, counter-Enlightenment visions of it as connected to power and emotion than to straightforwardly representationalist or correspondentist conceptions (2023). The problem with constructing an anthropological account of such a transformation is that populist critiques of representationalism and advocacy of a more relational epistemology echo countless anthropological arguments of the past few decades. Because our own roots are partly based in the same Romantic and counter-Enlightenment genealogy (one that Douglas Holmes masterfully described at the turn of the millennium in *Integral Europe*), this should perhaps not surprise us. But the implications of this overlap have yet to be confronted.

I hope the claims I make in this book regarding the distinct but related senses in which ordinariness has been important to Fascism, Predappio, and anthropology help spur such confrontation. The ordinary and the everyday have long been foundational concepts in our discipline and the wider social sciences, but their ubiquity should not blind us to the variety of uses to which they can be put. In politics, just as in academia, adjectives such as *ordinary*, *grounded*, *everyday*, *concrete*, and *real* are often wielded like weapons of war against those with whom we disagree, just as they once were, as I will describe, by Mussolini's regime (and see Langhammer 2018). Nobody ever wants to be on the side of the abstract, the detached, or the metaphysical, let alone of the elite. In the social sciences, a great deal of the responsibility for this state of affairs lies with Wittgenstein, whose ideas I have drawn on already in this introduction and who—because of his monumental impact on thinking about the

ordinary—will continue to loom over the rest of this book in somewhat spectral fashion.

Human life is, of course, messy, complex, contingent, and routine in any
number of ways, and I would be a strange sort of ethnographer if I thought
otherwise. But sometimes it becomes particularly important to people—Fascists,
Predappiesi, politicians, philosophers, or social scientists—that it be seen to be
so. The claims people make in pursuit of this goal can be powerful and seductive, and the hierarchy they produce—in which the good is always "down"—is
often disguised or naturalized. We will fail to understand such occasions, I suggest, if we do not take into account the ordinary life of concepts such as "ordinary life" themselves; and unless we attend to their instrumentalization, we
will fail to notice that such instrumentalization serves a range of political ends,
not all of which we may wish to see realized.

CHAPTER 1

Fascism and the Social Life of "Ordinary Life"

In June 1938, the king of Italy came to Predappio. Victor Emmanuel III was only five feet tall, and contemporary Predappiesi of the right age remember being somewhat bemused by his childlike stature. Nevertheless, thousands lined the streets of Predappio to welcome his motorcade, waving Italian flags and jostling for a view of the "king-emperor." The visit was filmed for propaganda purposes, and the archival footage can be viewed on YouTube.[1]

The king's motorcade went first to Palazzo Varano, the newly built town hall, located on the site of the schoolhouse in which Mussolini's mother taught. In the footage we see the king waving from its balcony to the crowds gathered below before getting back in the car, as children rush down the hill away from the building to get to his next destination before he does. This turns out to be the (also newly built) cemetery, where we see the king walking up the promenade toward the graves of Mussolini's parents to pay his respects to them. His final destination, before ascending to the Rocca delle Caminate, Mussolini's summer residence in which the king would be staying, was a small, nondescript, ordinary-looking stone house with some steps leading up to it (figure 1.1). This is Mussolini's birth house (*casa natale*), and as the king climbs the steps to go inside, we see him remove his military cap, as if to honor a place of holiness.

Just before this visit, though, Predappiesi had witnessed a different and rather strange sort of spectacle. On Mussolini's orders, the huge, ornate arch

FIGURE 1.1. The king of Italy visits Mussolini's birth house. Photo courtesy of Luce Historical Archive, Rome.

decorated with fasces that capped the gated stairway leading from one of Predappio's two main squares up to Mussolini's birth house, and which had been designed by renowned architect Florestano di Fausto, was removed, along with the stairway itself. Mussolini, it is said, felt that they were stylistically excessive in relation to their surroundings, the ordinary Apennine town of his birth.

Why did it matter to Mussolini that the king of Italy see the house in which il Duce was born without the adornments di Fausto created for it? To answer this question, in this chapter I want to narrate some of the ways in which very particular notions of ordinariness came to become important to the history of early Fascism, and thus to the history of Predappio, before going on in the following chapters to discuss the particular ways in which these notions matter there today. This is the history of a form of ordinary life that is in many ways very different from the form in which it is usually invoked in contemporary anthropology and the social sciences. That is part of my point: there is nothing essential to the form or category of ordinary life, just as there is nothing essential to its contents. That means that its invocation as a category can serve a surprising variety of ends. Fascism and a certain brand of anthropology are not the only two. Romantics, Marxists, vitalists, surrealists, and Oxford philosophers—all of these and more have employed the concept in varying ways and to varying ends, and in opposition to varying threats.

The story I am going to tell in this chapter is not intended to be a complete genealogy of invocations of ordinary life. Such a genealogy would take up several books rather than just one. There are excellent surveys of just fractions of the recent history of ordinary life as a form in the work of Michael Sheringham (2006), Ben Highmore (2002), and Michael Sayeau (2016), and we have already met Charles Taylor's genealogy of the modern concern for ordinariness (1989).

Nor am I going to attempt a complete survey of the ways in which ideas about ordinary life intersect and interweave with ideas about Fascism. The problem with attempting even this more limited narrative is not there are too few links but that there are too many. There is the obvious and broad path from Romanticism and the counter-Enlightenment to Nazism that a number of other scholarly works have trod and retrod (see for instance Berlin 1999; Sternhell, Sznajder, and Asheri 1989; Wolin 2006). There are linking streets such as those of surrealism and futurism: both are descended from Romanticism and pursued what Taylor calls "an unmediated unity" (1989, 417), but only one of them would become explicitly aligned with Fascism, while the other would go on to influence the theories of everyday life thinkers such as Michel de Certeau (1984). Then there are narrower alleyways like that of Jamesian pragmatism, an inspiration for both ordinary language philosophy and Mussolini, or at least so the latter alleged in interviews (e.g., O'Hare McCormick 1926).

Because Mussolini is so fundamental to the history of Predappio, what I am going to do in this chapter instead is to provide a very brief sketch of his origins and early life, in the village and beyond, and to focus in particular on the kind of socialism he espoused in his youth and his transition to Fascism at the outset of the First World War. In doing so, I want to draw out just one of the forms in which a specific vision of ordinary life emerged as a key concern in the early development of Fascism. Doing so will, I hope, help to illustrate my point about the variety of ways in which ordinary life as a marked category may be invoked and the variety of ends such invocations may serve, while also setting the stage for the next chapter, which will describe the impact of early Fascist conceptions of ordinary life on Predappio's construction as the "Disneyland of the Duce" in the 1920s and '30s.

It is also important to add here that the form of ordinary life I describe emerging as a concern in early Fascism is not a directly causal explanation of the importance of ordinary life to Predappiesi today. The relationship is much more complicated than that, as will emerge through the course of this book.

It is certainly the case that Fascism emerged partly in response to questions of life and ordinariness, and that Fascism, along with those concerns, played a large part in determining the history of Predappio and the concern with ordinary life there today that I delineate in later chapters. But, as I describe at the end of this chapter, the ordinary life that is marked for people in Predappio today is not continuous with early Fascist visions of ordinary life; if anything, in fact, the form ordinary life takes as an ideal in contemporary Predappio is marked precisely because it is an escape from Fascism and from its history.

The Boy with the Eyes of a Beast

Predappio has existed, in some form or another, since Roman antiquity, and its name is alleged to derive from the original Latin title given to the hill fort at the foot of the Apennines: Praesidium Domini Appi. Until its transformation into Predappio Nuova in the 1920s, Dovia, or Dvi, as it was known in dialect, was a tiny hamlet located around three kilometers down the hill from the original Predappio, a hamlet named for the two roads (*due vie*: Dovia) that it straddled, one to Predappio Alta (as the original village is now known) and one over the Apennines, toward Tuscany and Florence. In 1894, there were 503 inhabitants in Predappio Alta and 186 in Dovia (Proli 2013, 61).

The Romagna, the region in which Predappio is situated, had been under papal rule for centuries prior to its assimilation into the Kingdom of Italy during the Risorgimento and had cultivated a strong tradition of anticlericalism. The Romagna was also the agricultural heartland of Italy, and the latter half of the nineteenth century saw it hit by both economic crisis and by the impact of a developing capitalist farming industry. The combination of the two cast many of its sharecropping peasants into penury: dismissed from their lands by the established landlords, who were now forced to compete with the mechanized agricultural methods of big and small businesses, these sharecroppers were obligated instead to sell their labor by the day as *braccianti*, a sort of peasant proletariat. Malnutrition, tuberculosis, pellagra, and malaria were rife, and infant mortality rates were far higher than the Italian average (Proli 2013, 62).

For related reasons, also higher than average were the numbers of socialist and anarchist activists prominent in the Romagna, which remains famous today as a bastion of left-wing politics. Among the most prominent of nineteenth-century revolutionaries produced by the region was Andrea Costa, erstwhile anarchist internationalist and the first Italian parliamentary deputy elected on a socialist platform. Costa had another Romagnole colleague mustering votes for him in that election, a friend in whose house he stayed on at least one occasion, and who would give his firstborn son the middle name of Andrea in his honor: Alessandro Mussolini.

Born in nearby Collina on November 11, 1854, Alessandro was a blacksmith and a fervent and convinced socialist, who represented Predappio at the congress of Romagnole socialist groups in 1876. In 1882, Alessandro married Rosa Maltoni, a schoolteacher from Villafranca, a village near Forli, against the initial wishes of her parents, who did not approve of Alessandro's socialism. In 1883, they had their first child: Benito Andrea Amilcare Mussolini, named after Andrea Costa, Amilcare Cipriani (another prominent Romagnole socialist), and Benito Juarez, the Mexican revolutionary. At the time of his birth, the family were living in a small five-room house, which also served as Alessandro's workplace, a few steps from Dovia's only osteria (built as watering hole for travelers on the road to Tuscany—it remains in business today). A year later they would move to Dovia's schoolhouse, where Rosa worked as a teacher and where Benito Mussolini grew up. Both of these locations—the schoolhouse and the house in which Mussolini was born—would form central nodes of Predappio Nuova after its construction, as I will go on to describe in chapter 2.

In addition to his labors as a blacksmith, Alessandro was a moderately successful local politician and journalist, elected as a village councillor in 1889 on a joint socialist-liberal ticket, and eventually serving as deputy mayor of Predappio. After the 1902 local elections, however, he was—apparently rather unjustly (Bosworth 2002, 165)—arrested for participating in a riot led by socialists who believed their election victory had been stolen, and he was imprisoned for six months. The humiliation of incarceration and the death of his wife, Rosa, in 1905 seem to have ended the political career of Mussolini *padre*, who died running a small inn outside Forli in 1910. Originally interred in a cemetery near Forli, he was reburied during the Fascist reconstruction of Predappio alongside Rosa Maltoni, in the cemetery of San Cassiano, one level above what would become the tomb of his son. "Poor socialist Alessandro," my friend Carlo once said to me, "he must be spinning in his grave at the sight of all those black shirts."

Contemporary Predappiesi will tell you that their grandparents spoke of the boy with "the eyes of a beast," and much was later made by the Fascist regime of young Benito Mussolini's wildness and inability to conform to social rules. He got himself expelled from a prestigious Salesian school in nearby Faenza by pulling a knife on another boy, and one man I knew who attended the same school recalled a janitor who remembered the young Mussolini as, in his words, "a little madman."

Less was made by the regime of his fervent socialism, which was already evident in 1901, when he applied for—but failed to get—the post of secretary to the town council of Predappio after graduating from school. His first sustained forays into the journalism that would make him famous were with a socialist newspaper for Italian immigrants in Switzerland (of whom Mussolini was one himself between 1902 and 1904) called *L'Avvenire del Lavoratore* (The Worker's Future). By 1909, Mussolini had been appointed secretary to the socialist group in Austrian-ruled Trento, from which region he was then expelled later that same year because of his political journalism. In 1910, he was given the same job in Forli, the town nearest to Predappio, together with editorship of its weekly newsletter, *La Lotte di Classe* (The Class Struggle). A fervid internationalist, anticlericalist, and committed Marxist, Mussolini soon began to make a name for himself on the national stage, speaking at the Socialist Party congress in Milan of the "absolute intransigence" of his part of the country in favor of orthodox socialism (Bosworth 2002, 274), as well as in his village of Predappio, where (at least according to his own newspaper's report) he received a hero's welcome (276).

In this period, Mussolini was, as R. J. B. Bosworth puts it, "constructing himself, then, as 'the extremist,' the warrior of Romagnole socialism," itself already famous for its "intransigence" (2002, 279). The context of Italian socialism—and European socialism more broadly—at this time was one of serious crisis, however, and Mussolini's passionate commitment to an activist Marxism would soon lead him down a different path from that of the national party.

In 1895, a year after publishing the final volume of *Das Kapital*, Friedrich Engels died in London, thus passing the mantle of socialist leadership onto its next generation, and the two-decade-long economic crisis known as the Great Depression finally came to an end. The following year, Engels's executor, Eduard Bernstein, a prominent German socialist also living in exile in London, began publishing a series of newspaper articles that would set off what would become known in Marxist circles as the "revisionism debates."

Bernstein pointed out what others did not wish to acknowledge: that the crisis of the Great Depression, as it was then known, like other crises before it, had passed without apparently doing significant damage to the capitalist economic system; that, in fact, Marx's theses of the polarization of classes and the increasing pauperization of the working class did not appear to accurately represent reality or to be likely to do so in the near future; and that electoral success, rather than revolution, seemed to many socialists to promise the most likely path to a socialist future.

By this time, the German Social Democratic Party had been legalized for some years, and indeed Engels himself had advocated full parliamentary participation as a tactic in the struggle for revolution in his 1895 introduction to Karl Marx's *The Class Struggles in France*. What Bernstein sought to do however was to effect a much more drastic revision of socialist strategy and to reconcile, in his view, theory with practice: the party's policy, he argued in 1898, "has in every case proved more correct than its phraseology. Hence I have no wish to reform the actual policy of the party . . . ; what I am striving for, and as a theoretician must strive for, is a unity between theory and reality, between phraseology and action" (quoted in Adler 1954). Bernstein wanted to adapt Marxist doctrine to the exigencies of participation in liberal democracy.

The crisis of Marxism that would lead to Mussolini's split from the Italian Socialist Party was, in other words, at its origins fundamentally concerned with the relation between theory and practice, between the abstract and the concrete, between philosophy and life. The basic problem was that Marxist theory appeared to many prominent socialists of the time, such as Bernstein, to be an inaccurate representation of reality and thus a flawed guide to practical action.

There were three responses, very broadly speaking, to this crisis, each of which addressed this relationship in different ways: the first was the simplest and consisted of denying that such a gap between theory and practice existed or, if acknowledging that it did, claiming that it required only minor adjustments to the basic theoretical framework of Marxism. This was the solution adopted by the wing of European socialism that would go on to form the core of its communist parties, at the time exemplified in the works of Rosa Luxemburg, who virulently rejected Bernstein's arguments, and Karl Kautsky. The second type of solution followed Bernstein's cue in rethinking or rejecting some core aspects of Marxist doctrine, most obviously the strategic goal of revolution. This option would be taken up by the majority of European social democratic parties after the schism between socialists and Communists in the wake of the First World War.

The final option is the one of interest to us, for it is both the strangest and also that eventually adopted by Mussolini, broadly speaking. This solution consisted of acknowledging the theoretical failures of Marxism (though often insisting on socialism's usefulness as a motivating ideology), while continuing to give absolute primacy to the practical importance of revolution, thus reversing the standard means-end relationship in which revolution and socialism are placed by most Marxists: instead of revolution serving to bring about socialism, here socialism would serve to bring about revolution. This solution accepted the reformist point that material forces might not or would not lead to such a revolution and demanded instead that the proletarian revolution be brought about by human will and force of life—thus, again, reversing orthodox Marxist readings of causality, in which human will is secondary to material circumstances. This solution also accepted, in some senses at least, the substance of Bernstein's critique of the validity of core Marxist principles, while rejecting his conclusion from that premise that revolution was no longer a useful goal. It emerged from mixing Marxism with elements from other thinkers, most notably vitalist philosophers such as Henri Bergson and Friedrich Nietzsche, and with counter-Enlightenment narratives, which gave pride of place not to reason and science—as of course Marx had done, to a considerable, if debated, extent—but to the emotions, to the irrational, and to the spiritual.

In Italy, the revisionism debates had a significant impact. The Socialist Party was torn between a reformist wing—led by one of its founders, Filippo Turati, among others—and a maximalist, revolutionary wing, of which Mussolini was a vocal member. This conflict had been going on for some time before Mussolini made a name for himself in 1911–1912, on the occasion of the Italo-Turkish War. In contrast to the tepid response of the reformist wing of the party, Mussolini called a strike in his district to oppose the war, blocking troop trains from nearby Meldola and getting himself arrested (alongside his friend and contemporary Pietro Nenni, who would go on to become a prominent socialist politician after the fall of Fascism). Mussolini benefited considerably from the resulting notoriety, and at the Party Congress of 1912—held in Reggio Emilia, near Forli—he delivered a rapturously received speech and successfully demanded the expulsion of some reformist deputies. Later that same year he was made the editor of *Avanti!*, the Italian socialist national daily newspaper, a crucially important post in the party. Mussolini and his maximalist wing seemed to have won the battle for the soul of Italian socialism.

Life, Vitalism, Pragmatism

In Mussolini's early, maximalist socialism, we meet the beginnings of some of the ways in which a particular vision of ordinary life intersects with the histories of Fascism and Predappio. As I noted earlier, Mussolini's approach to socialism in the wake of the revisionism debates was not unique. Exemplary of it, in fact, is an intellectual who continues to be cited today, whom Mussolini referred to as his "master," and who acknowledged as his intellectual heirs, in the same breath, both Mussolini and Lenin (see Megaro 1938, 228; Meisel 1950).

Georges Sorel was a civil engineer for most of his life, before attaining celebrity in retirement as a philosopher and intellectual. A convert to Marxism by 1893, Sorel was at first inspired by Bernstein's revision of Marx but soon came to lament Bernstein's lack of revolutionary fervor (Sternhell, Sznajder, and Asheri 1989, 47). Significantly influenced by Bergson, as well as by Giovanni Battista Vico, Sorel recast fundamental Marxist concepts such as class and class war in mythical, voluntarist, and vitalist terms: what was really important about them was not that they were true but that they were motivating of political action (Sorel [1906] 1999).

Despite his education as a scientist, Sorel was deeply antitheoretical, declaring Marx's theory of surplus value, for example, to be uselessly arcane and uninspiring, except insofar as its obscurity might stimulate action in the same way as the mysteries of the Catholic Church had done (180–181). In his most famous work, *Reflections on Violence*, Sorel makes clear the difference between his own position and that of Bernstein and other revisionists: while they sought to harmonize theory and practice, he sought to transform Marxism from being any kind of theory at all into being a "weapon of war" (Sternhell, Sznajder, and Asheri 1989, 70). Other participants in the revisionism debates had missed the point, in other words, which was not whether or not Marx's theories were correct or predictive, but how effectively they functioned as "myths" in the service of the revolution. As Zeev Sternhell, Mario Sznajder, and Maia Asheri put it, "practice, for him, preceded theory, and only action really counted. The effectiveness of an act was much more important to him and its intrinsic qualities . . . In order for someone to throw himself or herself into action, 'the conviction' has to 'dominate the entire consciousness and to operate before the calculations of reflection have time to come into play.' That was why Sorel rejected any intellectual structure, which he called a utopia, and to which he opposed the power of the mobilizing myth" (1989, 75).

Sorel's concern with the power of myth is echoed today in some contemporary versions of neo-Fascism, as Maddalena Gretel Cammelli makes clear in her ethnography of CasaPound, a prominent Italian neo-Fascist group named after the poet Ezra Pound. She describes militants explicitly reflecting on the importance of a "'mythical past' that they draw on in order to mobilize participants and create new myths by invoking the eras of imperial Rome and the Fascist regime" (2017, 93).

Gretel Cammelli also describes the ways in which, for CasaPound militants, "the political program as such gives way to what activists feel is more important: lived experience, the emotional stance of a shared identity, community. Third-millennium Fascism is lived as a prerational experience, described as a style of life capable of grasping people's inner reason and meeting their need for identity" (2017, 98).

As we will see, this concern with "lived experience" is also crucial to an understanding of early Fascist ideology, or at least to what passes for ideology in early Fascism. As should already be becoming clear, the intellectual roots of Fascism lie in a disdain for departures from concrete experience, such as forms of theory, abstraction, or philosophy.

Perhaps unsurprisingly then, Sorel was also a convert to William James's pragmatism (Nye 1973, 422) and even published a book toward the end of his life titled *The Utility of Pragmatism*. His friend and a fellow inspiration for Fascism, Gustave Le Bon, the father of crowd psychology, shared this admiration, writing, "It matters little to science that an hypothesis be recognized as false after it has produced discoveries. It matters little, equally, that religious, political or moral hypotheses are judged inexact one day if they have assured the life and grandeur of the people who have adopted them" (Le Bon 1914, cited in Nye 1973, 423). As Hilary Putnam and Ruth A. Putnam write of William James, "his aim (as stated in his *Essays in Radical Empiricism*) is to produce a metaphysics and epistemology close to the natural realism of the common man. The 'common man' [*sic*] takes himself to perceive the ordinary objects of everyday life, whereas philosophers since Descartes have interposed certain types of private entities . . . between the perceiver and that world of things and events in a public space and time" (Putnam and Putnam 2017). Mussolini himself claimed to have read James and cited him approvingly in interviews (O'Hare McCormick 1926), and a number of scholars before the war argued that there was a certain affinity between Fascism and pragmatism (e.g., Elliot 1926, 1928; Stewart 1928; and Diggins 1966).

While historian John Diggins claims that Mussolini's knowledge of Jamesian pragmatism was only superficial at best, he also describes the ways in which the relationship between Fascism and American pragmatism was far from being only one-directional. Among those enamored with Fascism for a time was philosopher and student of James (James himself died in 1910, before the advent of Fascism) George Santayana, who admired the Fascist emphasis on hierarchy (Diggins 1966, 488). Prefiguring a point I will return to later in this chapter, Diggins also notes the antitheoretical affinities of both pragmatism and Fascism: "the Italian [pragmatist and later Fascist philosopher Giovanni] Papini was fond of saying that pragmatism was a method of doing without a philosophy. It might also be said that to some American liberals Fascism was a method of doing without an ideology" (496).

Diggins notes that the journal *New Republic*, founded by members of the American progressive movement, evinced some sympathy for Italian Fascism in its early years, arguing that no matter what its faults, it would surely be an improvement on the "stagnation" of liberal parliamentary politics (Diggins 1966, 495). Challenged by one more prescient scholar to explain how it could reconcile liberal progressivism with dictatorship, the journal replied, in a rather anthropological tone, "that the traditional 'formulas' of liberalism were inadequate to appraise developments either in Italy or in Russia" (496). "Alien critics should beware," it went on to argue in its unfortunately titled "Apology for Fascism," "of outlawing a political experiment which aroused in a whole nation an increased moral energy and dignified its activities by subordinating them to a deeply felt common purpose" (*New Republic* 1927, cited in Diggins 1966, 497). This emphasis on action at the expense of reflection is also echoed in later philosophical work on ordinary life, such as that of Wittgenstein, who suggested that Goethe's phrase from *Faust* ("in the beginning was the deed") could serve as a motto for his later philosophy (Monk 1991, 713). As Wittgenstein's biographer Ray Monk puts it, "the deed, the activity, is primary, and does not receive its rationale or its justification from any theory we might have of it. This is as true with regard to language and mathematics as it is with regard to ethics, aesthetics, and religion. 'As long as I can play the game, I can play it, and everything is all right'" (713).

The pragmatist notion of the "common man" also points to another aspect of both Sorel and Le Bon's thought with affinities to other ideas about ordinary life. Le Bon, famously the author of *The Crowd*, believed that the turn of the twentieth century was the era of "the unconscious action of crowds substituting itself for the conscious activity of individuals" (1896, 1). This fascination with "crowds" and "masses" would come to characterize the era of Fascism, as Stefan Jonsson has described with reference to Germany, where the masses became, in the words of novelist Alfred Döblin, "the most enormous fact of the era" (cited in Jonsson 2013, 7). Though Sorel disagreed with aspects of Le Bon's analysis in the book, both concurred on the unconscious and irrational aspects of crowd behavior and on the fact that this made crowds in some sense closer to "natural man" than any other social form. It was to the masses that Sorel believed his myths would appeal.

There is one fairly obvious and predictable outcome of Sorel's perspective: if it becomes clear that the subject one has taken to be capable of revolution, violence, and the general strike—in this case the proletariat—is not in fact inclined to such actions, then one will go in search of other subjects who are, since it is the end of revolution, and in Sorel's case the unraveling of the Enlightenment, that matter more than who actually achieves this end. By the time Mussolini was appointed to *Avanti!*, Sorel had lost hope in the consciousness of the working classes and was turning to antisemitism and the nationalism of *Action Française* and Charles Maurras.

From Red to Black

For Mussolini, a similar transformation to that of Sorel took place on the occasion of the First World War. Mussolini initially toed the party line of internationalist neutrality, writing after August 1914 that "the proletariat is not disposed to fight a war of aggression and conquest after which it will be merely as poor and exploited as before" (Bosworth 2002, 347). As Bosworth notes, however, "beneath the scatter of his words, he began to perceive that war could entail opportunity, the chance to destroy an old order, the possibility of imagining a new" (2002, 348). Like other socialist maximalists of this period, Mussolini started to see the war as a crucible of action through which Italian political life might be renewed and the cause of the revolution furthered. Soon such doubts would become public: on October 18, 1914, Mussolini wrote in *Avanti!* that a party "which wishes to live in history and, in so far as it is allowed, to make history, cannot submit, at the penalty of suicide, to a line which is dependent on an unarguable dogma or an eternal law. . . . Do we—as men and as socialists—want to be inert spectators of his huge drama? Or do we want to be, in some way and in some sense, the protagonists?" (2002, 351–352).

Note that what Mussolini, like Sorel, is opposed to here is what he sees as dogma and law—an interpretation of Marx that places fidelity to theory and principle above "living in history." As Bosworth describes, Mussolini even found a clinching argument against this interpretation with a quotation from Marx himself: "Whoever develops a set programme for the future is a reactionary" (2002, 352). Despite this sop to Marx, however, this particular heresy proved rather too unorthodox for the Socialist Party hierarchy; within a month of the publication of this editorial, Mussolini had lost his job at the newspaper and been expelled from the party.

The logic behind Mussolini's conversion to interventionism is complex—possibly even involving payment from the French government (Bosworth 2002, 350–353)—and much historiographical ink has been spilled on debating the consistency and rationality of Mussolini's intellectual position in this regard and more broadly. Some argue that a degree of coherency can be identified beneath the numerous alterations that Mussolini's political and philosophical position underwent through the course of his life, of which the abandonment of socialism was perhaps only the most startling (e.g., Gregor 1974, 1979a). Others, perhaps most famously Denis Mack Smith, make Mussolini appear as an opportunistic clown, far more interested in the achievement of personal power and success than in any particular intellectual program (1981).

An observer in 1920 described some of these consequences of Fascism's attitude to theory and everyday life in the following terms:

Despite the bombastic words of the programmes approved by their congresses, in which all the ingredients of the new or old revolutionary medicines were immersed, because the Fasci [di Combattimenti] lack a real and true political content and a doctrinal basis, they are obliged to accept the caprice of circumstances passively, and their vaunted *praxis*, which should have been the generating fluid of elasticity, becomes a solid cement which binds them together and fixes them in the iron framework of the facts of the everyday, until it transforms them, at first a little at a time and almost unknowingly, then suddenly consciously, into a real and true counter-revolutionary organism, the white guard counterplaced against the red guard. (Quoted in De Felice 1965, 660)

This critical observer's description of Fascism as "fixed" in "the iron framework of the everyday" is precisely what makes sense of Mussolini's transformation from red to black, just as it does of Sorel's transformation. To be "fixed in the everyday" is exactly the point of this vision of politics and ideology (if it can be called that); of course, fealty to a doctrine, a theory, a dogma, or a law (like Marxism) would come second to praxis, action, and lived experience. As Mabel Berezin notes in *Making the Fascist Self*, "Fascists did not believe in abstract values such as liberty, equality, fraternity. They believed in action and style—ideas that specify means and not ends and that make the ends of Fascist action extremely malleable. The Fascist belief in style has derailed attempts to codify Fascist ideology. Scholars' searches for doctrinal coherence have misread the issue of political style and drawn the incorrect conclusion that Italian Fascism was inchoate" (1997, 30).

In other words, like skeptical philosophers in the narrative of ordinary language philosophy, historians searching for an ideology of Fascism are asking the wrong question: it is in Fascist practice that its essence is to be found, at least according to its self-definitions (or lack thereof).

In the immediate aftermath of his sacking and expulsion from the Socialist Party, Mussolini founded a new paper, one that would go on to become the official organ of the Italian Fascist Party, *Il Popolo d'Italia*. In its pages, he continued to lobby for intervention into the war until 1915, when Italy finally joined the side of the Entente. Drafted that same year, he served as a Bersagliere until wounded by shrapnel and hospitalized in 1917.

In December 1914, shortly after his expulsion from the Socialist Party, Mussolini was already advocating for the constitution of what he called *Fasci d'azione rivoluzionaria* in order to spread "subversive, revolutionary, and anti-constitutional ideals" (cited in Bosworth 2002, 363), but his opportunity to put this idea into practice came with the end of the war. On March 23, 1919, he convoked a meeting of a range of ex-military groups in Milan, at which he assumed the role of their Duce, or leader, an event subsequently mythologized as the foundational moment of Italian Fascism.

"The Common Man"

Sorel and Le Bon, both important and well-documented influences on Mussolini (see Megaro 1938; Meisel 1950; Nye 1973; Payne 1995; Sternhell, Sznajder, and Asheri 1989), bring together the two key ingredients for the form that ordinary life would take in early Fascism: vitalism (life) and populism (ordinary man). Needless to say, this is a very specific vision of ordinary life. As Donna Jones argues, "inspired by Bergson, the French political provocateur Georges Sorel would deepen political disillusion with mechanistic and lifeless democracy, in which the sovereign abstract citizens are indifferent to one another and held together simply by an external mechanism. As Mark Antliff has recently shown, Sorel militated for disciplined, aestheticized violence for the sake of a palingenetic and organicist ultranationalism that promised to bring (at least Gentile) people together through intuitive, organic, and mutual sympathy" (Jones 2010, 8).

In other words, despite the fact that it might share with other visions of ordinary life an opposition to abstraction and mechanism, to theory and philosophy, this vision of ordinary life is an exclusivist one, as Jones shows in her account of early vitalism. Like Romanticism, as Charles Taylor has described (1989), it involves a turning inward as part of the valorization of ordinary life. But in the case of vitalism, that turn inward is in quest of a dynamic force, an élan vital, which all too easily became assimilable to race. Furthermore, as Jones shows, because race here came to function as a mysterious internal essence, it produced forms of racism in which race is not just a contingent product of Darwinian adaptation but a "noumenal" quality, not an effect but a direct cause of history (2010, 117–119). Race here is not just an accident of biology, but the basic driver of all history. Stefan Jonsson also notes this exclusivist vision of ordinariness in describing two Fascist visions of the masses: "the block," "the armored mass, drilled and disciplined, violently cut to shape," and "the swarm," "the Jewish mass and the gypsy mass or the mass of hysteric females" (2013, 46).

To return to comparisons with anthropology and the wider social sciences, it is worth noting in passing here that this is not the only exclusivist vision of ordinary life. Various invocations of it in academic literature—some of which also draw on vitalism and populism—make everyday life "the peculiar preserve of the subordinate, the weak, or 'the people': 'Dominant groups,' it seems, do not inhabit everyday worlds" (Crook 1998, 536). As Stephen Crook points out, there are in fact a number of affinities between early and reactionary vitalists such as Oswald Spengler and later, radical theorists of the everyday, such as de Certeau, Mikhail Bakhtin, Anthony Giddens, and Ulrich Beck. To this list one could also add James Scott's notion of "weapons of the weak" (1985), as well as a strain of Marxist theory on everyday life stretching from Georg Lukács (e.g., [1911] 1994) through Agnes Heller (1984) and Henri Lefebvre ([1947], [1961], [1981] 2014), up to the contemporary work of thinkers such as Franco Moretti (e.g., 1985, 2013), in which the everyday is by turns understood as the ultimate source of alienation and our greatest opportunity for liberation: "the privileging of the everyday proceeds through the construction of dualisms in which one side of the duality is assigned to established and pathological power while the other is assigned to resistant subordinates. This is so for Habermas's distinction between system and lifeworld, for Bakhtin's distinction between unitary language and heteroglossia, and for de Certeau's distinction between strategy and tactics" (Crook 1998, 536). The political valence is reversed in the vitalism of Spengler and Sorel, of course: "while Spengler directly celebrates the life-force embodied in the strong individual, de Certeau and Fiske celebrate the cunning of the life-force through which the individually weak achieve a collective strength" (536).

Spengler, incidentally, was a significant influence on Wittgenstein as he was developing what would become his "late" views on ordinary life (Monk 1991). Wittgenstein shared Spengler's pessimism and belief that western European culture was atrophied, no longer a "living organism" but "a dead, mechanical, structure" (698). Monk argues that Spengler's work is crucial to understanding the connection between this pessimism on Wittgenstein's part and his later philosophy (705). It was partly from Spengler that Wittgenstein derived his antipathy to law and theory, which Spengler associates with "dead," "mechanical" civilization, as opposed to "history, poetry, and life" (705).

There is an important difference though between the Spenglerian, Sorelian vision of the "life-force" of the strong individual and the contemporary social scientific work on the everyday that Crook points to above. For example, Le Bon's book on the crowd (subtitled *A Study of The Popular Mind*) was a highly conservative one. Crowds are irrational, uncivilized, and barbaric. In Le Bon's words, crowd beliefs "assume the characteristics of blind submission, fierce intolerance, and the need of violent propaganda" (Le Bon 1896, 64). As Sternhell puts it, "the masses move forward under the impulsion of myths, images, and feelings. They wish to obey and democracy is merely a delusion. For the founders of Fascism, the Great War was a laboratory where the ideas they had put forward throughout the first decade of the century were entirely vindicated" (1989, 31). This combination of ideas about how "ordinary men" behave, the power of myths, and the heroic leader capable of mobilizing them is what gives the form of ordinary life here its most distinctive characteristic: the masses require a kind of "modern Prince," as Le Bon—and Antonio Gramsci, for different if related reasons (Gramsci 1971)—believed, a "psychologist-statesman" who could make use of social scientific insights like those of Le Bon himself to ma-nipulate the masses as if they were an army (Le Bon 1910; Nye 1973). *Pace* Wil-liam Mazzarella's recent claim that populism is expressed "either as . . . the kind of clearing that a crowd can occupy . . . or as the radical fullness of the body of a leader in which the people may find a palpable image of their own substance" (2019: 52), early Fascism combined both at the same time. In Mussolini's case, many of the men he summoned to Milan in 1919 were indeed ex-soldiers, and the Fascist squads they formed modeled themselves quite explicitly on the mili-tary. In Mussolini they would find their heroic and exemplary leader.

"One Man Alone"

It is a truism in historiographical work on Mussolini and Fascism to worry about the relation between leader and movement. As Robert Paxton has strik-ingly put it, speaking of the idea that Fascism ought to be identified with its leader, "this image, whose power lingers today, is the last triumph of Fascist propagandists. It offers an alibi to nations that approved or tolerated Fascist leaders, and diverts attention from the persons, groups, and institutions who helped him" (Paxton 2004, 9). Indeed, as I will go on to discuss, this "alibi" of the myth of Mussolini is in many ways at the heart of the history of his home-town, just as he himself is.

This "alibi" has been offered as an explanation for Italy's failure properly to come to terms with its past and thus for Predappio's predicament as a center for neo-Fascist tourism: Fascism was a disease of one man and "one man alone," as Winston Churchill put it, not of the *bel paese*, thus no serious process of "defascistization" was required after the war. It has been deployed as part of arguments in favor of the town's recent initiative to build Italy's first and only "museum of Fascism" in the former Fascist Party headquarters: to counter this myth, and the distasteful tourism it inspires, Italy must confront its heritage openly. This "alibi" has also been deployed against that same project, by pub-lic intellectuals such as Carlo Ginzburg (Luzzatto and Ginzburg 2016): to this way of thinking, Italy may need to confront its heritage, but it certainly should not do so by building another potential shrine for neo-Fascists at a site that is fundamentally contaminated by its association with one man, not with the movement itself.

There are a number of reasons that the relationship between Mussolini and Fascism is a contentious topic. One, as Churchill's wartime propaganda speech to the Italians about Fascism as the invention of "one man alone" indicates, is about responsibility. If Fascism "was" Mussolini, then his Fascist cadres, his

conservative, socialist, religious, and military allies, his supporters in uniform
and out of it, and his old friends in Predappio can all be more or less absolved
of guilt for what happened in the twenty years between the "March on Rome"
and the fall of Fascism. This, in fact, was something like the position taken both
by the Allies and by new national administrations after Italy's liberation, a word
that already gestures to the idea of a people beneath an alien and unwonted
yoke. I will describe some of this, and what passed for "defascistization," in the
course of later chapters.

A second reason that it has often been difficult to separate Mussolini the person from Fascism the political movement relates to the curious nature of the
latter as an ideological phenomenon—or, rather, as an almost anti- or meta-
ideological phenomenon. Fascism's flexibility, mutability, and reliance on notions
of spirit, praxis, and life rather than doctrine are—rather paradoxically—among
its most defining features. Historians and political scientists have argued at significant length over how and whether to define Fascism, both in Italy and internationally, in part because of this chameleon-like quality. I will discuss some of
these arguments as they become relevant throughout this book; for now, I want
to focus on this striking quality of Fascism as a political phenomenon, that of
being self-consciously difficult to define or to pin down. As William Mazzarella
notes, quoting political scientist Cas Mudde, a populist politics like that of Fascism is a "'thin-centred ideology' (Mudde 2017), that can cohabit with any
number of political positions" (Mazzarella 2019, 47), a point that historian of
Fascism Roger Eatwell also makes, while nevertheless emphasizing that a valorization and defense of what he calls "plain people" is key characteristic of this
"thin ideology" (e.g., 2017, 366–367).

This quality is also partly indicated by Paxton's remark about "the last triumph of Fascists propagandists": if some things are characteristically Fascist,
then the attribution of almost divine authority and responsibility to "one man
alone" is surely one of those things. Indeed, this is one of the things that makes
Predappio, home to Mussolini's birthplace and grave, such a powerful attraction for contemporary neo-Fascists. But that such comingling of individual and
idea is possible is worth remarking upon. It will be a truism to historians of
Fascism, but perhaps not to anthropologists, nor indeed to others: we are not
usually wont to think of the *truth* of ideologies as standing and falling with
the person of a follower or even an originator. Marx, Vladimir Lenin, and Mao
Zedong qua individuals, for example, had an impact on the uptake of their
ideas by others as a matter of practical fact, and thus also on the appearance
and possibly the reality of those ideas as correct or otherwise; but the ideas
themselves were still ideas, intended to live beyond their creators (though see
Yurchak 2015 for discussion of Leninist "form" over substance). Rarely is that

relationship between doctrine and the actions of an individual or individuals itself inscribed explicitly in that doctrine and in those ideas themselves. Rarely does a movement say, in effect, "pay attention to what we do, not what we say." This is what I mean by anti- or meta-ideological: Fascist ideology—insofar as such a thing existed—refutes the importance of ideology; it contains its own commentary on the relationship between theory and practice. The substance of that commentary is that practice—often, but not always, that of "one man alone"—trumps theory. "Mussolini is always right!" was one of the Fascist regime's favorite catchphrases.

Thus was it possible for Italian Fascism to be born, like Mussolini, in the heartlands of Italian socialism, and to attract many of the latter's onetime adherents, like Mussolini, by drawing upon a particular selection of its truths; thus was it possible for it to champion female emancipation in 1919 and then spend the next twenty-odd years insisting that a woman's place was in the kitchen or the bedroom; thus could it draw on quasi-anarchist traditions such as syndicalism while also inflating the power of the state to previously unimaginable extents.

These are just a few examples of Italian Fascism's self-contradictions, often the results of the whims and vacillations of Mussolini himself, in response to changing circumstances. As a contemporary political scientist put it: "the ideology of Fascism contains a very queer *potpourri* of a sort of Machiavellian Pragmatism, Gentilean Idealism, Sorelian mythmaking and violence, and even the functionalism of the Guild Socialists and Syndicalists of Italy" (Elliott 1928, 10).

This was not a position that Fascism itself took, largely speaking, in its own, limited reflections on its self-contradictions. Fascism—for those Fascists who took the time to think about it—did not have to be ideologically consistent or systematic, because it had nothing but contempt for "intellectuals" and "rationalists" and for the virtues of abstraction or consistency that Fascists associated with systematic philosophizing. Fascism instead was about life, action, force, and practice—and often, of course, about violence. Unlike socialism, for example, which has produced an endless stream of attempts at self-definition or retheorization quite apart from the corpus of Marx's work, Italian Fascism was not self-reflexive (which is another reason why its contradictions were not often the subject of explicit reflection). Its closest equivalent to *The Communist Manifesto* is a brief entry in an encyclopedia in 1932, which appeared under Mussolini's name, but was in fact ghostwritten by Giovanni Gentile, one of the only examples of a Fascist philosopher. Even that text begins by rejecting the whole notion of the importance of doctrine in favor of practice.

All of this returns us to the key issue I wished to raise in briefly narrating the origins of Mussolini and Mussolinian Fascism. *Life, practice, action*—these are crucial terms in understanding what constitutes Fascist ideology, and they were understood by people such as Sorel and Mussolini in opposition to abstraction, theory, formalism, and transcendence. As Jean Comaroff puts it in relation to contemporary populism, "the fire of populism often excoriates the putative 'sophistry' of analysis, theorization, and complexification" (2009, quoted in Mazzarella 2019). At its heart, Fascism was an experiential, organicist, vitalist political movement, not an intellectual one. It was based on a moralized scale of politics in which ordinary life—albeit a very particular kind of ordinary life—trumped theory.

In Mussolini's transition from socialism to Fascism, we can see this in action. To what he perceives as the "dogma" of his opponents in the party, he opposes the voluntarism of force, action, and intervention, and a belief in the importance of understanding the contingency of historical events such as the outbreak of the First World War. Hence Fascism's immersion in what the critical observer quoted above calls "the iron framework of the everyday."

Needless to say, insofar as the everyday or ordinary life is invoked here, it is a highly specific vision of what that looks like (as I have suggested that any such invocation will be). It is a nationalist vision, a racialized, classed, and a militaristic one, as Donna Jones describes in her history of vitalism (2010). It will also, because of its need for a heroic leader to rise above the ordinary, become tied up with the exemplary figure of Mussolini himself, as I will describe in more detail in chapter 2.

William Mazzarella has recently argued in relation to populism that a concern for the ordinary is characteristic of both populism and anthropology: "One might . . . say that anthropology itself, methodologically if not always ideologically, tends toward a populist stance, aligning with the common sense of the common people" (2019, 46). The form that ordinary life took in the thought and practice of early Fascism is very different in many ways from the form it takes in anthropology and the broader social sciences. My intention here is precisely to highlight the diversity of forms in which the category may appear and of ends to which its instrumentalization may be directed.

It is undeniable, though, that there are some features common to many such invocations of ordinary life as a category (there is a family resemblance between them, if you will). As I noted in my introduction, many social scientific and political visions of ordinary life include a moralizing scale, for example, in which ordinary life is good and something else—something "less ordinary"—is bad.

Fascist invocations of ordinary life, according to at least one well-known account (Nolte 1965), also share with social scientific work a deep-seated "resistance to transcendence"; and while Fascist visions of ordinary life were specific and exclusionary (i.e., only certain sorts of people could be ordinary), some social scientific invocations have also been exclusionary, though along an entirely different axis (e.g., de Certeau 1984; Scott 1985). Likewise, Fascist visions of ordinary life were vitalist and in some sense radically so in absolutely distinguishing some lives from others; but some have read Wittgenstein's notion of "form of life" as vitalist, too (see Lash 2006; McDonough 2004; Moody and Shakespeare 2012), and, as Ray Monk notes in his biography, Wittgenstein's own thinking was sometimes unhappily inflected by ideas about race (1991, 277–279, 731–737).

My point here is that it is not just the contents of ordinary life—the contingent and conventionalized things we wish to point to when we invoke the category—that vary but also the characteristics of ordinary life as a conceptual category itself and its place in a broader galaxy of conceptual forms. For example, a great many invocations of ordinary life share Fascism's antipathy to abstraction, whether that abstraction is conceived of in the form of mechanism, strategy, law, or theory. But beyond the abstraction versus ordinariness dichotomy, there are other conceptual categories at play here, too, that reveal something about the specific forms that ordinary life takes.

As I will describe in more detail in chapter 2, in the early history of Fascism and Predappio, for instance, the category of ordinariness became tangled up with that of its heroic exemplary opposite. Mussolini was to be seen as both an ordinary man, from an ordinary Apennine village, and also as Il Duce, the man who was "always right." His hometown, likewise, became both a symbol of Mussolini's humble origins and a transfigured image of Fascist modernism through its reconstruction under the regime. In this history, in other words, unlike in contemporary anthropological discourse, the exemplary and the ordinary become intertwined. Similarly, the threat to ordinary life in contemporary Predappio does not come from skepticism (as in Cavell) or mechanism (as in early Fascism). Instead, it comes from the history and politics of Fascism itself.

The category of ordinary life itself has an ordinary life of its own: it appears at specific times and places and in response to specific needs and ends. One example of such a specific time and place is early Fascist thought, in which ordinary life emerges as a marked category in opposition to doctrine or philosophy, in the valorization of the common man in opposition to the bourgeoisie, but also in a highly exclusivist and racialized form, in which only some people could count as the right kind of ordinary people.

In Predappio today, ordinary life also appears as such a marked category. It takes "doing," in Sacks's terms, because in truth, in comparison to almost any other relevant context, life in Predappio is anything but ordinary, and its inhabitants are well aware of that fact. But the ordinary life that contemporary Predappiesi seek to produce is very different from the form in which it emerges in early Fascist thought.

Indeed, "doing being ordinary" is what people in Predappio do when they conspicuously and studiously refuse to engage with the politics of their history (Candea 2010). When Valentina tends to the graves of her relatives amid a sea of black-shirted tourists, and does so without complaint, she is not unaware of what these visitors are there for, and she knows why they all wear black. Nor is she so inured to their presence that it "goes without saying"; she has her own personal experience of the fact that people—some from her hometown—died fighting men wearing the same color; as I will describe, she lived through pitched street battles between neo-Fascists and Communists in the 1960s and '70s, and she knows that to a great many of her compatriots her home is anathema because of these tourists and the man they visit—"the Chernobyl of history," as its former mayor likes to put it, or a "toxic waste dump" in the words of one commentator (Wu Ming 2017). Nor does she have any sympathy with their politics, as she will explain to you if you ask, though probably not otherwise. She lives this as her ordinary life, and indeed does her best to categorize these visitors as doing the same, because to do otherwise is to conjure up political specters—black, but also red, as I will describe—who are best left undisturbed in their graves.

The category and form of ordinary life, not just its living, comes to life in Predappio in opposition to the politics of Fascism. By this I do not mean simply "Fascism," for it is not only Fascists who politicize Fascism. I mean simply what to almost anybody anywhere else would be a perfectly ordinary way of understanding Fascism, namely as one of the most controversial and ideologically divisive political experiments in recent Western history, to put it mildly. The utter domination of Predappio by the shadow of this experiment makes it impossible, I will argue in the remainder of this book, to live there without performing these operations of "ordinarification" on oneself, one's home, one's economic and ritual life, and one's politics.

CHAPTER 2

Ordinary Exemplars and the Moralization of the Everyday

Angelo Ciaranfi was born in Predappio in 1890. He must have known the young Benito Mussolini, only seven years his senior and, like Ciaranfi, active in the local section of the Italian Socialist Party (PSI). Unlike Mussolini, however, Ciaranfi remained loyal to the PSI throughout the years of the First World War and went on to become the last democratically elected mayor of Predappio in 1920, before the advent of Fascism forced his resignation in 1922.

After a few years under the regime, however, Ciaranfi, too, underwent a conversion and joined the Italian Fascist Party. In order to make the strength of his new convictions clear, he even rewrote his will to include a codicil requiring him to be buried in a Fascist black shirt.

Later still, "after the disaster and the tragedy of war, and the failures of Fascism," runs a local history book,

Ciaranfi, good old Ciaranfi, realized he had made a serious mistake, and turned on his feet politically again, joining the Italian Communist Party (PCI). After the liberation of Predappio, he served in the administration of the first postwar democratic mayor, Giuseppe Ferlini. But those tumultuous years had no doubt radically transformed Ciaranfi's existence, like those of many other Italians, and it is probably for this reason that he forgot to rewrite his will. So, when he died in June 1948, and his testa-

ment obliged him to be buried in a black shirt, there was much conster-
nation and embarrassment among his comrades, who were expecting to
send him off draped in a red flag with "The Internationale" playing. In
the end, and not without argument, it was decided that his body would
lie in an open casket, clad in the obligatory black shirt, for a brief private
ceremony with the family, before being buried with casket closed in a
civil ceremony, complete with the PCI band and the red flag. (Capacci,
Pasini, and Giunchi 2014, 219; all translations my own)

Many of my Predappiesi friends loved the story of Ciaranfi, his multiple
switches of political allegiance, and his awkward funeral. This particular rendition of it is to be found in a collection of oral histories and historical narratives, self-published by three local residents.

The book is titled *La fója de farfaraz*, local dialect for "The White Poplar's
Leaf," which can appear to change color with the wind by quickly flipping from
one side to the other. The expression in its title is used to denote a person who is
similarly prone to change allegiances depending on convenience, and the book
itself is filled with descriptions of *voltagabbana*, or turncoats, such as Ciaranfi,
who switched sides from socialist to Fascist in the interwar period and sometimes back again afterward. Yet it is an affectionate rendering of the town's history and treats this characteristic changeability largely not as a moral failing but
as a kind of necessary and pragmatic adjustment to reality.

Despite its title, however, most of the book is actually devoted to a hagiography of one particular—and comparatively politically consistent—local hero,
one who makes a brief appearance in the story above. This hero is not Benito
Mussolini. This fact in itself makes the book rather unusual, as almost all of
the limited number of publications that make mention of Predappio relate it
primarily to its most famous son, whose ideological inconsistency we have already encountered in the last chapter (e.g., D'Emilio and Gatta 2017; Gatta
2018; Zoli and Moressa 2007).

The figure on whom the book instead focuses is a man called Giuseppe Ferlini (figure 2.1). In addition to becoming the first postwar mayor of Predappio, as
the story above notes, Ferlini was also the commander of the local partisan brigades and helped to liberate the town from the Germans and Fascists in 1944.

It is not, of course, terribly surprising to find an ex-partisan and Communist politician being lauded by those who share his political views, broadly
speaking, as many on the left in Predappio do. Yet Ferlini is the subject of almost universal admiration, regardless of one's politics. He is regularly offered
up, by those on the left and the right, as the son Predappio should be most
proud of producing, in the place of his rather more famous co-citizen.

FIGURE 2.1.   Giuseppe Ferlini. Photo reproduced with kind permission of Nicoletta and Jara Valgiusti.

This chapter pursues the theme of the previous chapter—the instrumentalization of ordinariness in Fascist thought—by connecting it to the reconstruction of Predappio. I will try to show how this process of reconstruction mirrored the mythmaking around Mussolini himself, insofar as both involved the attempt to transfigure something marked as ordinary into something marked as extraordinary. Ironically, though, many Predappiesi, the actual inhabitants of the metonym of Mussolini and the place built to exemplify his transformation from the ordinary son of a blacksmith to Il Duce of Italy, could be rather cynical about Mussolini's transfiguration, given their intimate knowledge of his early life and changes of political colors. For them, in many ways, Mussolini remained ordinary, both in the sense of being the man they had known as a boy and in the sense of being just another *voltagabbana*.

I also explore the puzzle of contemporary Predappiesi attitudes to Ferlini, and the near universal admiration with which he is viewed across the political spectrum. I suggest that the explanation for this lies in the fact that Ferlini exemplifies a particular quality that is important to life in today's Predappio: ordinariness. But this is not the putative ordinariness of Mussolini, "the man like you," in the sense conjured up by the regime as a backdrop for other qualities associated with his greatness; it is, as I will try to show, precisely Ferlini's apparently unstudied humility, "good sense," and lack of ideological fervor that Predappiesi valorize. That is because it is these qualities that mark Predappiesi visions of ordinariness today, rather than those that inspired the Fascist reconstruction project that led to the town's creation. Ferlini concretizes these qualities in exemplary fashion.

Predappio's Greatest Son

Sergio is nearly one hundred years old. He nevertheless moves easily around his small house, refusing me permission to help him pour coffee, or grappa when we talk later into the evening. He speaks clearly and precisely, and possesses an extraordinarily detailed memory and a lively wit. Born in 1921, the year Mussolini came to power, in a small hamlet attached to Predappio, Sergio attended the same high school as Mussolini in the local town of Forlimpopoli. He and his family have run a small business in the town for decades.

Sergio has had an eventful life. After school and after working at a savings institute in Predappio for a brief period, he enrolled in the army, despite being blind in one eye and thus eligible for an exception to mandatory conscription. For a while, he had the unpleasant job of notifying the families of soldiers killed in action that their children, husbands, and brothers were dead. In part to escape this task, he volunteered for the Russian front in 1941. Fortunately for him—nearly eighty-five thousand Italian soldiers died fighting or in captivity on the Eastern Front—he was posted to North Africa instead. Wounded in 1943, he followed his battalion to Tunis, where he was captured by the British when the Eighth Army took the city. He is still annoyed that the British officer who captured him took his Longines watch and suggests he will keep valuables out of reach of whichever part of me is most English.

Sergio was in a prisoner of war camp in Mississippi when Mussolini was deposed in a coup on July 25, 1943. Almost instantly, he says, the majority of Italian officers in the camp—including those who had been fervent Fascists up until that moment—converted to the Royalist cause (King Victor Emmanuel III was now putatively in control of the Italian government and would soon bring Italy over to the Allied side). Sergio was asked to renew the oath he had signed when joining the army, pledging his allegiance to the king (the implication being that Sergio's allegiance would no longer be to Mussolini). He refused.

"It was a political question," he says, "and I was a fighter, a soldier, and I had done my duty. The Americans killed five men in my platoon, and now they were on our side? It's a matter of pride. In that moment, the Americans were bombarding Predappio, so they were my friends who were bombarding my parents? I would be cheating the memory of my soldiers, of my friends and relatives who died, and I would be giving in to harassment."

He was sent to a special camp for recalcitrant Italians, where, he claims, he and his fellows were given reduced rations and implicitly threatened with execution if they did not capitulate. "Gradually people gave in. We started with maybe around two thousand people. By August we had four hundred." Sergio never signed the oath.

Pressed on why he refused to sign, Sergio would say it was a combination of factors:

There was the pride of not cheating, betraying. The belief that if I switched to the other side I would be cheating, and cheating myself too because I was a volunteer. Look, I thought, I still think—though maybe I'm wrong—that wars are supposed to be won. Yes, it's true, I had seen things, including in Predappio, some things of the regime I didn't like at all, I'd say quite plainly. But who has the right to change things in a war? And there were many good things, too, because there was respect. You know, in my elementary school there was a girl and her brother, and we called them Libero and Libera. Know why we called them that? Because their father was an anarchist, and we all knew it. The boy played soccer with Romano Mussolini. Was this persecution? So, when they tell me about Fascism—yes, it's true, there were strict laws, but at the same time, there were ways of overlooking them.

Sergio was sent home in February 1946 and came straight to Predappio. He found a town that he felt no longer looked like his own. The Caproni airplane factory that had drawn thousands to live and work in Predappio had closed, and the vast majority of the tourism that brought enormous numbers of visitors to *il paese del Duce* had largely dried up. But according to Sergio, Predappio had changed in other ways, too.

I'll tell you an example—there was a man who was the uncle of my fiancée, he was, what would you say, the president of the national commerce association, and a personal friend of Mussolini. When I came back, he had adapted. He had become a little Christian Democrat. Those who have money are always safe. At first, I do it, and then I don't do it, you see? I repeat, it was a different town. People were not the same as in the past. I remember when we declared war, they summoned the people to Piazza Sant'Antonio. It was packed. Everybody was clapping. And all the chiefs were there, the big shots. So, I come back to Predappio, and many of them are dead, of course. But those who returned . . . there was this atmosphere of treachery, and the meanest of all were those who had been the most uncompromising Fascists. He who changes his mind, I don't respect this person—he who at 6 p.m. is a Fascist and at 6:01 is an anti-Fascist.

Toward the end of 1947, Sergio founded one of the first local sections of Movimento Sociale Italiano (MSI), the successor to the Italian Fascist Party. He was beaten in the streets by political opponents, and before the 1948 elections, in which the PCI came close to victory, was told that the local PCI chapter had specified the pole from which he would be hung in the event that the elections preceded a revolution. The local police told him to keep a gun on his person at all times.

Fortunately, there were some individuals who were not like this, because in all things there is some good. Ferlini, the first mayor of Predappio, was like this. They sang songs about him then and still now, because he was a partisan. He was a good guy, a good man, an honest man. I keep recordings of those songs, you know. They call him "the liberator" in the songs. He stepped in to protect me, it's true. They ousted him almost immediately though, the ones who had been Fascists and became Communists. He, poor man, was honest, too honest. One day, after the war and after he was ousted as mayor, I was seated there, and he called me. He says to me [in local dialect]:

"Sergio, come here, I want to tell you something—I've been to visit your friends!"

So I say, "My friends? Who are my friends?"

"Fascists, like you! I'm just coming back from there, I went to see them this morning."

So, who were these guys? They were Repubblichini [Fascist soldiers of Mussolini's post-1943 regime, the Italian Social Republic], and in the war they controlled the nearby mill, and the food that local people could access. So Ferlini had a deal with them to get food for people. He told me, "My problem was not fighting. They told you I fought against you and I liberated Predappio and so on, but really my problem was to give food to people who needed it. So, with the help of the priest and these guards, we brought flour to the town from the mill."

Many other Predappiesi share this admiration for Ferlini. Elena, for example, lives in the same building as Valentina. She is middle-aged and moderately conservative in her politics, and she has very firm opinions about many issues. One of them is Ferlini. While describing her father's experiences of postwar Predappio, Elena said to me:

> Ferlini was a truly great man, and he was great in spite of his background and education. . . . He was a simple man and he became our mayor, do you see? And I believe Ferlini is Predappio's greatest son, we need to tell others about him, and how he stopped all the fighting after the war . . . and you know he washed the stairs to the town hall when he retired? But they weren't all like our wonderful Ferlini, you know, he was on the left from before, and I admire people who were consistently on the left, even if I'm not.

Sergio is an unusual man in Predappio. His military and MSI credentials mean he is one of the few inhabitants of the town—souvenir shop owners excepted—whom other Predappiesi will definitely characterize as "extreme right." Yet he, too, along with Elena, shares the authors of *La fója de farfaraz*'s admiration for Ferlini.

I want to highlight two key elements in these narratives about Ferlini because they will form this chapter's focus. The first of these elements is the suggestion that ideology was of much less importance in one of the most politically turbulent periods of Italian history than one might imagine. As in the case of Fascist ideology itself, as I described in chapter 1, Sergio and the people he describes, as well as Ciaranfi, have little time for theoretical distinctions. Nor even does the regime in his telling, allowing the children of anarchists to play football with Il Duce's son, at least in Sergio's telling. Sergio himself is fairly consistent in his adherence to some version or another of the creed he signed up to fight for in 1941, but even he has no interest in justifying this adherence with reference to ideas. His refusal to change his colors after the July 25 coup is, by his own account, more about stubbornness and a sense of loyalty to his erstwhile comrades than any feeling that there was something politically wrong with deposing Mussolini. He helped to found the local MSI chapter in part because he came to believe his military service was leading to him being passed over for jobs at the expense of the newly dominant left. As for almost everyone else in his narrative—the former Fascist "big shots," the uncle who becomes "a little Christian Democrat"—they are far less ideologically consistent than he is: they are *voltagabbana*, turncoats, of whom everybody in Predappio has their favorite story, many of which are included in *La fója de farfaraz*.

Similarly, the authors of *La fója de farfaraz* argue that adherence to Fascism in Predappio did not stem from "political debates or ideology, but from normal citizens' adjustment to the new regime. So, unlike in other areas, Fascism did not produce deep longstanding personal hatred" (Capacci, Pasini, and Giunchi 2014, 55). On local Fascists, they claim that "local anti-Fascists agree that even the most visible Fascists in Predappio did not behave badly, all things considered. Some even behaved rather well considering their role. . . . The cases of really hated Fascists are very few, and are those who were informers. In such cases the odium is really severe, as to political sins are added the betrayal of one's own community, one's own people" (53). In this last remark, the implicit hierarchy is notable: "betraying one's own community" is more serious than any "political sin."

Neither Sergio nor the authors of *La fója de farfaraz* offer up these sorts of narratives of turncoats in an attempt to make serious moral claims about the behavior of the people they describe. They would certainly agree that such behavior is less than virtuous. But their point is not that people who engage in such behavior are particularly immoral. The point instead is to puncture an appearance of special probity given off by those who proclaim strong ideological convictions. The point is not that some people are extraordinarily immoral because they are ideologically inconsistent; it is that more or less everybody is perfectly ordinarily ideologically inconsistent, including those who might appear otherwise.

The other factor that both of these divergent political narratives share, however, is a fervent admiration for Giuseppe Ferlini. How is it, then, that a man whose political life was apparently spent firmly on one side of the barricades—as a partisan commander and a Communist mayor—ends up an exemplar to both the left and the right? The answer is partly wrapped up in the issue of how a kind of anti-ideological pragmatism relates to what being an exemplar in Predappio means, as I will try to show in this chapter and as is hinted at by Sergio's description of his fraternization with Fascist soldiers. But to get to those roots, we have to first return to the creation of Predappio as it is today, a monument to the biography of its other, more controversial, famous son.

Il Paese del Duce

Mussolini took power in 1922, three years after the first meeting of the Fasci di Combattimento in Milan described in the previous chapter. In Fascist mythology, this seizure of power was a "Fascist revolution" and followed the famous March on Rome on October 28, now one of the three key anniversary dates on which tourists come to Predappio. The reality was more mundane (more ordinary, perhaps) and, as Bosworth shows, "a change in government to be achieved by negotiation at least as much as by naked violence" (2002, 528).

Almost immediately after Mussolini became prime minister, he began the process of turning Predappio into a major site of mythmaking around his personality. He paid his first ceremonial visit there as head of government on April 15, 1923, accompanied by a selection of national dignitaries. For the occasion, the town's main street was renamed in his honor (a name it would retain until the end of the war), and the house in which Mussolini was born was gifted to him, decorated with garlands and flags. Indeed, in pictures of the visit, the whole town can be seen draped in banners and decorations, with crowds of people, their right arms upraised, filling Piazza Cavour in Predappio Alta to hear Mussolini speak from a balcony. Local and national newspapers celebrated the visit with extensive coverage, and commemorative postcards were printed. Within months, reconstruction work had begun, and over the course of the next fifteen or so years, Predappio was transformed from a hamlet of a few hundred people into an entirely new town of more than ten thousand.

It was Dovia, the small hamlet down the hill from Predappio Alta—the old town of Predappio—in which Mussolini was born, that was reconstructed as what is now Predappio (or Predappio Nuova), complete with a new municipal headquarters for the *comune* (in the schoolhouse in which Mussolini's mother used to teach); an impressively sized church in the main square; a hospital; a carabinieri barracks; a post office; a primary and secondary school; the local headquarters of the Fascist youth movement and of its official trade union; a cinema; an airplane factory and flight-testing facility; extensive accommodation for associated workers; and a flagship party headquarters for the Italian Fascist Party, also designed to host visiting dignitaries.

This was a huge urban engineering project—effectively the construction of a whole new town from scratch. The reconstruction process was attended by much pomp and circumstance throughout, usually focused, unsurprisingly, on Mussolini himself. In 1925, for example, Fascist Party national secretary Roberto Farinacci and Quadrumvir Italo Balbo attended the laying of the foundation stone of a church named in honor of Mussolini's mother in the town, declaring its inauguration an occasion for a "renewed oath": "Duce, we are always at your command, in both spirit and body" (Duggan 2013, 35). The centerpiece of this visit was the installation of a commemorative plaque at the house in which Mussolini was born, declaring him a great statesman and "savior of the nation."

FIGURE 2.2. Postcard depicting Palazzo Varano, Predappio.

The new town was constructed around two main squares, both of which were dominated by Mussolini's heritage: the first framed the house in which he was born, and the second the former schoolhouse in which his mother taught, which became the town hall (figure 2.2), in front of which was created a garden with an enormous fasces made out of topiary.

The local cemetery was also reconstructed in monumental style around the tomb in which the bodies of his parents were placed (his father had died apart from Mussolini's mother and had been buried in the nearby town of Forli, until his body was exhumed and transferred to Predappio).

As Sofia Serenelli has described, as early as 1919, Predappio had been a place of pilgrimage for Fascists, but from around 1926 such pilgrimages took on a national character, regulated and organized by the state and with a certain fixed form (2013, 94). Postcards depicting Predappio during and after the reconstruction process were mass-produced and sold throughout Italy. A propaganda office was opened in the new and monumental party headquarters building in the town, tasked with the organization of local tours and the publication of guidebooks and photo albums. Predappio, in other words, was from the outset at the very heart of the project of making Mussolini into a Sorelian myth.

In chapter 1, we encountered the relationship that thinkers such as Le Bon thought should obtain between "ordinary people" and their heroic leaders. Of course, in many respects, Mussolini fits this picture perfectly. As in other totalitarian regimes, the Fascist Party and government laid a great deal of emphasis on the exemplary qualities of its leader. Christopher Duggan, in a volume devoted to the "cult of the duce" (2013), notes that the notion of Mussolini as *l'uomo della providenza* ("the man of providence") had been around since the birth of the Fascist movement in 1919. But it was in 1925, after the crisis brought on by the assassination of socialist parliamentarian Giacomo Matteotti (after whom the main street in Predappio is now named) that its development began in earnest. Several failed attempts on Mussolini's life led to his being compared to Christ in parliament, to church bells ringing across Italy, and to the pope reportedly suggesting that Mussolini was being protected by God (Duggan 2013, 37). Though this was pragmatically convenient at the time for a regime suffering from a lack of ideological coherence and buffeted by the Matteotti scandal, later essays in the same volume attest to the persistence of the cult of personality both throughout the *ventennio* and into the postwar period, and it was in service of this cult that Predappio was transfigured into Predappio Nuova.

In a certain sense, then, Mussolini acted as what anthropologists might call an "exemplar" in the Fascist moral universe, as other dictators did in other totalitarian contexts (see Heywood 2022). In her landmark essay on exemplarity, Caroline Humphrey argues that ethics and morality in Mongolia inhere primarily in the relationship between persons and exemplars and precedents, rather than in rules or customs (Humphrey 1997, 25). More recently, Joel Robbins has suggested that exemplars may more broadly function as the embodiment of particular social values (2018). Perhaps unsurprisingly, though, this literature on moral exemplarity has not been put into sustained dialogue with that on ordinariness, though both share an interest in ethics. Surely if exemplars are anything, they are far from ordinary. They are military or political leaders such as Genghis Khan or Melanesian Big Men—or Adolf Hitler, Mussolini, Oswald Mosley, or Francisco Franco, as testified to by the personality cults that sprang up around them.

What I want to suggest in this chapter, however, is that, in different and particular senses, both Mussolini and Giuseppe Ferlini constitute what we might call "ordinary exemplars." They reveal, in different ways, which sorts of visions of ordinariness as a form were at work in historical Predappio and which are at work today.

The myth of Mussolini constructed by the Fascist regime was in many ways of anything but that of an ordinary man. Nevertheless, as Simona Storchi points out in her analysis of one of the first biographies of Mussolini, written by his then-lover Margherita Sarfatti, his humble roots were an important part of this mythology (2013a, 52). This was especially true when it came to Predappio, which became itself a sort of "ordinary exemplar," as I will try to show.

Predappio was built around Mussolini's own biography, as a sort of giant, open-air museum to his early life (and to the prowess of Fascist urban engineering). Given that this early life was spent as the son of the local blacksmith and schoolteacher in comparative poverty, it was ripe for exploitation in the service of constructing Mussolini, "the man like you, with your qualities and faults, with all that goes to make up the essential elements of that special human nature that is the nature of Italians" (Sarfatti, cited in Storchi 2013a, 52). As Serenelli notes, some of the first items of propaganda based on Predappio were postcards depicting Mussolini visiting "the 'humble' grave of his mother, and surrounded by his 'own people' in front of the house in which he was born" (Serenelli 2013, 95). In his speech, quoted earlier, at the inauguration of New Predappio, Farinacci stressed "the social rank of Fascism . . . which is proletarian, and, above, all rural." This, as Serenelli describes, "was the principle characteristic that Mussolini, who strictly supervised the quantity, quality, and location of the new buildings, intended to give to his home town" (2013, 97). In 1935, Mussolini personally unveiled a plaque at the house in which his father, Alessandro, was born that claimed the site would explain "what is meant by austerity of life" (Serenelli 2013, 102). This was a comparatively rare instance of attention paid to Alessandro, however, as his life as a local socialist politician made him a less than straightforward figure for the regime to draw on. Mussolini's mother, on the other hand, an "ordinary" schoolteacher with no such political complications, was the focus of much attention, and had a church and a nursery school named after her in Predappio.

Mussolini's birth house is a particularly interesting instance of the emphasis on Mussolini's humble roots. It sits directly above the second of Predappio's two large squares and is the central vista of an elaborate ceremonial gateway. It was isolated from surrounding houses by the construction of a tree-lined avenue around it and was originally reachable from the square by walking through an arch and a gate decorated with the Fascist emblem. Serenelli describes how it was "refurbished with its reassembled 'original' furniture . . . (Mussolini's only criticism was that the mattresses on the beds should have their wool stuffing replaced with more humble corn leaves)" and that, as I noted in chapter 1, before the visit to Predappio of King Victor Emmanuel in 1938, Mussolini "ordered the removal of the huge arch over the access steps to the *casa natale* [birth house] from the market square below" because he considered it excessively ornate (2013, 97).

So, much of the specific role Predappio had to play in the creation of the myth of Mussolini was focused on his humble, ordinary origins and proletarian, antibourgeois characteristics, and Italians were encouraged to see these—literally, by coming to Predappio to look at the corn leaves in his bed—

as part of his exemplary nature. Predappio Nuova was constructed as both the paradigmatically ordinary Apennine village home of Italy's humble Duce and also as a "cathedral in the desert" (Serenelli 2013, 99), a spectacular monument to one man and to Fascist urban planning and architecture. It was thus held up as an exemplar in two key senses: first, its reconstruction and transformation from a hamlet of a few hundred people into a bustling small town of ten thousand, a gem of Fascist architecture and urban engineering, the first of the Fascist "New Towns," made it worthy of exhibition as one of the marvels of Fascist modernism, alongside the new towns of the Pontine Marshes, EUR in Rome, and so on. Second, however, this whole project of reconstruction was premised on the fact that this was the ordinary town in which the great Duce was born, and this ordinariness was crucial to the reconstruction itself.

The mythmaking focused on Predappio thus had two dimensions: on the one hand, Predappio was intended to be seen as extraordinary, a modern Fascist cathedral in a desert of small medieval villages (Serenelli 2013, 99); on the other hand, the regime's determination to immortalize Mussolini's poor peasant upbringing meant that Predappio also had to be seen as fundamentally ordinary, an Italian village like any other, with which the tourists who came to see it could identify. Under Fascism, in other words, Predappio was exemplary of both something very special (Fascist modernism) and something very typical (an average peasant life in the Romagna). Just like Mussolini himself, Predappio Nuova was ordinariness transfigured into exemplarity.

Here we see the intermingling of ordinary and exemplary life that I noted would arise in chapter 1. While for thinkers like Le Bon, the exemplary leader is distinct from "the crowd," and it is this distinction that allows him to lead them, by the time we arrive at Fascism in practice and in government, that relationship between leader and masses has become more complex. Apparently "typical," "normal," or "representative" traits were deployed by the regime—as by other populist movements (Mudde and Kaltwasser 2017, 78)—in the production of the leader as an exemplary figure. It was not that Mussolini acted as an exemplar of ordinariness as a value in itself, but that his ordinariness formed the crucial backdrop to the exemplary traits (strength of will, masculinity, vision, and so on) that made him a cult figure and thus made that exemplarity all the more striking. So, here, ordinary life as a form becomes tied up with exemplary life, rather than fully opposed to it. This intermingling is reinforced by the regime's own commentary on its relationship to ideology that I noted in chapter 1, in which it explicitly elevates the practice of "one man alone" to the level of doctrine. This relationship between ordinary and exemplary life will become still more complex as we move to contemporary

Predappio, but before doing so I want to highlight one more feature of this vision of ordinary life, one that will return us to the question of how important (or unimportant) political ideology is to it.

"Historic turncoat number one in Predappio was Benito Mussolini, Il Duce of Fascism, son of Alessandro Mussolini, anarchist socialist, and blacksmith of Dovia," note the authors of *La fôja de farfaraz* (Capacci, Pasini, and Giunchi 2014, 212). Many in the cheering crowds in Piazza Cavour on the occasion of Mussolini's 1923 visit and the regular subsequent visits knew him personally. They remembered him as the firebrand socialist of his youth. They also knew that he had had many of his old comrades from the left in the village arrested in advance of the visit so that they would not cause him any inconvenience. So, the ordinary Mussolini conjured up in Fascist propaganda did not just mean, to Predappiesi, proletarian, rural, antibourgeois, and so on: he was also the first, and the greatest, of the turncoats who fill so many narratives of these years. Just as ordinary life in early Fascist thought was opposed to ideology or theoretical distinctions, so the ordinariness of Mussolini the local son in Predappio—and ordinariness more broadly, I will argue in later chapters—continued to develop in contrast to political principle or ideology.

La fôja de farfaraz contains a number of stories of locals making their feelings on this subject clear to Mussolini himself. They may or may not be apocryphal, but they illustrate the sense of intimacy with "ordinary Mussolini" to which Predappiesi feel they are entitled. In one such story, on a visit to the town Mussolini stops a local character he recognizes from his days in the PSI to ask him what he thinks of the political situation, and the man replies (in dialect), that he has never liked the white poplar leaf (*"La fôja de farfaraz"*) and turns pointedly away from Mussolini (Capacci, Pasini, and Giunchi 2014, 203). In another, a godson of Mussolini was baptized by Il Duce himself, when he was a socialist, with the name of "Rebel." After the Lateran Pact with the Catholic Church, Mussolini tells the child's father that he must change his son's name, and the father replies coldly that since, after all, Mussolini gave his godson the first name, Mussolini had better be the one to change it (214).

These and other stories that Predappiesi tell of the occasional knowing remark directed by locals at Il Duce have the same form and purpose as the stories we met at the outset of this chapter. In a strange twist of the regime's own narrative of Mussolini, "the man like you," the point of these stories is—usually—not to blame Mussolini for no longer being a socialist, but to "ordinarify" him, to reveal him as just as human, and just as inconsistent, as everybody else, in spite of his elevated status.

While exemplarity and the ordinary come to intertwine in the development of Predappio, in contrast to the distinction between the leader and the masses we met in chapter 1, the formal contrast between ordinary life and political ideology remains constant and indeed is reinforced by local perceptions of Mussolini in his ordinary guise as the greatest *voltagabbana* of all.

In sum, here again we can see the ordinary as a form taking on special and marked characteristics and being situated in specific relations to other concepts. Mussolini and his regime instrumentalize it in opposition to Italy's existing aristocratic parliamentarian leadership, and in the service of elevating him to the status of Fascism's prime moral exemplar, the man who is always right (*ha sempre ragione*). In addition, this very ordinary exemplarity of Mussolini itself also functions recursively, as I described in chapter 1, to undercut alternative, nonordinary or nonpractical visions of politics based on principle or ideas, because its whole point is that the actions of "one man alone" are the basis for political judgment. That recursiveness is intensified and takes on a particular character in Predappio, where the inconsistency of that one man's actions was especially plain for all to see. As in the story of Ciaranfi, and as Sergio might put it, everybody had seen Mussolini wearing red at 6 p.m. and black at 6:01.

"A Practical Man of Good Sense"

In the following section, I provide a brief summary of the life of Giuseppe Ferlini, drawn from oral histories and from *La föja de farfaraz* (Capacci, Pasini, and Giunchi 2014; all translations my own). The value of this narrative lies in its status as evidence for how contemporary Predappiesi relate to a man they are much more eager to celebrate than their more famous co-citizen. It also continues the story of Predappio's recent history through the war and immediate postwar period.

Ferlini was born to a peasant household seventeen years after Mussolini, in 1910, on land owned by Sergio's family. Ferlini's father was a socialist and was on at least one occasion apparently forced to drink cod liver oil in front of his family (a traditional Fascist punishment) by the regime's thugs (Capacci, Pasini, and Giunchi 2014, 122). Giuseppe shared his father's politics, joining the underground Italian Communist Party shortly before the war, though his actual participation in its activities was limited to distributing a few leaflets to close family and friends (126). Called up to fight in 1940, Ferlini was deployed in Rovigo in 1943 when the armistice was declared and, with others of his unit and like many Italian soldiers across the country, left his battalion in order to avoid capture and imprisonment by the German army. He then made his way, by train and by bicycle, back to his home in Predappio. There, at first, he simply returned to his old trade as a cobbler (129). Soon, however, he started to believe that the fall of Mussolini could finally augur his "dream of a free Italy" (130), and Ferlini began to try to convince others around him in Predappio of this, too (including Fascist acquaintances).

In late September 1943, Ferlini made contact with local representatives of the CLN (the National Liberation Committee, an umbrella organization formed to coordinate partisan resistance to the German occupation) and, soon after, left the town for the mountains west of Predappio. Billeted with an old friend who told him, "You'll be a great leader, Giuseppe," he is said to have responded, in an early hint of the modesty for which he is now renowned, "Gianni, you are far greater than me, to take me into your house like this" (Capacci, Pasini, and Giunchi 2014, 131). In the mountains, Ferlini worked in the fields and as a cobbler by day, while in the evening he sounded out locals for potential partisan support. Thus, for a period he lived "an almost ordinary life," as he himself put it (132).

Years later, when asked by his granddaughter why he had become a partisan, Ferlini responded by recounting the humiliations and beatings meted out to his father. "And all this because Domenico [Giuseppe's father], a peasant who didn't know how to read and write, was a member of an agrarian league, with a tiny band of five or six other peasants" (Capacci, Pasini, and Giunchi 2014, 133).

In 1944, Ferlini was made a lieutenant in the Eighth Garibaldi Brigade of the partisans and put in command of around fifteen men. By this point, more and more young men from the area, having escaped from the army or from German capture, were seeking to enroll in partisan units, and it was Ferlini's task to decide who could join and who could not. He was apparently a prudent man and took some pains over the selection of recruits. This was necessary in part because some of these men were former members of the Fascist militia and Black Brigades, and among the turncoats there could also have been spies. Later in life, Ferlini would claim that these former Fascists would go on to become the most bloodthirsty of his partisans, perhaps to demonstrate the strength of their new convictions: "They always wanted to shoot things, and I'd have to keep them in check, because the most important thing we were really doing was trying to feed everybody" (Capacci, Pasini, and Giunchi 2014, 135).

Sometimes Ferlini's men would capture Fascist soldiers from the area, whereupon, so locals claim, Ferlini would give them a good telling off, threaten them with death if they were captured again in uniform, and then "send them back to their mothers at home" (137). It is also said that Ferlini came to an arrangement with the marshal of the local Fascist militia, through a priest, to the effect that Ferlini would be warned about German troop movements and patrols and could thus avoid "useless and potentially fatal" conflicts (140) and the inevitable civilian repercussions that would follow from the deaths of German soldiers. A similar arrangement—the one recounted by Sergio above—led to the provision of grain to both civilians and partisans from a local mill under the guard of the Fascist militia.

By October 1944, the front had advanced to the Romagna, and Predappio was poised for liberation. By this point, Ferlini was in command of around seventy men from the Fourth Battalion of the Eighth Garibaldi Brigade and was advancing down the Apennines from the west. By the night of October 25, they were in Predappio, though so also were German and Fascist troops still, and the town was subject to significant aerial bombardment. On the morning of October 26, Ferlini took thirty of his partisans to the Caproni airplane factory, Predappio's biggest employer, where, in its wind tunnels, he found around a thousand of Predappio's inhabitants taking shelter from the bombing. At seven in the morning, Ferlini entered the wind tunnels, saying "I'm Ferlini, Giuseppe Ferlini of Predappio, the partisan. At last you get to meet 'Ferlini the butcher' [the name Fascist authorities had given him]":

> And the people of Predappio, who had heard Ferlini declared a dangerous killer and a bandit by the Nazi Fascists, looked him in the face, knew him, and went to meet him and his men with open arms. 'It's me, it's me, Ferlini,' he said. Giuseppe Ferlini, peasant until the age of twenty-six, simple worker and artisan, anti-Fascist, Communist, and partisan fighter, became a symbolic character for the changes to come in Predappio. . . . Among those who came to him then was Augusto Moschi, one of Mussolini's closest relatives in Predappio [and known for his affiliation to the regime]. Moschi greeted Ferlini with pleasure, saying, "Come here, look at me, I've been persecuted, too!" In fact Moschi had been exiled from Predappio for a brief period by the regime, but certainly not because he was an anti-Fascist! But Ferlini accepted his greetings nonetheless. (144)

Fighting continued in Predappio for two more days, until its liberation on October 28. Local legend has it that Ferlini waited deliberately until the anniversary of the Fascist March on Rome to liberate Mussolini's hometown, but according to the authors of *La fòja de farfaraz*, the reality is that he was simply waiting for the arrival of Allied troops, being, as he was above all else, "a practical man and of good sense" (Capacci, Pasini, and Giunchi 2014, 145).

On December 9, Ferlini was declared the mayor of Predappio by the British commander of local Allied troops, with the support of the CLN and local Predappiesi dignitaries. Among his local councillors was Angelo Ciaranfi, whom we met at the beginning of this chapter, by now a member of the Italian

Communist Party. Ferlini would serve until the first postwar democratic elections were held in Predappio in 1946. The stories of his pragmatism as mayor begin almost immediately:

> In this period a number of Predappiesi Fascists were arrested and imprisoned in the Carabinieri barracks. . . . Ferlini came to them and reassured them: "Stay calm; if you haven't done anything wrong, no one will do anything to you." By this he meant that if they weren't guilty, they would be treated with respect. And so it was . . . other Fascists were in hiding, afraid of what the partisans would do to them. . . . Ferlini went to their wives and told them to tell their husbands, "If you want to eat and live in peace, you mustn't hide but come out with a shovel and a pickaxe instead, to help repair the town." Thus it was that in those days, Fascists worked alongside partisans to help repair the damage of war. (Capacci, Pasini, and Giunchi 2014, 154)

Other stories of Ferlini's postwar mayoralty reiterate this theme of pragmatic beneficence to representatives of the defeated regime. He is said to have set some of the prisoners to work moving wood into the town to keep locals warm. Among these was Mussolini's godson, Rebel, now rebaptized and a Fascist army officer, who thought himself too important to carry wood like his men. Ferlini is said to have simply smiled at him and set him to work overseeing the operation (Capacci, Pasini, and Giunchi 2014, 155). Another story relates Ferlini's visit to the former Fascist *podestà* (mayor, in effect) to request some of his cattle to feed locals. The *podestà* agrees without hesitation, afraid of repercussions, but Ferlini treats him with courtesy and pays him for the cattle from the town coffers (155). Another tells of him approaching two captured *repubblichini* and, to the astonishment of his comrades who have been screaming insults at them, offering his hand, saying, "You fought on one side, we on the other, you lost and we won, but now enough, the war is over" (158). In another story, he saves the life of a Black Brigade leader from Predappio who is set to be killed by a mob (160–161).

Another favorite theme of stories about Ferlini is his modesty and humility. One that Predappiesi enjoy telling is of his visit to Milan to see Count Caproni, the owner of the Caproni factory, in autumn 1945. Caproni is said to have lived in a splendid and large house, with a reception room complete with waxed marble floors. Ferlini, wearing, as he always did, poorly made studded boots, takes two steps into this room and immediately slips on the floor and ends up beneath the desk at which Count Caproni sits.

In the elections of March 1946, Ferlini chose—"with perfect discretion" (Capacci, Pasini, and Giunchi 2014, 164)—not to stand as a candidate for mayor:

"He wanted no public honours or payments. Perhaps he had also been some-what marginalized by some leading Communist partisans, who were upset by his magnanimity toward Fascists. Ferlini, a practical man of good sense, dedicated himself to his artisanal work and to his family" (164). The man who replaced him, ironically, was another of Mussolini's godsons from his time as a socialist. People say, as I noted of Elena earlier in this chapter, that Ferlini spent the mornings of his retirement washing the stone staircase that leads up to Predappio's town hall.

An Ordinary Exemplar

In this brief summary of Ferlini's hagiography, we meet a number of elements that recur again and again in contemporary accounts of Ferlini's exemplary status: his humble origins as a peasant and a shoemaker; his lack of ideological pretense (though a Communist, he had no real involvement in politics before the war and his justification for becoming a partisan centered on the treatment by Fascists of his even more humble father); his "good sense and practicality" as a soldier (he was focused more on feeding people than fighting and avoided armed conflict where possible); and his pragmatism and magnanimity in dealing with representatives of the regime, with whom he made deals when a soldier and whom he pardoned and "sent home to their mothers" as a mayor.

Admiration for Ferlini among contemporary Predappiesi transcends the political gulf that divides Sergio and those on the left because it does not center on his military or political abilities. One could easily imagine his celebration as the Communist equivalent of Mussolini, the heroic partisan leader, and its first post-Fascist mayor. Instead, this admiration is focused precisely on the quality I argue that Predappiesi work hard to produce: his ordinariness, as "a practical man of good sense." Yet the form this ordinariness takes, Ferlini's character as an ordinary exemplar, is not the same as that of Mussolini under the regime. Rather than act as a backdrop for other exemplary qualities, in Ferlini's case it is the value of ordinariness itself that he exemplifies.

Contemporary Predappiesi spend very little time talking about Mussolini. Aside from the special case of the souvenir shops (see chapter 5), images or mentions of him in public discourse are hard to find in the town. One or two small street signs point the way to the *casa natale* (Mussolini's birth house), but until recently it was an empty exhibition space (see chapter 4). Nothing advertises the location of the family crypt, which is why one is very likely to be stopped on the street to be asked for directions to it by visiting tourists. The only person in the town who regularly talks of Mussolini is its mayor, and that is, as the last incumbent of this position was wont to point out to me, because the mayor is obliged to do so as the public face of "extraordinary" Predappio, the man to whom the news networks and journalists go for a quotation.

Earlier on in this chapter, I argued that despite its extraordinary status, ordinariness was an important dimension of Predappio's exemplarity under the Fascist regime: Mussolini's putatively ordinary origins helped frame both him as an exemplary leader and Predappio as one of the jewels in the crown of Fascist urban engineering. While vestiges of this interest in ordinary Mussolini remain today—for instance, in a focus on "young Mussolini," when he appears in public discourse—for the most part, ordinariness has shifted in meaning and focus. What had made Predappio a positive exemplar under the regime is now what makes it a negative exemplar to many outsiders. Its spectacular appearance and extraordinary heritage are now deeply problematic, symptoms of Italy's "difficult heritage" (Macdonald 2009), not objects of pride. It is this extraordinariness that is now the backdrop to the ordinary that Predappiesi reach for in contrast to it: stories of Ferlini's pragmatism, poverty, and humility do not serve to set the stage for greatness; instead, they serve to scale him and his town down and away from grand ideological and historical narratives that focus on Predappio's relationship to Mussolini. These stories do, in short, exactly what many anthropological arguments about the ordinary and the everyday do. They concretize ordinariness in particular phenomena—nepotism, petty crime, marital disputes—or figures such as Ferlini, so as to set them against some putatively "larger" class of phenomena—politics, ideology, great men, transcendence—or figures such as Mussolini.

Ferlini, by contrast to Mussolini, is thought to be ordinary because he is humble, he is pragmatic, he lacks political ambition—because he retired to wash the town staircase. But the reason he is exemplary is that these are anything but ordinary (in the sense of "typical") characteristics in Predappio, in which ordinariness itself has come to take on a particular salience. Predappio's entire existence depends on its original mythical status as the ordinary town in which "humble" Mussolini was born, yet that same fact now marks its existence as quite extraordinary: it is a Fascist "cathedral" in a desert of medieval architecture, an island of black in the political sea of Romagnole red, and its inhabitants are habituated to outsiders defining them almost entirely with reference to the high politics and ideology of debates around Fascism, for good or for ill. In an extraordinary place, whose very urban fabric seems to demand that one take a position on Fascism, being thoroughly ordinary may itself be seen as extraordinary and indeed exemplary for this reason. Ferlini is not exemplary in spite of his ordinariness, but because of it. Again, I emphasize this is an ethnographically specific vision of ordinariness, as any will be: to be ordinary in Predappio today means to be—like Ferlini—somehow outside of and apart from ideological debates about Fascism.

Most Predappiesi take no public pride in their town's status as the birthplace of Il Duce. Neither, however, do they contest this status, for example by inhabiting the opposite pole of political exemplarity: they do not trumpet their socialist heritage any more than they do their Fascist heritage, as we will see in more detail in chapter 3. Instead, for the most part, they deal with this extraordinary heritage, their equally extraordinary place in the Italian popular imaginary, and this unique form of "cultural intimacy" (Herzfeld 2016 [1997]), by scaling themselves down, and out of history, in all the ways that they can. Ordinariness, as exemplified by Ferlini, is a prized virtue in this context.

The notion of exemplarity has been helpful to anthropologists in showing how particular values are seen to be concretized and instantiated in specific individuals and thus rendered tangible (e.g., Humphrey 1997; Robbins 2018). In my account, however, what takes the place of a value such as leadership, strength, or generosity is ordinariness, something we are more wont to think of as a given property of something or someone. Indeed, there is something unlikely about the category of the "ordinary exemplar," in that one might well assume that ordinariness should require no exemplification.

I have argued, however, that it does, and sought to describe two different instances in relation to Italian Fascism in which the ordinary and the exemplary have intersected. In the first and more straightforward case, both Mussolini's "ordinary" peasant upbringing and Predappio as an "ordinary" Italian town served to frame the work done by the regime to turn both into quite extraordinary objects of attention. Mussolini, of course, became Il Duce, the object of a cult of personality. Predappio, meanwhile, was transubstantiated into Predappio Nuova, the *paese del Duce*, rebuilt as a monument to him and to the regime's modernity.

In this first, historical case, Mussolini's ordinariness was defined by its generic nature. He exemplifies the ordinary in the sense of a general, typical, type: "rural," "impoverished," "working-class," and so on. His ordinariness in this sense is quite distinct from his exemplarity as a cult figure; it is the background against which his status as *l'uomo della providenza* emerges, rather than the cause of it.

In contemporary Predappio, however, things are somewhat different. It is impossible for locals or outsiders to take any putative ordinariness about Predappio as a backdrop for granted, because it is clearly not very ordinary at all. Its place in the popular imaginary is completely founded upon its extraordinary status as the place of Mussolini's birth and the site of his tomb, and this is constantly reinforced by Predappio's appearances in popular culture, in the press, and on television, which all tie it to this status, as do interactions Predappiesi have with outsiders, who make assumptions about them on the same basis. In this context, a sense of ordinariness takes a great deal of work to construct and sustain. One form that work takes is exemplification through the figure of Ferlini. Unlike in the historical case of Mussolini, it is precisely Ferlini's ordinariness that makes him exemplary. Here, ordinariness is a concrete value: it is not that Ferlini is exemplary because he stands for or is typical of some set of other things, but because, like Humphrey's Mongolian exemplars, he is taken to exhibit certain specific (and unusual) characteristics of ordinariness that can be drawn on by those around him, used to concretize the idea that their home—despite its history, its architecture, and its place in contemporary political polemic—is really just another ordinary Italian town, filled with ordinary Italian people. He is, in a sense, a "scaling-device" (Summerson Carr and Lempert 2016), whom Predappiesi can deploy to scale their home and themselves "down" into the everyday and out of the grand historical narratives of Fascism into which they have been unwillingly enmeshed.

I want to close this chapter by returning to the question I raised at its outset, namely the relationship between ordinariness and ideology, through one last comparison between Ferlini and Mussolini. Both Ferlini's and Mussolini's ordinary exemplarity function in opposition to ideology. Mussolini is an exemplar of ordinariness in a manner that is anti-ideological both in his self-proclaimed pragmatism and also in the sense in which Predappiesi know him concretely to be ideologically inconsistent, "historical turncoat number one." This is thus a continuation of the points I made in chapter 1 about early Fascism's framing of ordinary life as in opposition to ideology; but contextualized in Predappio, Mussolini's childhood home, that framing takes on a particular salience, because Predappiesi in the 1920s and '30s had an intimate (one might say ordinary) knowledge of just how unimportant ideology seemed to be for their socialist-turned-Fascist compatriot.

Ferlini's ordinariness is also, in some sense, opposed to ideology. This is evidenced in the fact that the ordinariness he exemplifies appeals to Predappiesi across the political spectrum; in the way in which, despite their own politics, the authors of *La fója de farfaraz* consistently downplay Ferlini's Communism; in the ways in which he himself repeatedly understates his role as anti-Fascist liberator and claims only to have been trying to feed people; in the stories people love to tell of his work rebuilding Predappio with former Fascists after the war; in the insinuation that other Communists—the implication is often that these "other Communists" are *voltagabbana*, those who switched sides and thus needed to demonstrate the strength of their convictions—punished him for this practical attitude to ideological difference.

Yet there is an obvious difference between the ways in which Mussolini and Ferlini are ordinary, as opposed to "ideological": Ferlini's pragmatism is admired, while Mussolini's is ridiculed. This is for a range of reasons. One difference is that Mussolini's pragmatism—like that of other "turncoats"—is usually cast as self-serving, in a way that is not true of Ferlini. Indeed, this is arguably another reason for Ferlini's status as an exemplar. While he is not ideologically driven, neither is he a *voltagabbana*: his "good sense" is cast as a form of moral, rather than political, consistency, directed at the well-being of his home instead of himself. Yet there is a more complex distinction at work, too, I suggest.

This difference, between Mussolini's pragmatism and Ferlini's "good sense," mirrors the distinction we met in the introduction, between "ordinary life" (the formal category, deliberately invoked) and ordinary life (the things the category is supposed to capture). Mussolini's pragmatism is not the unmarked pragmatism of "a practical man of good sense," just as invoking the notion of "ordinary life" is actually far from the realm of ordinary language; Mussolini's pragmatism is a deliberate stance. His Fascism is ideologically anti-ideological, committedly uncommitted to principle. In contrast, Ferlini is the quintessential "practical man of good sense": he has no theory for why he ought to be practical, he simply is. He is not, as it were, "a pragmatist," he is pragmatic. His lack of ideological commitment is described in a manner that leaves it unmarked and unstudied, natural rather than cultivated.

This, I suggest, is another reason why Ferlini is so easily cast as exemplary in contemporary Predappio: his ordinariness, unlike the semblance of "ordinary life" that contemporary Predappiesi reach for through him in studied and deliberate fashion, seems to take no work.

Of course, this is not really true; as we know, it takes work to do all the things that people might count as ordinary life. But that is not the same as the work Mussolini and early Fascists had to do, and the work many contemporary Predappiesi do, to pursue the form of ordinary life, in which the quality of ordinariness itself is at stake. In other words, and ironically, the very fact that Predappiesi require an exemplar of ordinariness is indicative of the chasm that separates him and them.

I hope that, by now, the historical reasons for this have become clear. Predappio's urban fabric, its economy, its ritual calendar, and its people are all inextricably tied up in a history that makes it anything but an ordinary place, a history of which its inhabitants and outsiders are fully conscious. Having described some of this history, in the next chapter I discuss some of the ways in which this life continues to intertwine with the afterlife of its most famous son.

CHAPTER 3

The "Carnival of Mussolini" and How to Pretend It Isn't Happening

In a technical sense, life under the Fascist regime ended in Predappio on October 28, 1944, when it was liberated by Allied troops of the Polish II Corps and Giuseppe Ferlini's partisans. The date is significant, for it was the anniversary of Mussolini's March on Rome in 1922, the much-mythologized occasion for the Fascist seizure of power. Some locals suggest that the occasion for the liberation was chosen deliberately (though Ferlini's biographers dispute this, as we have seen). If indeed the intention behind the choice to march into Predappio on October 28 was to give new meaning to a sacred date in the Fascist calendar, it cannot be said to have been very successful.

Today, the Sunday that falls nearest to October 28 is one of three key dates for neo-Fascist pilgrims who visit Predappio every year (the others are the anniversaries of Mussolini's death and birth, April 25 and July 29, respectively). October 28 is by far the most significant of the three and is usually the occasion for thousands of people to march from Piazza Sant'Antonio, in the center of the town, to the cemetery of San Cassiano around two kilometers away, where Mussolini is buried. After the march, they disperse to buy memorabilia in one of the three "souvenir" shops in Predappio (see chapter 5), to continue their celebrations over food at one of Predappio's restaurants, or to return home.

In this chapter, I describe the history and development of these pilgrimages, as well as the history of Predappiesi responses to them and what those responses look like today. My aim in doing so will be to show how ritual life in Predappio—structured, whether its inhabitants like it or not, around the three major Fascist anniversary days—involves the same kinds of operations of "ordinarification" we met in the case of moral exemplars in chapter 2 and of mythmaking around Mussolini in chapter 1.

These marches are in many ways the most notorious aspects of Predappio's heritage. Every year, photos of them are splashed across the pages of national and even international newspapers, and journalists and television crews from around the world come to see the "carnival of Mussolini," as some call it. It is practically impossible for Predappiesi to forget their home's history, thanks to its urban fabric, the souvenir shops on its streets, and the regular flow of "nostalgic" tourists. But on these three days in particular, it becomes even harder than usual to pretend that Predappio is just an ordinary Italian town.

As with choices of moral exemplars, opportunities for "resistance" to these rituals in Predappio abound and have abounded throughout the decades since the return of Mussolini's body in 1957. Just as one could, but few Predappiesi actually do, tell the story of Ferlini's exemplarity as the story of a noble Communist partisan celebrated for his politics and his military prowess, so one could, and some people do, tell the story of Predappiesi responses to the Fascist ritual marches as one involving at least occasional acts of heroic anti-Fascist resistance, as we will see. But the truth of the story, as in Ferlini's case, is that most Predappiesi do not attempt to "resist" the marches by fighting one kind of politics with another or by celebrating one ritual rather than another. Nor do they look back, as I will describe, on the political violence between left and right that characterized the 1960s and '70s with nostalgia for an age in which Fascists and left-wing militants fought on the town's streets. Nor do the townspeople particularly welcome contemporary initiatives from outside the town that aim to "take it back" from those who "invade" it every year in April, July, and October. Instead, Predappiesi respond to the anniversary marches much as they respond to the ways in which their home is interwoven with the biography of Mussolini and his regime: by seeking to transform something that to others appears utterly strange and extraordinary into something banal, ordinary, and everyday.

Predappiesi do so, I will suggest, by conspicuously continuing with "ordinary activities" amid the strange carnage of the carnivals of Mussolini that go on around them: they do their shopping, go to church, visit their families, and lay flowers in the town cemetery, while surrounded by marching men in black, and journalists and TV cameras trying to capture the worst of the carnival's excesses. Like a particularly condensed and concentrated version of what "normal" life is in Predappio, this takes work and effort: you have to raise your voice to order a coffee at the bar while men next to you are singing Fascist anthems; you have to shoulder your way through crowds of them at the cemetery in order to tend your parents' graves. This results, I suggest, in a curious inversion of some standard anthropological assumptions about ritual and everyday life: here it is the ritual of the "carnival of Mussolini," not everyday life, that weighs on Predappiesi in its triannual rhythm, and it is to the practices of everyday life—practiced in part precisely because they are everyday—that many Predappiesi turn for respite.

The Body of Il Duce

I have already described the extent to which Fascism as a political movement was interwoven with the character and personality of its founder and leader. This was no less true of his body, as Sergio Luzzatto has shown in detail (Luzzatto 2014). Fascist propagandists obsessed over his masculine virility and tried their best to underplay his aging and becoming a grandfather. Anti-Fascists, meanwhile, were equally concerned with his body in attempting his assassination, identifying, as Fascism did as we saw in chapter 1, the body of the man with the power of the regime (Luzzatto 2014, 13–52).

On April 28, 1945, Mussolini and his mistress Clara Petacci were shot by a partisan firing squad outside the gates of the Villa Belmonte, having been captured trying to flee to Switzerland the day before. The next day their bodies were dumped in Milan's Piazzale Loreto along with those of other executed Fascists. The choice of location was deliberate: Fascists had executed fifteen partisans in Piazzale Loreto in August 1944 and left their bodies in the square as a warning to others. After being similarly dumped without ceremony in the midst of a crowd in the square, Mussolini's corpse was strung up, upside down, from a gas station roof, as masses of people thronged to see the proof of his death and to visit their own minor punishments on his remains.

The black-and-white pictures of Mussolini on display in Piazzale Loreto are the most famous image of the fate of his body and served as a rallying cry for the Italian left for some time afterward. Yet the strange story of Mussolini's body only begins in Piazzale Loreto. It would end, in some respects at least, twelve years later, when the remains were returned to the Mussolini family crypt in Predappio.

After being displayed in Piazzale Loreto, Mussolini's corpse was buried in secret in an unmarked tomb in Milan's Musocco cemetery. Luzzatto claims the only attendant ceremony was a group of partisans dancing on top of his grave (2014, 82). The secrecy attending the burial was clearly rather less than absolute, however, because shortly thereafter, the location of the body became known to a young neo-Fascist and member of the "Democratic Fascist Party [sic]," an underground reincarnation of Mussolini's Italian Fascist Party (PNF). On the day after Easter Monday, April 23, 1946, Mussolini rose again: along with two collaborators, Domenico Leccisi broke into the Musocco Cemetery under cover of night and stole Mussolini's casket, leaving a statement from the Democratic Fascist Party in its place. For three hundred days, the body remained missing and the subject of intense public speculation, eventually turning up in a monastery outside Pavia, where it had been taken by a Franciscan Abbot to whom Leccisi had entrusted it. To get the body back, the Milanese chief of police had to agree to provide it with a Christian burial, so it was subsequently interred in a different convent, Cerro Maggiore near Milan.

Religious ritual focused on Mussolini's body began even in its public absence, and indeed Leccisi's escapade is a testament to the continued power Mussolini's body exerted over his neo-Fascist inheritors. Secret masses were held on the anniversary of his death, with the ones in Rome 1947 drawing so many people that the police became involved (Luzzatto 2014, 147). In Predappio, one local amateur historian told me that people remember flowers appearing at the Mussolini family crypt as early as 1946. In 1950, a campaign was started called "Buried in Italy," in which a substitute tomb for Mussolini was supposed to be created in each and every Italian town and city (149). Later in the decade a "spiritual confession" emerged, purporting to be written by Mussolini shortly before his death and attesting to the strength of his Catholicism at the time, though most historians consider it to be a fake (125).

Meanwhile, in May 1957, Predappio achieved the notable distinction of seeing a second of its native sons elected prime minister of Italy. Adone Zoli's family were landholders in Predappio; Mussolini's father-in-law had worked on these lands, his wife was born on them, Zoli's own family tomb is just a few yards from the Mussolini crypt in the local cemetery, and I have toured the old family wine cellar beneath one of the town's restaurants.

Zoli's Christian Democrat government of the time was extremely precarious. To survive, it required the parliamentary deputies of the Movimento Sociale Italiano (MSI) not to vote it down, thus obliging a democratic government to come to some agreement with the neo-Fascist contingent in parliament for the first time since the war. Ironically, the deciding vote in parliament fell to Domenico Leccisi, who had first been elected as an MSI deputy but then left the party as it attempted to make itself more respectable.

As part of the deal with the MSI, Zoli agreed to have Mussolini's remains reburied in the family crypt in Predappio. A story contemporary Predappiesi love to tell is of Zoli telephoning the then-mayor of Predappio, Egidio Proli, to ask his permission for the reburial. "He didn't scare us when he was alive," Proli is alleged to have responded, "so why should he scare us now that he's dead?"

On August 30, accompanied by a substantial police escort and some of the monks from the Capuchin convent in Cerro Maggiore, Mussolini's body arrived back home. Also awaiting his return were the national press corps and a small group of family members and devotees, who were photographed giving the Fascist salute at the cemetery.

Just a week later, three and a half thousand neo-Fascists turned up on Sunday to pay their respects, with several arrested by the local police for making the same salute. A week after that, a further seven thousand arrived. The police forced anyone wearing a black shirt to take it off, leaving the cemetery full of men in undershirts (Luzzatto 2014, 213). Egidio Proli may or may not have been afraid of Mussolini, dead or alive, but Predappio was certainly not prepared for the impact the posthumous return of its most famous son would have on its future.

"Di Chi Vegna"

In 2017, tensions had been running high in the region for some time in regard to Predappio before October 28, largely due to heated debates that had been taking place over the proposal to build a museum in the town's former Fascist Party headquarters, the Casa del Fascio, debates that I discuss in chapter 6. A large number of prominent local politicians, dignitaries, and intellectuals had taken one position or another regarding this proposal (or one position after another, in some cases), and much discussion was taking place over exactly where various people and organizations stood.

The Associazione Nazionale Partigiani d'Italia (ANPI) is the largest and most politically powerful of a number of organizations that represent partisan veterans from the Second World War. Formed in 1945 and originally intended to act on behalf of partisans from a range of different political formations (Communist, Catholic, Liberal), ANPI soon became much more closely affiliated with the powerful Italian Communist Party and has since remained firmly on the left of the political spectrum. ANPI now admits members of any age, provided they are willing to declare themselves to be anti-Fascist and in agreement with the organization's aims. Today the majority of its membership consists of younger volunteers, with fewer than 10 percent being veterans of the war. Its lobbying power continues to be substantial, though; for example, it was credited with playing a considerable part in the defeat of former prime minister Matteo Renzi's proposals for constitutional reform in a 2016 referendum.

After a period of vacillation and internal discussion between its national and local leadership, ANPI would come out in opposition to the Casa del Fascio project in December 2017, but already by October its provincial chapter, based in the nearby town of Forlì, had decided that some display of anti-Fascist sentiment in Predappio was important in light of the town's ubiquity in the media.

So, on Saturday, October 28, 2017, Predappio—or, more precisely, the provincial chapter of ANPI, in Predappio—hosted an event in celebration of the anniversary of the town's liberation, for the first time in living memory, as far as I could discover. The plan settled upon was to hold a series of speeches and musical performances in the local cinema, before moving to the local left-wing social club (Casa del Popolo) for dinner, and so the evening was entitled a "Tagliatella anti-Fascista." Even the planning for this event had already caused some degree of controversy, however: the original scheme had been for the music to take place outside in a public square, but ANPI was strongly advised by local and provincial authorities that this would risk problems of public order, given the likely presence of visiting neo-Fascists that same weekend, and so agreed to move the event indoors.

I arranged to attend with my friend Carlo, the technical director of Predappio's Casa del Fascio project. Carlo is a tall man with slightly wild, Albert Einstein–like hair and a quiet demeanor that conceals a sharp mind and deep-seated political convictions. His biographical relationship to Predappio is rather singular and begins with another calendrical irony: October 28 is also his birthday.

Carlo was born, like most of my own family, in the nearest town to Predappio, Forlì, in 1950. He became politicized, like many other young Italians, in 1968 and was a leading member of the Forlì section of Lotta Continua, a famous left-wing extraparliamentary autonomist movement led by Adriano Sofri. Though at first Carlo's Lotta Continua group paid little heed to the local neo-Fascists of 1968, things changed in 1969 when a bomb exploded in a bank in Piazza Fontana, Milan, beginning more than a decade of political violence in Italy that came to be known as the "years of lead." The bombing has been the subject of three separate trials, the first identifying anarchists as the culprits and the second and third neo-Fascists. Sofri, the leader of Lotta Continua, would later be convicted of inciting the murder of a police officer who was himself suspected of murdering an anarchist in the course of interrogating him over the bombing (this latter murder was then famously dramatized by the Nobel laureate Dario Fo as *Accidental Death of an Anarchist*). Though no trial has produced a clear result in the Piazza Fontana case, it remains a widespread and credible belief in Italy that neo-Fascists, with the possible collaboration of elements within the

Italian state, were responsible for the bombing, and in its wake "Fascism" suddenly became a critical political rallying call for young people like Carlo on the left. With the specter of Fascism awoken, the nearby town of Predappio also became, unsurprisingly, the focal point for a series of clashes between neo-Fascists and militants such as Carlo.

Things came to a head a few years later in the spring of 1971, when local media reported plans for a large neo-Fascist gathering in Predappio. Carlo and his Lotta Continua group, urged on by other extraparliamentary movements, planned a national counterdemonstration in the town on the anniversary of Italy's liberation, to which two hundred or so militants came. Carlo chose as the title for their demonstration a phrase in local dialect (*di chi vegna*) that can be roughly translated as "bring it on." Carlo and his men took the same route Predappio's contemporary visitors take, marching from the square to the cemetery, where they had a violent encounter with a party of neo-Fascists that ended with the latter's ejection from the town.

This was on April 26, the anniversary of Italy's liberation. April 28 is the anniversary of Mussolini's death, and so three days later neo-Fascists came to Predappio again, only this time they came in force. They launched a planned assault on the Casa del Popolo, the same building in which Carlo and I would eat our "anti-Fascist pasta" forty-six years later. At the time of the attack, there were only seven or eight elderly locals inside, who nevertheless managed to fight off their aggressors, but not before arranging a rematch later that day at the Rocca delle Caminate, Mussolini's old summer retreat on the hill above Predappio (and, so some claim, the site of the first government meeting of the Republic of Salò), where his widow, "Donna" Rachele, as she is often called, still owned a restaurant. Such was the anger at the attack on the old men in the Casa del Popolo that around three hundred people turned up at the Rocca, from Predappio and farther afield, to fight the neo-Fascists. In Carlo's recollections, Rachele Mussolini's restaurant turned into something like the scene of a Western movie, complete with flying bricks and glasses. The restaurant has never opened again since. Most of the Fascist contingent had to be taken to hospital by police, where they were beaten up again as soon as their escort had disappeared. They retaliated later by bombing Lotta Continua's Forlì headquarters. Later still, someone else set off a small bomb in the Mussolini family crypt itself.

People in Predappio have different memories of this period, though all are united in describing it as a contested and violent time in Predappio's history. Ivo Marcelli, mayor of Predappio in the 1990s, told me he remembered the 1970s as a decade of beatings, roadblocks, and raids every weekend. Like Carlo, Ivo thought it was all necessary to send a message to the Fascists that their violence was not welcome. Franco, however, an entrepreneur who sat on the local council during this period, describes Lotta Continua and the Fascists as "idiots on one side and idiots on the other":

> I mean, there were those two factions that had nothing to do with the real world. When they put the bomb in the tomb, there was a city council meeting, four hundred people came to the meeting who wanted to reopen the tomb, nobody was of the right wing, very few of them. They were just working people who understood that there was damage and tourists wouldn't come. A member of the MSI [Movimento Sociale Italiano—a reincarnation of the Fascist Party], Sergio Moschi [kin to the Fascist Moschi who greeted Ferlini at the liberation of Predappio—see chapter 2] intervened and said, "Let's keep the tomb closed—he fed us for so many years when he was alive, do you want him to feed us even when he's dead?" The situation was strange: the left wing wanted to reopen it, and the right wing wanted to keep it closed.

But Franco also remembers the attack on the Casa del Popolo as a moment of unity: "Everybody mobilized, even people who were not left-wing or anti-Fascist. When they beat those old men, the whole town united." To Franco, then, the politics that inspired both neo-Fascists and left-wing militants were redundant, detached from "the real world." Beating up somebody's grandfather, on the other hand, was something everybody—setting aside their politics, in some cases—could unite to oppose and punish.

Giorgio Frassineti, mayor of Predappio from 2009 to 2019—and thus during much of my fieldwork—remembers Predappio in the 1970s as a "militarized town," with armored police appearing on the streets periodically and his parents afraid of letting him play outside. Giorgio, like every other postwar mayor of Predappio until 2019, is from the party of the left, but he does not share Carlo's nostalgia for the violence of the 1960s and '70s: "I met this guy a few years back, a big Lotta Continua guy from Milan, who says to me with pride, 'Yeah, I remember Predappio, I came to fight there.' And I thought, 'Wow, thanks: you came to my town to play war so I couldn't go outside to play football.'"

The 1970s were a decade of political turmoil more broadly in Italy, and Predappio was a unique context for simmering tensions to boil over. But both nationally and locally these tensions would ease by the beginning of the 1980s. The centenary of Mussolini's birth was 1983, and a very large gathering of neo-Fascists was expected to mark the July anniversary in Predappio. Despite the fears of some locals, the event passed without violence and is widely credited with ushering in a new era of peaceful—if still distasteful, for many—"nostalgic" tourism. The only interruption of this peace that I have heard discussed was an occasion in the 1990s, amid internecine disputes within the far right over the move toward the center of Alleanza Nazionale (AN; the inheritor of the MSI), in which Domenico Leccisi—then still living and still firmly opposed to any form of "defascistization"—is supposed to have punched an AN parliamentary deputy in the face during one of the anniversary marches.

Meanwhile, an illicit trade in Fascist souvenirs had sprung up in Predappio to serve the visiting tourists. Mostly this was men selling antique postcards out of the back of their cars in the cemetery parking lot, but throughout the 1980s it grew to include food and wine stamped with Mussolini's face. In the early 1990s, Ivo gave a license to open a print shop to a man who would go on to become one of the biggest entrepreneurs of the so-called souvenir trade: "The problem is, this kind of license allows other things. From the very first day they started selling souvenirs. I went to the police and the prefecture, and I told them what was happening, and they said, 'Mayor, you're worrying for nothing, let them do it, they're doing no harm . . . and aren't you interested in making some money?'"

Ivo remembers his decision with some regret for its unintentional consequences, and Carlo remembers it with anger: "They were so stupid not to understand that the shops would come to be important for far more than just economic reasons."

Carlo himself had more or less left the world of politics when Lotta Continua dissolved in 1976. He had become a cultural operator of sorts, helping to organize conferences, exhibitions, and concerts across the region, developing a reputation as a successful manager of such projects. He continued to follow news and developments in Predappio, including the periodic resurgence of debates over what to do with various neglected buildings in the town. He knew Giorgio before he was elected mayor of Predappio in 2009, and when Giorgio ran for reelection on a platform including the Casa del Fascio project, he recruited Carlo as the project's technical director. So, forty-five years after his battles with neo-Fascists in the town, Carlo returned to Predappio to live and work. Now, however, he was fighting battles on two fronts: with the "nostalgic" tourists he still despised but also with his erstwhile friends from the left, who came to Predappio on October 28, 2017, in part to signal their opposition to the Casa del Fascio project he led.

Anti-Fascist Pasta

I arrived with Carlo by car that day, and as we drove down Predappio's main street on our way to the ANPI event, it was clear that some people had already

FIGURE 3.1. ANPI's national vice president speaks. Photo by author.

arrived in the town for a very different purpose. Groups of men dressed in black wandered between the souvenir shops and greeted one another in advance of their own anniversary celebration, which was scheduled for the following day. We turned off the main street and parked near the cinema, in front of which was gathered another kind of crowd. The color black was still in evidence but far less dominant, and a number of people sported red handkerchiefs around their necks. There were also considerably more women present, and three police cars were parked in front of the cinema. Inside, Giorgio was giving a speech, one with which I was more than familiar, as it was his standard media pitch in defense of the Casa del Fascio project: Predappio, as he liked to put it, was "the Chernobyl of history," a town suffering unjustly from *damnatio memoriae*, and as a consequence of this silence about its history and the history of Fascism there were young men wandering around outside in black shirts; "culture" and "education" were the answer to this problem, and these were what his vision of the new museum would provide.

Giorgio was followed by ANPI's national vice president (figure 3.1) and by Miro Gori, the president of its provincial chapter, who had organized the gathering. Miro spoke warmly of the continued need for anti-Fascist vigilance and then—somewhat less warmly—thanked Giorgio for hosting them, before making clear that ANPI's position on the museum was that it needed to take a much clearer line on the evils of Fascism.

Carlo and I greeted some acquaintances from Forli outside the cinema, as the band struck up and a choral group from Bologna began singing partisan songs. Many of those who had come were prominent opponents of the museum project, and discussion turned swiftly to the speeches, as a few people complained that Giorgio only ever said the same thing and never bothered to address any of their criticisms. The discussion was not especially friendly. Carlo had known many of these men for decades, having worked with them in Lotta Continua in the seventies; the Casa del Fascio project had produced a significant political rupture, however, and though they spoke politely together, they no longer saw one another much socially. While we stood and talked, one younger ANPI member told me the story of how in the 1970s, his Communist father would lock him in his room and tell him, "Do your homework. I have to go to Predappio to beat up the Fascists."

We soon moved to the local *circolo* (the site of the neo-Fascist attack in 1971) for some anti-Fascist pasta, and I sat, amid around a hundred others, with Giorgio, Carlo, and two other members of the local council. Giorgio was clearly uncomfortable and ill at ease—except when being interviewed by a German documentary crew who were making a film about Predappio.

Though the evening broke up with backslapping and apparent geniality and without any encounters with the black-shirted visitors outside, I had the strong sense throughout that nobody present that night really wanted to be there. Visitors I spoke with from ANPI and other left-wing groups felt as though they had entered a foreign country, and the sooner they could leave, the happier they would feel. Meanwhile, Giorgio and his local entourage were hosting them on sufferance and out of obligation and resented their visitors for the sense of moral superiority they brought with them. Some of these sentiments would spill out into the open the following year, when, to Giorgio's fury, ANPI refused him permission to speak at the same event.

Back in 2017, on the day after ANPI's event, I arrived in Piazza Sant'Antonio early in the morning to find it was already teeming with men (and some women) in black, some holding flags with Celtic crosses and fasces on them. Later estimates would put the number of people at around three thousand. A few carabinieri vans were parked in the square as well, and officers stood around them, talking and watching the crowd. Giorgio has told me with a knowing nod that another group of people who descend on Predappio on October 28 are Italian secret service agents, who are quite happy to find a whole host of people in whom they are interested gathered in the same place. That day I found Giorgio himself almost immediately—he was fairly easy to make out in a bright white shirt amid all the black—and we strolled up to the town hall together to get a more expansive view of the crowd. He told me it takes him a week to recover emotionally from this event, though he seemed focused on checking the opinion pages of various newspapers for their responses to his speech from the day before. I asked whether he could see any locals in the crowd, and he shook his head emphatically, barely even looking up: "There are no Predappiesi here," he said definitively.

The marches begin with a crowd that gradually coalesces in Piazza Sant'Antonio, the square that hosts Predappio's church and the former Fascist Party headquarters building and sits beneath the town hall (figure 3.2). The theoretical start time for the march is 9 a.m., but in the several years I have witnessed it, it has never begun before 10:30, and most of the early hours are spent with people aimlessly milling around, sitting in bars and drinking coffee, and taking photographs, until eventually a loose sort of cortege is formed out of the mass of people. There are usually a few men present wearing tricolor armbands whose job it is to corral the visitors into something resembling the right shape for a march, but beyond this they take no particular leading role. At the head of the cortege walk the most enthusiastic of the visitors; these are almost all men (unless a female member of Mussolini's family is present). They usually carry a range of wreaths that they will go on to place on Mussolini's tomb, or wave Italian flags or flags with a Celtic cross, which has become symbol of the far right across Europe (see Shoshan 2016) (figure 3.3). Almost all will be in some sort of uniform, either in all black clothes or in a Fascist military or party uniform of some sort (figure 3.4). Throughout the cortege will be various banners, more Italian flags, and placards with political slogans printed on them; these are rarely overtly pro-Fascist slogans, but more often calls to be proud of Italy's history or attacks on censorship. Not all such slogans are quite so anodyne, though. In 2018, the national and international press focused their coverage of Predappio on a prospective parliamentary candidate for the far-right Forza Nuova who was wearing a T-shirt she had printed with a mock-up of the Disneyland logo, but with Predappio's skyline and the word 'Auschwitzland' printed below. She seems to have thought this an attempt at humor, but it earned a public rebuke from the Disney Corporation and condemnation in the Italian parliament and senate.

The marchers proceed along the road from Piazza Sant'Antonio to the cemetery of San Cassiano, where they gather in the large parking lot immediately outside it for brief speeches in celebration of Mussolini, punctuated by Roman salutes from the crowd (all illegal, strictly speaking—see Heywood 2019). Afterward, a sort of flag-bearing guard of honor is formed along the pathway to the Mussolini family crypt, and visitors queue up to descend into it to leave a wreath, flowers, or a message in the visitors' book (figure 3.5.).

These days, that is mostly the end of things, as the era of violent clashes with the left is gone. Most of the marchers return to the town in straggling

FIGURE 3.2. Marchers begin to arrive. Photo by author.

FIGURE 3.3. The march begins. Photo by author.

FIGURE 3.4. Uniforms on display. Photo by author.

FIGURE 3.5. At the cemetery. Photo by author.

groups, perhaps stopping to eat at one of its few restaurants, before heading home, as there is very little else for them to do. I have been told that a very hardcore group of attendees is hosted for lunch at the nearby Villa Carpena—which I describe in the next chapter—but nobody I knew in Predappio knew much about this or expressed any interest in it.

The marches in Predappio have a particular place in the galaxy of contemporary neo-Fascist Italian politics. They are primarily associated with Forza Nuova, a direct descendant of Mussolini's PNF. Forza Nuova emerged as a political force in Italy in the early 2000s, having splintered off from Fiamma Tricolore, itself the product of a sectarian split within the MSI over the centerward drift of Alleanza Nazionale. Forza Nuova was founded by Roberto Fiore—presently the party leader and an erstwhile Member of the European Parliament—and Massimo Morsello (who died in 2001), two former members of violent far-right activist groups from the 1980s who were alleged to have played a part in the bombing attack on a Bologna train station in which eighty-five people died. Both of them spent time in exile in the United Kingdom after warrants were issued for their arrest, but returned to Italy in the late 1990s. Since its founding in 1997, Forza Nuova has failed to elect a single representative to either of Italy's houses of parliament, but it is among the most prominent of Italian neo-Fascist political groupings and is linked to other European far-right movements such as Hungary's Jobbik and Greece's Golden Dawn. Members of the group are known to have taken part in violent criminality, and in 2021 they were in the news for rioting against compulsory COVID vaccination certificates.

Forza Nuova differs somewhat from another of Italy's most well-known extreme-right political parties, CasaPound, named for poet and Fascist sympathizer Ezra Pound, and the object of a fascinating ethnography by Maddalena Grettel Cammelli (2015, 2017). CasaPound began life as a social movement, rather than a political party; it was founded by a far-right activist called Gianluca Iannone, who had once been jailed for punching a policeman at a march in Predappio. Today, however, Iannone and CasaPound have distanced themselves from those they call the "clowns" who come to Predappio, with one leading CasaPound member describing the marchers as "monkeys trained by anti-Fascists" (La Repubblica 2018). They have set themselves in opposition to what is perceived to be Forza Nuova's more conservative, nostalgic politics and cast themselves as "third millennium Fascists," inspired more by Fascism as a style of life than an ideology or a specific historical period. As we will see, this perception of the marches in Predappio as "clownish" and "folkloristic" is not confined to CasaPound alone. Indeed, Italy's government at the time of writing is led by the Brothers of Italy, a cousin of Forza Nuova formed mainly by former members of Alleanza Nazionale. Its leader, Giorgia Meloni, has been careful to separate herself from Predappio's visitors, declaring the marches "politically something very distant from me in a very significant way" (ANSA 2022).

I left Giorgio to his newspapers and followed the marchers along the route to the cemetery. On the way I found Sergio, whom we met in chapter 2, sitting in a chair outside of the gas station he owned, watching the crowd go by. I greeted him and he responded, asking politely after my work. I asked him what he thought of the march—given his background in the MSI—and he made a face, saying, "This isn't my sort of thing at all. If you have strong political opinions, that's fine, but live by them on your own, keep them to yourself. You don't need to do all of this to make your point."

October 28, on which fall these two anniversaries with very different connotations and during which two very different sets of people make their presences felt to the inhabitants of this tiny Apennine town, nicely encapsulates some of the contradictions that characterize both contemporary Predappio and its history. There are literally two Predappios, one old and one new, one high and one low; but more than this, Predappio is also a place in which two opposite poles meet—again literally, as on this weekend and other similar occasions, but also symbolically—and, depending on one's perspective, clash or blend. To their participants, an anti-Fascist pasta dinner and a march to commemorate Fascism's one-time triumph could not have been more distinct from each other, heirs to the time when the two sides would physically clash in the town; but to many Predappiesi, they were in some senses two similar incursions into their ordinary life, distinguished by their scale and, sometimes, by the color of the clothes on display.

The Carnival of Mussolini

It would be easy to cast Predappio and its inhabitants as unfortunate victims of history and the fetishes of the far right, and in many respects they are exactly that. Carlo would make this point to me forcefully by calling Predappio an "abandoned place," gesturing to the same images of desolation called up by Giorgio in his favorite Chernobyl analogy. On this view, Predappio has been deliberately forgotten by most of Italy, left in embarrassment to its fate in the dustbin of history along with those who march in its streets. The implication here is that there is a certain convenience to Predappio's existence as a kind of "Fascist parenthesis," as if by condensing Italy's Fascist heritage and depositing it in a single place, the rest of the country will somehow escape its taint. This is a travesty, to Carlo, because Predappio is not just a sad monument to the nation's shameful past but a living place with real inhabitants, people like Valentina, who do not deserve to meet neo-Fascists on the streets while they do their shopping. Carlo's political passions have evidently been tempered by the years, but he remains sincerely anti-Fascist in his convictions, and it is clear that he feels that Predappio's fate is an injustice to its inhabitants. "Where are they?" he would ask rhetorically of the regional left. "Why aren't they here? They never come. Predappio is an hour's drive from Bologna [the pride of the Italian left] but you never see them here." He was particularly frustrated by the friends of his youth and others on the left who were happy to speak up in opposition to the Casa del Fascio project but unwilling to show their faces in Predappio or to do anything else to rescue the Predappiesi from their plight beyond staging anti-Fascist pasta evenings.

But this narrative of a left-wing heart beneath Predappio's Fascist skin does have its limits. We have already met them in some of the memories Predappiesi themselves have of the 1960s and '70s, when Carlo and other outsiders would come to Predappio to fight off the visiting neo-Fascists. It is very easy for an outsider to imagine—and perhaps to sympathize with—the intentions of Lotta Continua and other such groups in these endeavors. But many Predappiesi, like Franco and even Giorgio, an erstwhile Communist politician, remember these visits as traumatic incursions, not heroic rescues. Suddenly their home was not only a pilgrimage site for one political extreme but also a battlefield, thanks to the other. Predappiesi themselves seem to have taken little to no part in the fighting, hiding out at home instead and waiting for things to die down. The only exception to this, so far as I can gather, was the battle at the Rocca delle Caminate, and this, as we have seen, was prompted largely not by political feeling but by anger at the beating of elderly locals—not outsiders—by neo-Fascists. Giorgio sums up local attitudes to this period neatly in his anecdote about meeting the old Lotta Continua militant: like any ordinary Italian boy, all he wanted to do was play football, not look through his windows at the armored police cars outside.

As we have seen already in this chapter, this feeling of resentment at the hyperpoliticization of their home—as if it were not politicized enough to begin with—continues today. The ANPI event I have described, billed as a modern-day liberation, a re-creation of the partisan victory over Fascism, and composed of many of the people who came to Predappio with Carlo in the 1960s and '70s, was not attended as far as I could tell by a single local resident, beyond the councillors present as somewhat uncomfortable guests. At the anti-Fascist dinner afterward, it was as if a bubble enclosed us at the table; all around there was singing, cheering, embracing, people moving between friends, and in the midst of this our table sat quietly, no one approaching, its own little dark parenthesis amid a sea of partisan red. At one point, one of the local officials present turned to me with a look of disgust on his face and said, sotto voce: "These people come here once a year and think they can teach us about democracy, and then they go home and leave us to deal with the guys who'll come tomorrow. Look around you—the people on this table are the only people present who are actually from Predappio. This is practically colonialism." I asked him whether he felt the same way about the black-shirted *nostalgici* who would arrive the day after, and to my surprise he told me that he thought these visitors were worse: "At least the *nostalgici* don't come here because they think they can teach us anything."

So, while it is no doubt true that Predappio constitutes a sort of island, abandoned to history by a long succession of Italian governments without the willpower or the inclination seriously to confront Italy's Fascist heritage, it is not the case that its inhabitants seek refuge or liberation in some other, more palatable form of ritual politics. Anti-Fascism has always been a potential source of solace for Predappiesi, and some few have embraced it. But the majority have found alternative solutions to their problem, ones involving, not a different form of political ritual, but an attempt to escape from it as far as possible altogether.

No one I have ever met in Predappio has anything positive to say of the Fascist ritual marches or attends them. Even Sergio, as we have seen, whose politics are far to the right of most Predappiesi, sits and watches them go by with disapproval. Those more politically moderate remember with pleasure how, when tensions were running high in the 1960s and '70s, they would deliberately misdirect anyone dressed in black asking for directions to the tomb. Valentina, whom we met in chapter 1, is offended by their use of Christian symbols: "They come with wooden crosses, but it was him [Mussolini] who put us on the cross! It makes the blood boil in my veins." Elena, whom we met in chapter 2, along with many others, dislikes the ways in which they behave in the cemetery: "Three days each year they come and cause chaos in the cemetery, among the dead who should be respected." Many object to the presence of uniforms or overt Fascist paraphernalia. Angela, a middle-aged woman who owns a small café in the town, remembers tanks and soldiers in the streets every weekend in the 1970s and being kept at home by her parents: "It was so annoying, such a pain in the ass. . . . Those people [neo-Fascists] would deliberately provoke violence. Like, they'd go into the Casa del Popolo and order a *black* coffee very loudly. My parents would say, 'Stay home, the bad people are coming again,' because we lived near the cemetery, too. And I just wanted to go out and play. They should have just made his [Mussolini's] body disappear."

Despite the economic benefits she might accrue from tourism as a café owner, Angela retains her disgust at those who come for the marches:

> I try not to look at them because it makes me angry. One of the ritual days, I was sitting with some friends outside my café, and this man arrives. He's a dwarf and old, over sixty, and he's dressed in the uniform of the Balilla [Fascist Youth Organization], shorts and all! And he gives the Roman salute to everyone and clicks his heels, and says "We will be back!" Normally I'm very respectful to the elderly and disabled but that time I couldn't contain myself. I said, "You should be grateful they're gone, what do you think they would have done to you? You'd have been the first to die, and where would you have come back from then?"

Massimo is another restaurateur, originally from Forlì, the owner of a surprisingly grand and rather chic eating house on the road from the town to the cemetery. Because of its proximity to Mussolini's tomb, Massimo's restaurant takes in considerable trade from the tourists who visit the tomb, and unlike Angela, he has no intention of turning this trade away. He takes bookings for coach parties months in advance of October 28 and remembers his shock when ten thousand people descended on the town that day the first year in which he opened. "They all ask me, 'Which side are you on? Are you one of us, comrade [*camerata*—the regime's preferred form of address]?' Obviously, I just grin and bear it. 'Yes of course!' I say, but only because I can't say no."

Massimo is an outsider, having been born and brought up in Forlì, and unusual in his willingness to pay lip service to his customers' ideology, but his generally pragmatic outlook is typical, in spite of the equally widespread distaste and dislike of the ritual marches. As we saw with Mussolini himself in the last chapter, the most characteristic Predappiesi response to the marches is simply to ignore them as far as is possible. This is true for most of the year, in which they are simply not discussed, even in the run-up to the anniversaries when the press is, in any year, full of speculation about what outrage to public decency will take place in the town.

Predappiesi are prepared for the questions of outsiders like me and naturally unsurprised to find the marches are an object of extreme curiosity. Predappiesi are fully aware of the extraordinary status of their home as far as the rest of Italy is concerned. Nobody is under any illusions about whether or not the sight of a dwarf in a Fascist youth uniform is an ordinary occurrence. In response to questions, Predappiesi will likely express some sense of disapproval or dislike of the continued existence of the marches. They may well also recall the violence and chaos of the 1960s and '70s as a time in which the ritual marches made a real difference to their lives. But they will usually do so in order to draw a contrast between the past and the present: then, the marches were a serious inconvenience because of the associated violence and public disorder (not because of their political implications); now, the typical Predappiesi response to the marches is to treat them as a joke and a minor inconvenience, at worst, as if an English village were temporarily occupied by an army of Morris dancers.

Angela's story of the dwarf in the Balilla uniform is characteristic. Even more so is the idea that the ritual marches constitute a sort of "carnival," a typical feature of life in Italian towns and villages. "Folkloric" is another ubiquitous term locals use to describe the neo-Fascist marches. Gianni, a well-known local artist in Predappio, put it this way: "It's just like a carnival: instead of being in the Carnival of Viareggio [a well-known event in the adjacent region of Tuscany], we're in the carnival of Mussolini. Let them be and they'll just go home afterward. They're ridiculous: forty-year-old kids dressed up as senior Fascist officers."

The carnival is a particularly apt notion to use to discuss the relationship between the ritual marches and ordinary life in Predappio, given its extensive role in social scientific debates about everyday life. Perhaps its most well-known invocation is in Bakhtin's work on Rabelais (1984), but it has also been employed by other theorists writing on the everyday, such as Henri Lefebvre (1947) and Georges Bataille (1949), among others. The point such writers often make about the carnival is that it is an inversion, or subversion, of everyday life: the world turned upside down, a time for a king of fools instead of a king, and of potlatch and excess instead of hunger and want. Though in Lefebvre's use it is supposed to be in some sense both external to but also arising from the everyday, it is nevertheless a moment of radical promise, of hope for those alienated by the normal rhythms of capitalist life ([1947] 2014). For that promise to be fulfilled, the carnival must become more than just a moment and itself become integrated into everyday life. Bakhtin is more insistent on a distinction, arguing that the carnivalesque "is outside of and contrary to all existing forms of the coercive socioeconomic and political organization, which is suspended for the time of the festivity" (1984, 255). In any case, and as in some of the other writing on the everyday we met in earlier chapters, the carnival is invoked in this literature as a special form of human action, a kind of willed and ephemeral escape from the strictures of an everyday life that by contrast is simply there, with all the weight of oppressive regularity.

In Predappio, however, the situation is exactly the other way around: it is the carnival of Mussolini that weighs on its inhabitants, and it is in a cultivated sense of ordinariness that Predappiesi find respite (see Heywood 2023a).

"We don't let it bother us," Silvana says of herself and her husband, who are agriculturalists living just up the hill from Predappio on the way to the Rocca delle Caminate. "Sure, in the old days we would lock ourselves in, but now it's just a day like any other day. I'm not going to stop doing my shopping because of them!" Andrea, an office worker whose parents live in a hamlet a few kilometers on from the cemetery and who visits them every Sunday, makes a point of sitting in his car waiting for the police to allow traffic to pass when the march is finished: "Why should I not see my parents on this Sunday, like any other Sunday? So I have to wait for a bit while they waste their time on this stuff, I don't care."

The most striking demonstrations of this attitude are visible on the days of the ritual marches themselves: the café on Piazza Sant'Antonio is open for business, its taciturn proprietor equally silently polite to all customers; it is packed with men in black, standing or sitting in groups, eating and drinking, waiting for the march to begin. Yet amid this mass of black sit the café's regular Predappiesi customers, quietly talking among themselves, reading the newspapers, and generally behaving as if there is nothing unusual going on at all by avoiding interaction and exchange with the outsiders, while nevertheless pursuing their normal routines. On one occasion as I sat with my friend Marco, an agricultural worker, we saw a group of black-shirted visitors standing at the bar break out into a rendition of "Giovinezza," the official hymn of the PNF. In the midst of the song Marco got up from his chair, walked calmly up to the bar until he was standing next to the group, and ordered an espresso at a volume calculated to supersede that of the singing, which faltered briefly before continuing on. Beyond making his coffee order heard, he paid absolutely no other form of attention to the group next to him.

The same attitude is visible in the cemetery. During the tense years of the 1970s, most locals would have avoided going to the cemetery on the days of the ritual marches, even though they take place on a Sunday, a day on which many would normally go to tend the graves of their relatives. Now, on the other hand, locals are as likely to go on these Sundays as on any other. Elena visits her father's grave, despite her strong disapproval of the behavior of the marchers in the cemetery. I have seen her push her way through a crowd gathered on the cemetery steps to listen to speeches, seemingly oblivious to the fact that she stands out in a floral dress instead of black. Valentina, too, goes to visit her parents' graves. As we have seen, she reasons that tourists who go to the Mussolini crypt are there to visit a dead person, just as she is, and there is nothing out of the ordinary in that. She is far less understanding of the ritual marchers, however, with their uniforms, their speeches, and their singing. But that will not stop her from doing her regular duty to her parents, even though their graves are only steps away from the Mussolini family tomb.

Predappiesi also have other rituals and festivals, including church festivals and others focused on food and on wine. In these, many Predappiesi participate with enthusiasm. Such festivals are common throughout Italy (and so are in that sense perfectly ordinary), whereas the carnival of Mussolini happens only in Predappio. One might also wonder whether Predappiesi attitudes to the ritual marches are simply a consequence of the fact that this is not "their" ritual; but that would beg the question of why exactly that is the case. One could, as I noted in the introduction, very easily imagine a different Predappio, in which its most famous son was an object of pride and anniversaries associated with him were the subject of celebration for his fellow citizens. Instead, even Sergio frowns as he watches the marches pass.

In Predappiesi attitudes to the carnival of Mussolini, in other words, we find the reverse of what we might expect from the standard narrative about the relationship between a carnival and everyday life. It is not everyday life that weighs heavy, but carnival time: three times a year, regular as clockwork, people in Predappio know that what passes for a sense of normality in a place so very far from normal will be punctured by thousands of men and women carrying out a ritual that will splash Predappio across the pages of newspapers once again. Their response to this, in line with the broader argument I have been making in this book, is often to reach for precisely that sense of ordinariness that the ritual marches so obviously disrupt.

The specific literature on the opposition between the carnival and everyday life is also echoed in a broader distinction to be found in recent anthropological writing on the relationship between ethics, ritual, and everyday life. On one side of this distinction are authors such as Veena Das (e.g., 2007) and Michael Lambek (2010), who, as we have seen, tend to locate ethics in the tacit, more or less unreflective practices of everyday life; on the other side are those, such as Robbins (2016), who point to the ways in which rituals express and to some extent realize collective moral values in transcendent fashion. Meanwhile other authors point to situations in which this distinction appears to hold less purchase: thus, James Laidlaw and Jonathan Mair describe a Buddhist religious retreat in which the contingencies and shortcomings of everyday life are incorporated into an intensively ritualized environment (2019).

In the case of Predappio, there is clearly an operative distinction between the ritual marches and ordinary life. But ordinary life here consists of anything but tacit and unreflective practices. It is not a level of existence to which one can descend, nor is it something one might want to escape. A sense of ordinariness in Predappio is not the basic ground of existence, but the outcome of the kind of work I have been describing so far in this book: it takes effort to make ordering a coffee look normal when people next to you are singing a Fascist hymn; you have to consciously decide to go to visit your parents, even if it means sitting in your car watching black-shirted marchers stream past you, or to tend the graves of your relatives on the same day in which their cemetery is turned into a parade ground.

All of this is also why ANPI's anti-Fascist pasta dinner failed in its attempt to "rescue" Predappio from the Fascists. Predappiesi reactions to anti-Fascist ritual are just like Predappiesi reactions to Fascist ritual. Just as Predappiesi do not, by and large, reach for heroic exemplars of anti-Fascism to counter the cult of personality still evident around Mussolini, neither do they welcome left-wing rituals to counter the right-wing rituals associated with that cult. Instead, just as they counter Mussolini's personality cult with Ferlini's pragmatic common sense, so they counter the ritual marches with the practices of ordinary life. But this is not the ordinary life that we find in social scientific literature. It is not an unmarked category, or unthinking and unreflective routine, or marital disputes, or petty crime, or any other thing that an analyst has decided is ordinary. The practices of ordinary life opposed to ritual here are not so much ordinary because they are practices, but practiced at least in part precisely because they are ordinary, defined in opposition to the politics of Fascism. They constitute a category that exists in opposition to ritual, not in an abstract analytical sense, but in the life of Predappiesi themselves.

CHAPTER 4

Everyday Space and Walking in the Fascist City

The Rocca delle Caminate is a medieval castle, built on a hill looking over Predappio. It was given to Mussolini by local authorities to use as a summer residence in 1923, and at the top of its tower is a massive spotlight that could project the Fascist emblem onto the night sky when Mussolini was in residence. The emblem was visible from almost forty miles away, as far the Romagnole coastline.

The view from the top of that tower is breathtaking. Its platform is almost exactly the same height as the 110th floor of the original World Trade Center, from which Michel de Certeau famously described New York transforming into "a text that lies before one's eyes" in *The Practice of Everyday Life* (1984, 92). The text that lies before one at the Rocca is very different from the "endless labyrinths" of New York City (92). Yet de Certeau's point is that from the "Icarian" heights of the Twin Towers, such labyrinths became legible and knowable, as one looked down on the city "like a god." The height "makes the complexity of the city readable" (92). Most of what one sees from the Rocca is a patchwork landscape of Romagnole countryside. But in the midst of this landscape is the town of Predappio, built to a grid plan, like New York and unlike all of the town's older neighbors.

De Certeau's point in placing the reader far above the streets of the city is that this god's-eye view creates a fiction: "a 'theoretical' (that is, visual) simulacrum, in short a picture, whose condition of possibility is an oblivion and a misunderstanding of practices. . . . The ordinary practitioners of the city live 'down below,' below the thresholds at which visibility begins" (1984, 93). This argument thus belongs within the family of arguments about ordinary or everyday life I have been describing, which find in everyday activities (walking and other spatial practices, in this case) something more real and more alive than the abstractions of theoretical fictions and other such simulacra.

The comparison with Predappio is almost too easy. Built to be a modernist paradise, it was self-consciously designed to look like the kind of "ideal picture" of a city that de Certeau describes (unlike, in fact, New York City; see Maulsby 2014a for a comparable account of the modernist transformation of Milan). While de Certeau's "god's-eye view" was at least putatively available to anyone who wished to pay the entrance fee to the World Trade Center, the Duce's-eye view from the Rocca was only ever available to Mussolini and the select few who lived and visited with him. Mussolini built Predappio to look well planned, so it is no surprise that the perspective from which it most appears so was his own summer castle.

Today, the Rocca is closed to visitors, unless with special permission of the local authorities, and while it is theoretically a sort of business space, a potential home for new tech companies in the region, only one company has offices there, and they are sparsely populated. The Rocca is empty for most of the year, a panopticon with no one to enjoy the view. Predappiesi live "down below," as de Certeau puts it, as ordinary practitioners of a space without a god to watch over them.

It would, in other words, be very easy to dichotomize two forms of experience of Predappio, as de Certeau does of city life more generally: on the one hand, a picture or simulacrum of modernism's dream space, viewable as such by the man who created it; and on the other hand, everyday Predappio, the space as it is really lived in by those who see it not from above but from within and who create it as such through "murky intertwining daily behaviors" (de Certeau 1984, 93).

In many respects, the comparison is apposite. Predappio is "read" as a single text not only by those few who have been able to observe it from the Rocca but also by most of those who have heard of the town or encountered it. In the wider public imaginary, Predappio looks very much as it does from the tower of the Rocca or in Fascist-era picture postcards: a strange island of Fascist monumentalism, set apart both spatially and temporally from its neighbors and from the present day. Its urban fabric and its place in history make this narrative a compelling one. But Predappiesi work very hard to escape this story, and the ways in which they relate to the space of their home are no exception.

So there are also crucial differences between the case of Predappio and the argument of de Certeau. One is the part that history and memory have to play in experiences of Predappio. As Michael Sheringham describes, "for de Certeau (following Lefebvre) the 'lieu pratiqué' of the city street is a locus of accumulated, compacted histories" (2006, 234). In Predappio, by contrast, the situation is more akin to that described by another sociologist of the ordinary, Michel Maffesoli: "everyday space is associated with the attenuation or abolition of time: the *quotidien* is a haven from history" (Sheringham 2006, 234). There are spaces in Predappio that are suffused with the sort of "accumulated, compacted histories" to which de Certeau refers. But, as we will see, these sorts of spaces are actually far from being ordinary, and they are spaces that Predappiesi themselves, in general, avoid. By contrast, the public spaces most would accept as ordinary have been largely emptied out of their histories, purged of their connections to Fascism and indeed to any specters of the *ventennio*, as the two decades of Fascist rule are often called.

Another, and more fundamental, difference is one we have encountered before in this book in juxtaposing theories of the ordinary with its experience in Predappio. That difference resides in the fact that ordinariness is a marked category in this context. In other words, ordinary experiences of space in Predappio are not just ordinary because they are certain sorts of experiences that a theorist has categorized as ordinary ("walking, organizing living space, reading, telling stories" (Sheringham 2006, 230); these things exist, of course, but there are also experiences of spaces and spaces themselves that have been *made to be* ordinary.

The Rocca itself is an excellent example of this: once the summer residence of Il Duce and possessed of the most splendid views in the region, it is now a barely occupied business park, while local scouts use its grounds to camp in. Despite being reconstructed and remodeled in recent years, only a single plaque in an out-of-the-way spot marks its history. In this sense, it is not a ruin; it is more akin to what Marc Augé, drawing on de Certeau, has called a "nonplace": a place without history, which is geared to the production of anonymous, "average" subjects (1995, 100). But, as I will argue, this and other places like it in Predappio are not (or at least not wholly) made such by the forces of "supermodernity," as they are in Augé's account. Insofar as some aspects of spatial life in Predappio are like the experience of existence in an airport lounge, that, I will suggest, is for many Predappiesi because life in an airport lounge is preferable to life in a living museum to Fascism.

Mussolini's Ghost

"Wait, are you telling me you only got your driving license a year ago? And to drive on the other side of the road?"

Edoardo seemed to shrink back in the passenger seat next to me as we took the hairpin turns up the mountain road to the Rocca from Predappio. This road used to be a racecourse in the 1950s, and every hundred yards or so there is another extremely sharp bend.

This was my third visit to the Rocca. The first two were in the company of Giorgio, the mayor; Carlo, the director of the Casa del Fascio project; and two different groups of dignitaries. On the first visit, we went with some potential funders for the museum, and on the second with a pair of BBC journalists. On both occasions, Giorgio extolled the Rocca as an example of how Predappio could make good use of its past, though these speeches rang somewhat hollow given that the Rocca was almost completely empty, and after each visit Carlo would complain to me privately about nobody making any use of the space, despite its costly remodeling.

On this third visit I was with Edoardo, who owns a very small bed-and-breakfast in Predappio along with his wife. Short, balding, and in his late fifties, Edoardo was the custodian of the Rocca for a period of time and has managed to retain the keys to it (mainly because nobody bothers enough about the place to ask for them back). His father was a guard at the Rocca while Mussolini was using it and then a member of Sergio's local chapter of the MSI. Edoardo tells me that he idolized his father, though he does not excuse the crimes committed in Fascism's name. Growing up, he was an altar boy at the chapel in San Cassiano, where Mussolini is buried, and he would serve at masses for the "nostalgic" tourists and even for some senior and still-living Fascist hierarchs, come to pay their respects to their old Duce.

We were on our way to the Rocca because Edoardo had promised a family of tourists staying in his bed-and-breakfast that he would give them a tour of the place. They were disappointed to have arrived in Predappio the day before only to discover that the Mussolini crypt was closed to visitors, after a spat between Giorgio and the Mussolini family (see chapter 5). They were a young family, the husband and wife in their thirties, together with their daughter. They had long hoped to visit Predappio, they told me, because they were from Latina, another famous Fascist new town in Lazio, and felt a kinship for Predappio as a consequence (on Latina, see Miltiadis 2022). They had no interest in politics, the father insisted, and would never come for the marches. They just wanted their daughter to understand her history.

FIGURE 4.1.   Saint Alexander with the fasces on his shield. Photo by author.

Edoardo had suggested I drive him while the visitors followed in their own car, and as we were halfway up the mountain I made the mistake of telling him that I had only recently acquired a license and that I was used to driving on the left-hand side of the road. Despite these impediments and the stomach-churning turns, we made it to the Rocca unscathed.

The Rocca was a rather ominous sight in February fog. At least a thousand years old, it is a squat, square stone building with a tall tower in the middle, barely visible from the road, surrounded by its own grounds and a high stone wall with two access points. It rises through the mist only as you come through one of these gates. Before doing so, you pass several outer buildings that housed Mussolini's bodyguards, a now-deconsecrated chapel, and a prison in which a number of partisans were tortured and murdered during the last months of the war. The chapel is decorated with images of Saints Rosa and Alexander (Mussolini's parents' names), and Saint Alexander's shield is adorned by a fasces (figure 4.1).

The only acknowledgment of the Rocca's recent history is a plaque, set behind a building and locatable only if you know where it is or stumble upon it by accident, which notes that the Rocca was the site of the deaths of "noble spirits who courageously resisted brutal torture and gave their lives for a free Italy." This plaque was first erected in 2009 in front of the Rocca's main gates, before being defaced by persons unknown and subsequently relocated to its present position of obscurity near the prison itself.

Edoardo's tour of the Rocca was notably different from those I had been on before. When I had come with Giorgio, we had been whisked straight past the outer buildings, and no mention was made of the chapel, the prison, the guards' barracks, or the murdered partisans. Giorgio's focus was on impressing our guests with the extensive remodeling carried out on the interior of the castle itself and its potential to host companies from a burgeoning Romagnole tech sector. There is no visible reminder of Mussolini's occupancy in the interior of the Rocca after this remodeling. We were shown plush-looking conference suites, offices, and reception rooms, all filled with standard leather and aluminum seats and modular desks, and none of which were occupied. As long as you averted your eyes from the views through the window, you could imagine yourself in any modern office building. The only mention of the past came when Giorgio described how he used to play in the ruins of the grounds as a child and how happy it made it him now to see the castle "restored."

Edoardo, on the other hand, told us rambling stories of his father's time as a guard at the Rocca and recounted the tale of Antonio Carini, a well-known local partisan tortured in the Rocca's prison and subsequently murdered. Edoardo went out of his way to show us the plaque in memory of fallen partisans and to point out the fasces on Saint Alexander's shield. Edoardo's tour was rather strange and disorganized, jumping from story to story with no discernible narrative arc, but partly for that reason it felt a great deal more like what de Certeau describes as the "anti-panoptic" experience of everyday life: "The dispersion of stories points to the dispersion of the memorable as well. And in fact memory is a sort of anti-museum: it is not localizable. Fragments of it come out in legends. . . . Haunted places are the only ones people can live in— and this inverts the schema of the Panopticon" (1984, 108).

By contrast, Giorgio's tour proceeded "as if space had been trapped by time, as if there were no history other than the last forty-eight hours of news, as if each individual history were drawing its motives from . . . an unending history in the present" (Augé 1995, 104–105). Like the foreigner Augé describes as feeling at home "in the anonymity of motorways, service stations, big stores, or hotel chains" (105), with Giorgio, our guests (and I) had no trouble identifying the form of an upscale office space: standardized desks with holes in them for wires to connect to telephones and computers, LCD TVs and projectors for displays, long conference tables surrounded by leather chairs, and the smell of carpet cleaner.

Which of these is an ordinary practice of experiencing space? The temptation is to see in Edoardo's fragmented memories of his father's stories and his conjuring up of the ghosts of the Mussolinis and dead partisans a more everyday experience of the Rocca, as de Certeau's narrative suggests. Yet Edoardo was not simply "practicing everyday life" as if that were a natural exercise: he was performing for a very specific audience. His guests were not other Predappiesi, they were tourists, people he was in part dependent on for his livelihood but from whom most Predappiesi would distinguish themselves sharply. The tourists were there "to understand their history," as the father put it to me. They had come to see Mussolini's tomb, and instead they got his summer residence. In other words, Edoardo's tour of the Rocca and its Fascist past was anything but ordinary in Predappio, where most people try to have as little to do with history as possible. Much more ordinary, in fact, was Giorgio's fleeting reference to his childhood playing in its ruins, and his otherwise overwhelming focus on the Rocca's transformation into a nonplace, outside of history, as something worthy of pride. As we will see in this chapter, this pattern is replicated in the case of a number of other Predappiesi public spaces.

"A House of Memories"

This contrast, between a historicized Predappio experienced by outsiders and the ordinary spaces of the town from which history has largely been exorcised, is echoed elsewhere. The Villa Carpena is a little way outside of Predappio, on the road to Forlì. Its association with Predappio stems from the fact that it was the postwar home of Mussolini's wife, Rachele (see Heywood 2024a).

The Mussolinis first bought the house in 1914 when Benito Mussolini was made editor of *Avanti!* It was one of the regular family residences during his time in power, and in 1957, after a period of time in confinement and with the return of her husband's body to the area, Rachele Mussolini moved there permanently. It remained in family hands after her death until 2000, when it was bought and transformed into a "museum" by an entrepreneur who already owned a "souvenir" shop in Predappio.

The word *museum* is enclosed within quotation marks on the sign on the front gate of the Villa Carpena, as if to warn the visitor of what is to come (figure 4.2).

Below, without the quotation marks, are the words *house of memories*. The villa is advertised by large signs on a number of main roads around the area, all of which have been defaced by anti-Fascist graffiti (figure 4.3).

FIGURE 4.2. The "museum" at the Villa Carpena. Photo by author.

FIGURE 4.3. Every advertisement for the Villa Carpena on surrounding roads has been defaced. Photo by author.

The villa is a vast and almost entirely uncurated collection of objects related to Fascism and to the Mussolinis. Like Edoardo's stories of the Rocca, it seems to have no guiding thread. The villa's grounds are filled with stone plaques commemorating Fascists fallen for their country, busts of Mussolini of various sizes, some extremely unhappy-sounding peacocks, a haphazard and seemingly random array of agricultural machinery that Rachele Mussolini is said to have collected, a replica of the glider used by German troops to rescue Mussolini from imprisonment after the coup of 1943, and a life-size model of Father Christmas wearing Fascist black (figure 4.4).

FIGURE 4.4.   Fascist Father Christmas. Photo by author.

To get in you have to pay an entrance fee, and to see the interior of the house you have to go on one of the regular tours; when I visited, the tour was run by a skeletal man in his eighties with a shaven head.

The interior of the house, he claimed, has been preserved as a shrine to the domestic life of the Mussolinis. If this is true, then Rachele Mussolini must have found it difficult to throw things away, because almost every wall and surface in the house is occupied by an object or a photograph with some tangential relationship to Fascism or the Mussolinis. During our visit, the guide picked up a perfectly ordinary man's shoe from a shelf and told us simply, "This was Romano [Mussolini]'s shoe," as if that was all we would need to know to understand its importance.

The trope of the museum (especially the biographical museum) as a space the subject has only just left, as it were, a preserved reminder of the ordinary traces of an individual life, is not in itself uncommon (see, e.g., Reed 2002). Fictionalized or literary versions of it can also be found, as in the Sherlock Holmes museum in London, for example. Yet the Villa Carpena is not quite the same sort of phenomenon. While it contains elements of this genre (for example, one of Mussolini's uniforms laid out on his bed, as if he were just about to get dressed), its enormous range of hodgepodge objects is too excessive for one to imagine the house as an actual dwelling. Some of the walls are covered almost from floor to ceiling in pictures, plaques, and framed Fascist slogans; kitchen surfaces are nearly invisible beneath a plethora of cups, plates, and crockery of all forms. Yet the aesthetic of ordinariness is very much the target.

On my visit, our guide claimed to have known Rachele and spent a great deal of time extolling her merits as an ordinary Italian housewife, pointing out her inexpensive clothes and kitchenware. The whole point of this "museum," he noted repeatedly, was to show visitors the "real," private lives of the Mussolinis, as normal, ordinary people, away from politics. This did not stop the guide from also engaging in spirited debate with some on my tour group over broader political and historical questions regarding the merits of Fascism: he repeatedly claimed that the Holocaust was a myth and that more people were killed by partisans after the war than by Fascism in twenty years. He lamented the erasure of Fascism from Italian history, at one point holding up a street sign from 1930s Predappio, decorated with the fasces: "Why would you throw this away?" he asked rhetorically. "Look at how well-made it is!" he said, knocking it with his fist to demonstrate its durability. Unknowingly echoing some of de Certeau's remarks on the affordances of street names as tools of power, he added, "Just so that everybody had to learn new street names!"

He was also very keen to suggest that the house was haunted by those whose memories it contains: one of his proudest exhibits is a mirror in which he claimed you could see the outline of Mussolini's face. I could see only smudges, but an Italian TV program called "Ghost Hunters" has filmed an episode at the villa based on this mirror.

In the attic of the house is what the guide called a "documentation center," full of pro-Fascist pamphlets and newspapers (most of them still in plastic wrapping) and decorated by amateurish murals of Fascist soldiers. Our guide argued that schoolchildren should be brought here to learn about their "real" history.

After the tour, one is gently guided toward a shop selling souvenirs of the sort one can find in Predappio, alongside Fascist-leaning history books and even some of Romano Mussolini's paintings (though many in Predappio insist that these are forgeries). On the tour I attended, a special guest was wheeled out to meet us at its conclusion: a ninety-four-year-old woman with one of the most strikingly blue pairs of eyes I have ever seen. I had read about her in the local press before my visit: she had been a volunteer for the RSI (the Italian Socialist Republic, the puppet regime installed by the Nazis after Mussolini was deposed in 1943) in the last days of the war, and her continued devotion to the cause was so strong that she had decided to live her final days at the Villa Carpena. The owner and his wife were evidently proud of this living addition to their collection and encouraged me to talk to her in English. To my surprise, she spoke the language perfectly and with a cut-glass accent. This, she told me, was a result of having lived in England for a few years in the 1950s ("in exile," she called it). She said she had decided to die at Villa Carpena because her happiest memories were of the RSI, and it brought them all back to her.

The Villa Carpena is not in any genuine sense a museum, as its owners themselves seem to acknowledge when they put the word in quotation marks. It is far more like de Certeau's "anti-museum," or, in the language of the owners, a "house of memories." It is an uncurated assemblage of objects related not by any kind of master narrative but by fragmented associations ("This is Romano's shoe"); the ghost of Donna Rachele, the ordinary housewife; and Mussolini's outline in his mirror. This ordinariness, like others we have met, is created and constructed, and obviously so: if indeed Rachele Mussolini was a master of household management, she would certainly have disapproved of her kitchenware being strewn around her space as it is. The haphazardness and disorganization, whether deliberate or not, sit strangely beside the clearly reverential attitude of its staff, evoking an impression of bathos: Fascist slogans about Mussolini always being right sit oddly amid the chaos of what we are supposed to see as his ordinary life.

If there is anything ordinary or everyday about the Villa Carpena, it is not an everyday that most Predappiesi would recognize. When they speak of Villa Carpena, they will often snort or raise their eyebrows at what they perceive to be a cynical, money-spinning enterprise of the same genre as the souvenir shops (see chapter 5). Furthermore, the content of Villa Carpena's everyday memorialization, like that of Edoardo's tour of the Rocca, is geared toward tourists and outsiders because it is exactly what many Predappiesi go to considerable lengths to avoid. As I suggested at the outset of this chapter, in Predappio, *pace* de Certeau, ordinary and everyday public spaces are often not accumulations of microhistories and memories; they are public spaces—like the Rocca—in which history can be forgotten.

The House of the Fasces

Unlike the Villa Carpena, only a couple of signs point the way to the house in which Mussolini was born in Predappio, and they are small and colored brown for heritage, again unlike the large advertisements for the Villa Carpena that dot the roads around the town, which are banded by the Italian tricolor.

The house itself is completely unmarked on the outside, unless there is an exhibition inside (I am aware of three since it opened for this purpose, in 1999), in which case a small A-frame sign may be placed by the door, or a poster on the wall. To get inside, one climbs a stone staircase and enters through a door, in front of which is a reception desk manned by a municipal worker (the house is owned by the municipality). The house gets few visitors, largely because there is nothing to see inside of it. It is completely empty. Before my fieldwork in Predappio it had once hosted an exhibition about Mussolini's early life, and while I was there it was briefly used to display the plans for the Casa del Fascio (see chapter 6 and below).

Similarly empty is the Casa del Fascio itself. This is the most famous building in Predappio. It dominates the main square of Sant'Antonio, and its tower is one of clearest sights from the top of the Rocca (figure 4.5).

Built not only to host the local party headquarters, the Casa del Fascio e dell'Ospitalità also originally held a theater, a library, and a bar and was used to provide facilities for the many visitors who flocked to Predappio under the regime (Storchi 2019; Tramonti 2014). With the fall of Fascism, it became state property along with all party-owned buildings (see Maulsby 2014b on the national legacy of Case del Fascio), and, as Simona Storchi has documented (2019), the subsequent seventy years saw a constant tug-of-war between the municipal authorities and the state over who should be responsible for the building's upkeep. In the 1960s and '70s parts of it played host to a manufacturing company and a socialist working men's club (*circolo*), but already by 1968 the Casa del

FIGURE 4.5. The tower of the Casa del Fascio in Predappio. Photo courtesy of Hannah Malone.

Fascio was beginning to fall to pieces (Storchi 2019, 144), and that decline has steadily continued.

To enter the Casa del Fascio today you have to be accompanied by someone from the municipal authorities, and you have to wear a hard hat. That is because the interior of the building is a wreck. There are piles of rubble everywhere and holes in the walls and ceilings where water comes in and forms pools on the floor. Bits of corrugated iron block access to various corridors, and in one of its main rooms the huge iron flagpole that used to fly the tricolor lies abandoned on the floor. Pigeons have made their home inside, and the hard hat protects one from more than just collapsing ceilings (figure 4.6).

Storchi has demonstrated that various municipal authorities have, over the years, sought to intervene in this process of decay, restore the Casa del Fascio, and put it to some kind of public use (2019). In chapter 6, I describe the most recent such attempt, namely the proposal to transform it into a museum (or documentation center) on Fascism. None of those attempted interventions, however—including, as of the time of writing, the museum project—have met with any success, and the building remains in a sort of spectral state: despite

FIGURE 4.6. The remains of the iron flagpole of the Casa del Fascio. Photo by author.

its ruined interior and apart from some graffiti and broken windows, it appears more or less undamaged on the outside, allowing it to blend relatively unremarkably into its surroundings.

Storchi's extensive archival research has shown that the problem of what to do with the Casa del Fascio preoccupied a number of successive municipal administrations over the decades. Yet part of the reason Storchi's account is so valuable is that it flies in the face of everyday wisdom in Predappio, which holds that nobody has ever really cared for the fate of the building. Some people remember the manufacturing company, or the socialist bar, but nobody that I knew spoke of the Casa del Fascio as a great missed opportunity, with the exception of those involved in the planning of the present museum project. Most Predappiesi will pass the building on a day-to-day basis or sit at one of the two bars directly opposite it on Piazza Sant'Antonio, but they will do so without paying it the least attention. It has long become part of the fabric of ordinary life in the town, but what has become ordinary and taken for granted about it is that it exists in a kind of liminal state: not nearly ruined enough in its exterior to be noticeably different from its surroundings but utterly desolate inside, the whole building exists as a facade. Without any explicit trappings of Fascism on the outside or any marks of history bar a tiny plaque (erected only in the past few years), and with the inside safely empty and thus attracting even fewer visitors than Mussolini's birth house, the building can pass as unremarkable.

In other words, though there may be no grand strategy behind the Casa del Fascio's present status and though some few in municipal administrations may have wished things otherwise, its existence as a facade emptied of history is perfectly in tune with the wider Predappiesi attitudes to their history I have been describing.

Hannah Malone (2017) has shown in comprehensive detail how confused and inconsistent strategies for dealing with Fascist urban heritage have been at a national level in postwar Italy. While some aspects of this heritage, such as Predappio's street names and signs (see Storchi 2013b), were marked for destruction in the immediate aftermath of the regime's fall, much of it has since been simply neglected or recycled without attention to its past (see also Arthurs 2010; Mitterhofer 2013; Hökerberg 2017 for a counterexample; and Fuller 2007 on Fascist architecture in former Italian colonies) in what Nick Carter and Simon Martin call "uncritical preservation" (2017, 355), "which allows Fascist sites to blend into the urban landscape" (Malone 2017, 452).

This is in contrast to postwar Germany, where Sharon Macdonald has described the fate that befell the Nazi Party rally grounds in Nuremberg (2006, 2009). Macdonald notes the ways in which the Nuremberg grounds were designed by Albert Speer with their own ruination in mind, intended to look to a thousand-year posterity like the classical ruins of ancient Greece and Rome (see, e.g., Arthurs 2012 and Kallis 2014 on the importance of Rome to Fascist architecture). This led to an impasse in postwar debates over what to do with this material heritage of the Nazi regime: repair it, and you risk returning it to its former glory and resurrecting it as a site of pilgrimage for the far right; but abandon it altogether and you accomplish exactly what its Nazi planners intended, and risk imbuing it instead with the allure of ruins. Macdonald explains the solution arrived at by then–state culture minister Hermann Glaser:

> What should be done, he suggested, was to let the buildings fall into a state of semi-disrepair but not total ruin. They should be allowed to look ugly and uncared-for. And they should be used for banal uses, such as storage, and leisure activities like tennis and motor-racing. Such uses were already underway, but they had been put in place unreflectively and for pragmatic reasons. In Glaser's new vision, however, they became something more significant and subtle: they became forms of material resistance to the Nazi meanings and potential agency of the architecture. That is, their very

form made them into modes of neutralising Nazi agency. Calculated ne-
glect was understood as blocking the two dangerous potential triggers.
Glaser called this strategy *Trivialisierung*—trivialization. (2006, 19)

The parallels with the fate of the Casa del Fascio are clear: "semi-disrepair"
nicely characterizes its condition. Like the Nuremberg rally grounds, the more
or less healthy condition of the Casa del Fascio's exterior leaves it without the
"allure of the ruin" and indeed allows it to blend in perfectly well with the rest
of Predappio's urban fabric; when it has been put to use, it has been to utterly
banal purposes—a small manufacturing company and a bar; and its present
emptiness makes it even less worthy of notice. Indeed, the term for the Nuremberg strategy, *trivialization*, in some ways echoes the notion of ordinarification
I have occasionally been using here to describe other Predappiesi strategies of
nullifying their past.

There are interesting contrasts between the two cases, however. The most
significant of these contrasts is one Macdonald points to in differentiating Glaser's strategy from previously "unreflective" and "pragmatic" usage. By making trivialization into an explicit strategy, Glaser transformed pragmatism into
resistance.

We should not, by now, be surprised to find that Predappiesi have not taken
this step. As I have been describing for other aspects of the pursuit of ordinariness in Predappio, the point of this pursuit is not simply resistance to Fascism as a movement but resistance to everything associated with Fascism and
in some ways to history itself. Put another way, trivialization in Nuremberg
was a means to an end (resistance); in Predappio, ordinarification is both means
and end. The point is not to disarm a specifically Fascist historicization, one
that ends in the splendor of classical ruins, but to disarm any form of historicization whatsoever.

The Tomb of Il Duce

By contrast to the birth house and the Casa del Fascio, but like the Villa Carpena,
Mussolini's tomb is outside of the control of Predappio's citizens, as it remains
the formal property of the Mussolini family. Indeed, the inability of the municipality to exercise its authority over the tomb has been demonstrated on occasion
when the family chooses to close the tomb to visitors in order to "punish" Predappio or its council for perceived slights, as I describe in chapter 5.

While there are official signs pointing the way to the local cemetery (it
houses the relatives of many living Predappiesi), none of them name its most

famous inhabitant. There is a small sign on the outside of the crypt itself, within the cemetery, placed there by the family. The crypt is at the end of the cemetery's central path, in pride of place. All other graves in the cemetery are small standing mausolea or stone plaques.

As with the Villa Carpena, Mussolini's tomb far more closely resembles de Certeau's characterization of ordinary space and memory than any of the buildings over which Predappiesi or their elected officials have any control. It is a sort of a parody of a state-sanctioned mausoleum like the Pantheon.

The colors of the Italian *tricolore* are everywhere, as are the fasces of the regime. The sarcophagi of various close relatives of Mussolini are surrounded by somewhat incongruous photographs and busts of the relative in question: Rachele Mussolini is pictured holding a pair of birds, and her bust makes her resemble George Washington in a blouse. Mussolini's own bust is the most prominent, in the center of the tomb and behind a wrought iron barrier in which can be seen a stylized version of the letter M (figure 4.7). Surrounding it are a number of relics in glass cases, which are impossible to identify from behind the barrier, and to its right is another, larger, stylized M, seemingly sited with no eye to symmetry or design.

Again, as in the Villa Carpena, small and uncontextualized objects related to Fascism are scattered about the tomb in seemingly haphazard fashion. In fact, an anteroom of the crypt could well pass for a storeroom for the Villa Carpena's additional stock: it is filled with a jumble of pictures of Mussolini, of his father, flags, banners, scarves, Christian imagery, and a wooden statue of a priest in black that looks like it could have been—and perhaps was—carved by the same hand that made the Villa Carpena's Fascist Father Christmas.

Leaving the tomb, one ascends another staircase, this one lined with plaques donated by visitors (figure 4.8). Once again, no single order or form of organization dominates the display: plaques of every size and shape have been nailed next to one another, seemingly in an attempt simply to jam as many of them in as possible, with no attention to their aesthetics or relationship. Some are cheap-looking gold plate; others are Fascist black; still others are made of clay, iron, or marble. Some include a photo of a deceased "comrade," others a poem written in honor of Mussolini.

Directly in front of the bust in the center of the tomb is an open visitors' book, often placed on top of an Italian flag. Entries in the visitors' books express, like the tomb itself and the Villa Carpena, an odd assortment of sentiments. The majority involve some short endorsement of Mussolini or of Fascism ("Come back to us Duce!," "Dear Benito, my faith and honor to you forever," "History has proved you right!"), and many compare Mussolini to Christ ("Mussolini, you died for our sins!," "Dongo [where Mussolini was executed] is our Calvary!,"

FIGURE 4.7. The tomb and visitors' book.

FIGURE 4.8. Commemorative plaques. Photo by author.

"You founded my religion: Fascism," "This is not a tomb, it is the repository of the holy grail") or ask him to save Italy from some enemy or other ("Come back and rescue us from the dirty Communists who have ruined our country," "You alone can save us from the pigs in government").

Amid these more orthodox sentiments, however, other curiosities emerge:

"Duce, please help Napoli to win the cup tomorrow!"

"One day in Predappio is better than ten days at the seaside."

"You are our Mohammed, and Predappio is our Mecca, except we are not Muslims."

Some comments in the book depart substantially from Fascist orthodoxy, occasionally provoking responses from other visitors:

"You know, your original ideas weren't so bad, but then you made some pretty serious mistakes."

"You died but you left us with the spirit of Fascism. Please come and take it back to hell with you and leave us in peace with democracy."

"Can I say something? Have any of you idiots ever read a history book or do you only listen to what your Fascist granddad tells you?"

"You should have died sooner, piece of s***!"

"Here lies a murderer with his symbols of death and shame. [Underneath:] Stay at home then idiot, instead of coming here!"

"I am utterly ashamed to be here! [Underneath:] Then don't come, you ****"[1]

Like the rest of the crypt, the visitors' book appears uncurated, simply a repository of fragmented and at times incoherent feelings about Fascism, which sometimes even—as above—become a dialogue between opposing viewpoints.

Walking in Predappio

The examples I have been describing thus far in this chapter illustrate two key points about Predappiesi public space. The first is that, *pace* de Certeau, ordinary spaces (at least public ones over which the municipality has control) in Predappio tend not to be spaces suffused with history and memory; quite the opposite, they are spaces that have been emptied of history and memory. The second, related, point is that such places are not ordinary in this way by nature. The Rocca, Mussolini's birth house, and the Casa del Fascio have all had history and memory extracted from them during the seventy years since the end of the war: the Rocca has been rebuilt and transformed into what local authorities imagine a globalized business space ought to look like; the birth house has been emptied of its contents; and the Casa del Fascio has been left to its pigeons on the inside.

None of these spaces has anything individual or idiosyncratic left to it. Even the Casa del Fascio's rotting interior has been stripped of anything that marked its former uses, leaving only gray stone and peeling plaster.

Yet for most Predappiesi, it is these dehistoricized public spaces that are ordinary, not the Villa Carpena, or Mussolini's tomb, despite the fact that these latter spaces, in their haphazard and disorganized failures at curating some form of Fascist memory, look much more like de Certeau's "anti-museums" and "haunted places," the opposites of the panopticon.

But what of Predappio's more private, more intimate space, or of normal life beyond these particular public spaces? After all, it is not only spaces of memory that de Certeau opposes to the simulacrum of the grid-plan imaginary of city life; it is also the simple quotidian experience of walking the streets.

Yet we have already seen in my depiction of Valentina and her shopping trip in chapter 1 that walking the streets of Predappio is a far from straightforward experience. In many ways the perspective on the town it generates is just as much a simulacrum as the god's-eye view one gets from the Rocca. Predappiesi have cultivated an ability to ignore aspects of the urban fabric of their home that would leave an outsider open-mouthed.

This is not simply a question of habituation, because what is at issue is not merely aesthetics. After all, the urban fabric in question is simply not one to which one could easily become unwittingly habituated. For example, I am writing this chapter at my desk in my home in Cambridge, England. Cambridge is a city to which tourists flock from around the world and throughout the year. King's Parade, the site of the iconic King's College Chapel, can be hard to navigate in the summer because of the sheer quantity of people stopping to photograph or simply stare at the inescapably striking Gothic architecture. I have often felt frustration as I weave between tour groups and families and spare hardly a glance for the fabric of a city in which I was born and in which I have lived for most of my adult life.

I know, however, that it is there, and I know that if I stopped to speak to some of these visitors, I would no doubt share their feelings as to its beauty and majesty. Sometimes, particularly if the sun is setting and if I am not in a rush, then I might even stop myself and bask in the pleasure of the same sight that outsiders to my home are enjoying, aware that I am fortunate to have the opportunity to do so on a daily basis, even if I do not always take advantage of it.

None of that is possible for most Predappiesi. Of course, many of them are habituated to the aesthetics of their home, just as I am to those of Cambridge. But what they have to learn to "unsee" that I do not are the political connotations of those aesthetics. They cannot stand and share in the admiring gaze of a black-shirted visitor at their church or at the Casa del Fascio, because they know or guess that what is being admired is not, or at least not wholly, aesthetic. They know that the aesthetics of their home are iconic of a politics that most of them want nothing to do with.

To illustrate the potential perils of walking in Predappio, take the case of Elena, whom we met briefly in chapter 2 as an admirer of Mayor Ferlini. Elena is not, however, such a fan of Predappio's present-day mayors.

She has had a rather complicated personal life, and although her father and her father's family come from Predappio, she herself moved to the town only in the early 2000s, making her a relative outsider as far as others are concerned. She moved to Predappio, despite never having lived there previously, because of the way it made her feel close to her now-deceased father. She feels that she is still sometimes unjustly treated as an outsider, given her family's roots in the town. But she also feels that her father was poorly treated by some in the town, too, largely as a consequence of his right-wing political leanings. Her memories of her father, and the narratives of her father's memories she cherishes, often revolve around this fact and around a changing sense of place and space in Predappio after the war. For instance, she recalls him telling her of an episode from his boyhood immediately after the war. Locals were busy removing door signs and street signs with the fasces on them (some of which presumably ended up in the Villa Carpena), and Elena's father came across the father of one of his friends from the Fascist youth movement chiseling the sign from outside the family house. He stopped to stare, and the man asked him what he thought he was looking at, pointedly calling him a Balilla, as those in the youth movement had been known. Elena's father replied that the man's son had been a Balilla, too, whereupon the man descended from his ladder and proceeded to give Elena's father a beating, the recounting of which still causes Elena to turn red with indignation.

A few years before my fieldwork, Elena decided to put her recollections of her father's memories to use and organize cultural walking tours of Predappio. She would not go to the cemetery, she decided, because that was too politicized, but she would show people around the important sites within the town and tell them of her father's stories of Predappio in the war and after. She arranged the walks in cooperation with a representative of a Romagnole tourism association. The arrangement sounds a lot like Edoardo's tour of the Rocca, only somewhat more formalized and focused on the town itself (cf. Reed 2002 on walking tours and memory in London).

Within a short period of time, however, she says that the association received a telephone call from the mayor's office claiming that they required official permission to operate this sort of tour (permission the association claimed to Elena it had never required elsewhere). "I understood," she says, "They never said it, but I understood: 'You're touching too sensitive topics,' they meant. All I was doing was talking of my dad's memories, and I was with someone with an official tax number, no funny business, so they couldn't have stopped me even with the police, but to avoid the arguments I stopped myself anyway. I would never have talked about Fascism; instead I would have talked about what Predappio represents, as the beginning of the history of this statesman, who would later become Mussolini. Who knows that Mussolini lived with Rachele nearby, that he would get drunk and play the violin? Who talks about that? Nobody."

Elena's project and her reaction to the attempt to shut it down perhaps explain why she may still be perceived as an outsider by many in the town. As a project, it seems to condense a lot of what de Certeau approves of in the ordinary experience of city life: a bottom-up, personal initiative led by an individual in collaboration with a local association, designed to allow tourists to walk in the footsteps of an everyday man of Predappio and to hear about his memories of quotidian life in the town. But, as the reaction to the project suggests, this is not the sort of "walking in the city" that many Predappiesi wish to encourage.

The sort of walking in the city that most Predappiesi engage in involves, instead, as in Valentina's shopping trip, a sort of studied avoidance of exactly the sorts of memory that Elena wishes to evoke. People do not, as a rule, have any desire to reminisce about the days when the flowers in front of the town hall were shaped to look a giant fasces or to pick out the place where a miniature fasces used to sit in the facade of the old hospital. Predappiesi know these things are there, just as I know that King's College Chapel is there; and they know, as I do of King's, that tourists will come to take pictures (or, in some cases in Predappio, stare in horror at some still-present reminder of the regime). But Predappiesi are not habituated to these facts; they are highly attuned to them (cf. Candea 2013). A really ordinary Predappiesi walking tour is like those Giorgio gave me at the Rocca, when he walked straight past the guardhouse in which partisans were tortured and murdered without a word, heading instead straight for the Rocca's newly anonymized interior.

The problem with Elena's walking tours, with Edoardo's unofficial trips to the Rocca, with the Villa Carpena, and with Mussolini's tomb, is not that they are not "really" ordinary. In their fragmented, haphazard, and uncurated form, as we have seen, they much more closely resemble what theorists of urban space such as de Certeau assume is ordinary than, say, the passionless remodeling of the Rocca and Mussolini's birth house, or the spectral life of the Casa del Fascio, normal on the outside and ruined on the inside.

The problem is that the form of the ordinary is not enough. Left to itself, uncurated and uncultivated space and its experience in Predappio might share the formal properties that social scientists are wont to attribute to ordinary or everyday space, but there is in truth nothing in those properties alone that is sufficient to make something ordinary. Indeed, there is very obviously a great deal that is extraordinary, astonishing, and grotesque about spaces such as the Villa Carpena and Mussolini's tomb and even, at least for some, in Elena's walking tours and her desire to remember the Mussolini who would get drunk with his wife and play the violin. Making space ordinary in Predappio, as with the other aspects of Predappiesi life, takes work. In this case, the work involved may take the form of an emptying out of history and memory, the transformation of public spaces into "nonplaces," empty like Mussolini's birth house or reconstructed to resemble an image of an anonymous office space. Or it may take the form of a practice or experience of space, a learned avoidance of those aspects of home that conjure up the ghosts of history.

The ordinary Predappio produced by all of this is certainly not the same Predappio as the one you can see from Il Duce's perch at the top of the Rocca's tower. But in many ways it is just as much of a simulacrum, to be achieved rather than discovered.

In this chapter and in chapter 3, we have looked at how a sense of ordinary life in Predappio emerges in relation to ritual and to space. In the next chapter, we turn to language: What, after all, could be more ordinary than language? Yet ordinary language too, as we will see, may be a strategic choice and an object of cultivation, rather than simply a fact of existence, particularly when it comes to debates about how exactly to define Fascism. Such debates have a fraught history in general and particularly in Italy. One easy way out of them is to take the view that there simply is no single definition of Fascism and that it is a sort of "family resemblance" term, an argument put forward by Umberto Eco among others (1995). It is a mistake, though, to see this as a resolution to such debates, rather than the intervention it actually is. In Predappio in particular, taking this sort of ordinary language position on Fascism serves the broader project I have been describing: of ordinarifying a place that is anything but ordinary.

CHAPTER 5

Ordinary Skepticism and Fascist Family Resemblances

Many politicians are habituated to receiving hate mail or abuse, perhaps due to their gender, ethnicity, or sexual orientation or because of some particular policy they espouse. Giorgio Frassineti, mayor of Predappio during most of the period of my fieldwork, received regular postcards from different holiday destinations while he was in office, all from the same anonymous individual and all beginning, "Dear Fascist Dickhead." Another regular writer would address all his correspondence to Giorgio as the "Podestà" of Predappio, the official designation for a mayor under the Fascist regime.

Predappio and Fascism are indissolubly linked in the minds of most outsiders who have heard of the town, for obvious reasons. So, it is not only Giorgio, as Predappio's most public citizen, who falls victim to this association. I was told on countless occasions that it was a common habit for Predappiesi to lie about their origins when traveling outside of the town, in order to head off the inevitable assumptions that outsiders would make about them. Not that such assumptions always lead to negative consequences: many Predappiesi have stories of discounts or other forms of preferential treatment at hotels when they show their passports, and the Italian police are famous in the town for displaying leniency to Predappiesi caught speeding, as are the military for giving an easy ride to Predappiesi conscripts.

Gianni, the local artist we met in chapter 3, has a story of visiting a bar in Rome ("They're all Fascists there, you know," he says) and being overheard to pronounce his *s*'s in the idiosyncratic fashion of Emilia-Romagna. Upon revealing to his new Roman friends that he is from Predappio, he was instantly taken to be a *camerata* and directed to a variety of restaurants in the city in which the mention of his hometown would earn him a very cheap dinner.

Gianni is not, in fact, a Fascist, or at least not according to any criteria that would make sense to anybody in Predappio or to most people elsewhere. He has no compunction accepting a cheap dinner from self-proclaimed Fascists because he is an easygoing man with almost nothing to say about politics, preferring instead to devote himself to his paintings. Giorgio, the mayor, might possibly be a "dickhead" in the opinion of some Predappiesi who did not vote for him in mayoral elections, but nobody except an outsider going only by his place of residence would call him a Fascist. He has been a member of Italy's mainstream left-wing party throughout his political career.

The association between Predappio and Predappiesi on the one hand, and Fascism on the other, is not really dependent on the thought that everyone in Predappio is actually a Fascist. Rather, in cases like these, Predappio and Predappiesi are indexes of Fascism to those around them. That is, the town, or the appearance of its inhabitants, seems to do the work of making Fascism itself present to others, for good or for ill, in the same way in which a swastika indexes the presence of Nazism (Shoshan 2016). In providing a discounted room rate or restaurant dinner or in forgiving someone's speeding ticket for no other reason than that the person is from Predappio, one is somehow— among other things—doing a favor for Fascism. In addressing the mayor of Predappio as a dickhead one is striking a blow at Fascism, even if this particular mayor, like all his postwar predecessors, is an erstwhile member of the Communist Party. More obviously, Predappio also clearly has long had an iconic as well as indexical relationship to Fascism, from the early days of Fascist picture postcards of Predappio under the regime, to the woman with the "Auschwitzland" T-shirt I described in chapter 3, who mocked up a representation of the Predappio skyline in place of the Disneyland logo.

Seeking out indexical or iconic signs of Fascism is a common response to the problem of how to actually identify it, as I will describe in this chapter. But it is not the only such response, and it is not the response that Predappiesi themselves adopt, largely speaking. Trying to define Fascism has long been a fraught problem for historians, journalists, political actors, courts, and ordinary people. George Orwell once called "What is Fascism?" the most important unanswered question of our time (1944), and in recent years that question has suddenly seemed relevant to many across the world once more, as a flurry of new or familiar answers have emerged in response to the perception of an international resurgence of the far right. In Predappio, it is a rather particular problem, unsurprisingly, and its relevance has never been purely historical.

It is possible to pick out two broad families of responses to this question. One sort of response seeks to provide a definition of some sort, a "Fascist minimum," in the words of one well-known such attempt (Eatwell 1996). This sort of response has been attempted by a number of historians and politicians, as well as by jurists, who have, in contexts such as postwar Italy and Germany, been charged with the task of identifying and rooting out the remains of Fascist regimes.

The second sort of response is one with which anthropologists and social scientists may well feel more at home. It is neatly encapsulated in an essay by Umberto Eco for the *New York Review of Books* (1995). Though the piece is in part an attempt to enumerate a list of basic features of what Eco calls "Ur-Fascism," it is most notable for the argument that Fascism, like "game" in Wittgenstein's writings, is a family resemblance term. That is, in ordinary language it is used not with the intention of picking out a definable and essential characteristic, but to draw together a set of phenomena none of which in fact share any single quality: "Fascism became an all-purpose term because one can eliminate from a Fascist regime one or more features, and it will still be recognizable as Fascist. Take away imperialism from Fascism and you still have Franco and Salazar. Take away colonialism and you still have the Balkan Fascism of the Ustashes. Add to the Italian Fascism a radical anti-capitalism (which never much fascinated Mussolini) and you have Ezra Pound. Add a cult of Celtic mythology and the Grail mysticism (completely alien to official Fascism) and you have one of the most respected Fascist gurus, Julius Evola" (1995).

Anthropologists and other "soft" social scientists are often wary of definitions (Needham 1975; Heywood 2023b). Definitions, by definition, elide complexity, variety, and the gray areas of everyday life with fiat-based assumptions. An argument such as Eco's—and the Wittgensteinian claims on which it is based—feels a great deal more fine-grained and more ethnographically sensitive. Unlike definitional arguments, it reads not as an assertion ("Fascism is X") but as a description of fact or ordinary language use ("This is just how we talk about Fascism").

Things are not quite so simple, however, as is obvious from the fact that Eco's intervention competes with the sort of definitional interventions others have made. If Fascism is a family resemblance term, then the search for such a single definition of it is foolhardy. In this respect, at least, it is assertive as well as descriptive.

Another related feature of this sort of claim, one it shares with other arguments about ordinariness we have met in this book, is the way in which it seems to naturalize everyday language. "Linguistic habits are frequently important symptoms of underlying feelings," Eco tells us, in justification of his focus on linguistic usage. This is undeniable, but to say simply that Fascism is a family resemblance term does not actually tell us anything about the content of those feelings. It is to evade, rather than answer, the question of why it might be that people use the word in this or that way. To call such usage ordinary is to make this question seem even less plausible: it is just a matter of fact, like ordinary life itself.

But like ordinary life itself, such ordinary usage of Fascism in Predappio is far from neutral or simply given. When everyone around you takes you and your town as themselves indexical or iconic signs of Fascism, being fuzzy about what Fascism is accomplishes particular effects, ones in line with others I have been describing throughout this book: it muddies the waters of that taken-for-granted relationship between Predappio and Fascism. Just as there may be no distinctive characteristic of Fascism, so there may be no distinctively Fascist characteristic of Predappio.

In this chapter, I describe some of the ways in which Predappiesi talk about Fascism. How they do so, I suggest, often demonstrates the same characteristic of scaling down and ordinarifying as other aspects of life in Predappio I have discussed. For though there exists no shortage of potential candidates to be called Fascist, Predappiesi often employ various strategies to avoid doing so: neo-Fascist marchers are called "folkloric" or "nostalgic," those who sell Fascist-themed merchandise are said to be simply rapacious and interested only in money, and even the Fascism of Mussolini's relatives can be blurry as a consequence of their (unchosen) kinship links. The result of this, I suggest, is a particular kind of ordinary language about Fascism, one which in fact resembles that of the skeptical philosopher: Fascism is much more often the object of doubt than it is of certainty.

Dogs, and I Do Not Know What Else

Historical and political arguments over the proper meaning and definition of Fascism have been taking place since it first emerged as a phenomenon in the 1920s and show no immediate sign of abating. A range of definitions have been proffered by eminent historians of the subject in search of that so-called Fascist minimum (Eatwell 1996), while at least one prominent scholar became so frustrated by the ambiguous use of the term that he famously called for it to be banned from historical discourse (Allardyce 1979; see Holmes 2000, 13). Orwell, in raising the question of what Fascism is, was making nearly the same point in remarking that he had heard the word applied to "farmers, shopkeepers, Social Credit, corporal punishment, fox-hunting, bull-fighting, the 1922 Committee, the 1941 Committee, Kipling, Gandhi, Chiang Kai-Shek, homosexuality, Priestley's broadcasts, Youth Hostels, astrology, women, dogs and I do not know what else" (1944). Historians and other academics have defined Fascism as, among other things, a class-based response to the development of socialism (see, e.g., Poulantzas 1974; Trotsky [1944] 1993), a psychological phenomenon resulting from a kind of mass hysteria (Reich 1933), a species of "developmental dictatorship" (Gregor 1979b), a palingenetic type of ultranationalism (Griffin 1991), and a form of religion as a political movement (Gentile 1990), to name only a few such definitions.

Recently these debates have become yet more fraught by, as it were, coming alive. They have moved from residing largely or entirely in the realm of scholarly journals and academic conferences (from being about the intension of the word, as it were) into the world that such journals and conferences aim to investigate, from the abstract to the concrete, from analysis to object (to being about potential extensions of the word). *Slate*, for example, recently printed an excerpt from Passmore's *Fascism: A Very Short Introduction* as part of its academy series on Fascism, suggesting readers consult the extract to determine whether or not they were living in a "Fascist state" (Passmore 2017); the *Atlantic*, noting the "elusiveness" of definitions of Fascism, interviewed historian Robert Paxton in search of a checklist of features with which to assess the extent to which Donald Trump is a Fascist (Green 2016). The pages of international news and commentary have recently been filled with speculation as to whether and how far France's National Front, Germany's AfD, or Austria's Freedom Party count or do not count as Fascist, and the word was even in the running to be Merriam-Webster's "word of the year" in 2016.

The problem of definition is exacerbated by a number of factors in the case of Fascism, including the lack of any clear doctrinal text, inconsistency of practice and policy on the part of "Fascist" regimes (as I described in chapter 1), an apparent aversion to ideological or theoretical self-definition on the part of self-declared Fascists themselves, and the fact that Fascist movements have been, if they have been anything, usually ultranationalist in character, while also—arguably—forming a supranational object of some form.

All of these factors, as well as more traditional problems of definition, combine to make it extremely difficult to define Fascism, while apparently doing nothing to dispel the appetite of historians, political scientists, journalists, commentators, and ordinary people for attempting to do so.

These attempts have an especially complex history in Italy, where Fascism became, in effect, a criminal category after the fall of the regime. Article 30 of the Long Armistice between Italy and the Allies, signed on September 29, 1943, obliged the Italian government to "carry out all directives which the United Nations may call for, including the abolition of Fascist institutions, the dismissal and internment of Fascist personnel, the control of Fascist funds, the suppression of Fascist ideologies and teachings" (Domenico 1991, 22). At this point, Italy was the first major Axis power to surrender to the Allies and was thus in some ways a testing ground for what would take place in Germany two years later. Unlike the German case however, and—for different reasons—also unlike the case of France, Italy in 1943 was perched uncomfortably between the status of a vanquished enemy and that of a cobelligerent against the Axis. On the one hand, Italy had been at war with the Allies since 1940. On the other, Italians themselves had deposed Mussolini, and the new regime surrendered to the Allies and joined the war against Germany.

Furthermore, given the fact that most of the new, pro-Allied regime's leaders had at some point or another held prominent positions under Mussolini, abolishing "Fascist" institutions and dismissing or interning "Fascist" personnel were in no sense simple proposals. These tasks were further complicated by the fact that the Allies were still fighting a war in Italy against Germany and the puppet regime of the Italian Social Republic (RSI), while also attempting to administer their own occupied territories in the country. Many of the initial Allied efforts at what was called "epuration" were haphazard and disorganized, as Roy Domenico recounts, targeting confused categories such as "Fascist sympathizers" or "those potentially dangerous to the security of the Allied Armed Forces" (1991, 27), while administrators also—with varying degrees of knowledge and satisfaction—collaborated with former Fascists in their efforts to govern the country (31).

An attempt was made to clarify matters somewhat in 1944 when a survey (*scheda personale*) was issued to all Italian state employees listing forty-three categories of questions (including asking respondents to declare whether or not they had ever held the position of national secretary of the PNF) regarding exactly how deeply the respondent had been involved in Fascist activities and for how long, in an effort to determine who should be prosecuted by tribunals. Again, because this was 1944, and the Allies were still fighting the Germans and the RSI in the north of the country, a crucial concern in the questionnaire was to establish whether the respondent had been a member of the Fascist Party until Mussolini's fall from government in 1943 (more or less acceptable for the de facto reason that almost every state employee had been obliged or strongly encouraged to hold a party membership card during the regime) and had subsequently repented or whether they persisted in support of the RSI, which made one not only a Fascist but also a traitor to the legitimate Italian government in the south. This distinction and the effective definition of a Fascist as a *repubblichino*, as RSI supporters were called, became entrenched in both Italian and United Nations policy, despite the derisory attitude toward the questionnaire that many Italians held. The result was that epuration efforts were directed at a subset of individuals whose loyalty to the regime persisted after 1943, rather than at those whose participation in the movement ended—for whatever reason—with the coup against Mussolini in July 1943. That this particular definition served a number of purposes is well documented: it focused punitive efforts on those who were still hostile to the Allies (this was obviously the category which most concerned British and American administrators); it rescued the Allies from the need to purge the entirety of the Italian bureaucratic apparatus and the chaos that would result; and it allowed the royal government to avoid difficult questions about the relationship between Mussolini and the monarchy, the Catholic Church, and a range of other interests with which he had cooperated.

The twelfth disposition of the 1947 Italian constitution forbids the reorganization, "under any form whatsoever" of "the dissolved Italian Fascist Party." This disposition was then clarified and somewhat extended in a 1952 law known as the Scelba Law, which forbids not only the reorganization of the dissolved Fascist Party but also "apologia" for it, as well as public demonstrations in favor of it. Yet these measures, too, have been undermined in a number of ways, most obviously by the 1946 Togliatti amnesty for convicted Fascist criminals and associated legal reforms, which led to the release of between twenty and thirty thousand people, as well as the electoral successes of the neo-Fascist MSI in 1948 (Domenico 1991, 212–214; Parlato 2006; Parlato 2017, 44).

Moreover, several Italian courts have, over the years, issued a number of decisions that very much restrict—or simply confuse—the scope of the application of the Scelba Law and its constitutional antecedent, as I have described elsewhere (Heywood 2019). For instance, already by 1958, at the trial of three men—two of whom were indicted for performing the Roman salute and wearing a black shirt at Mussolini's tomb in Predappio—Italy's constitutional court ruled that the law could apply only in situations in which there was a realistic and intended prospect of the reconstitution of the PNF, not simply in cases in which demonstrations were made in favor of it. Similarly, in 1994, the Consiglio di Stato ruled that use of the fasces as a political symbol could not in and of itself constitute a breach of electoral law, given the symbol's longer historical association with ancient Rome (Maestri 2017). More recently, the criminal section of the Corte di Cassazione condemned two CasaPound militants for giving a Roman salute at a memorial day gathering and then, in 2016, absolved seven other militants for performing exactly the same gesture at a larger such memorial event. In Predappio, where Roman salutes are a regular occurrence, often in full view of police or carabinieri agents, no one expects intervention from the judicial authorities.

Policemen may not consider themselves experts on identifying Fascists, but other outsiders to Predappio do. On one October 28 anniversary march, I was watching a small group of men of varying ages wearing black Fascist military uniforms, led by a shaven-headed man in his forties. As the troop neared Mussolini's mausoleum, its leader called out to the group to begin marching in military step. After a brief and obvious moment of confusion, a young man toward the rear of the group began to goose-step, before being instantly reprimanded by the troop leader: "No! That's their [the Nazis'] thing! We're Fascists, not Nazis!"

I was reminded of this minor display of technical discrimination (goose-stepping makes you a Nazi, not a Fascist, and the difference is important to some) a little later on the same day as I stood on the street with some anti-Fascist acquaintances of Carlo who had come to Predappio from Forlì to witness the extent of the turnout and to take their dog for a walk. As we stood and watched individuals and groups of people pass by, some of whom were returning to town from the mausoleum, on foot and by car, one of Carlo's acquaintances began reeling off ostensive definitions of her own: "That one's Fascist . . . that one too . . . probably that one . . . that one might not be . . ." I asked how she was able to tell who was a Fascist and who was not, and she listed some of what she took to be indexical signs: black clothing (not an essential criterion, because anarchists wear black, too), leather (also not essential), biker paraphernalia, shaven head (also not an essential criterion), Fascist slogans printed on T-shirts, and origin of car license plate. Later on, Carlo gave me another example of a comparable practice from the 1970s, one adopted by leftist militants from Forlì looking for visiting Fascists to attack: a volunteer would wait by the side of the road below a local hilltop for a bus to pass by; when it did, the volunteer would raise his arm to give the Roman salute, and if the busload of visitors did the same in response, he would signal to comrades at the top of the hill, who would promptly begin dropping rocks and boulders on the bus from above.

Ordinary Skepticism

The search for a "Fascist minimum" has an established history both in Italy and abroad. One might well imagine that Predappiesi would have elevated this search into a science: Where would one be more likely to find experts on what constitutes Fascism than in the birthplace of its founder and the Mecca for neo-Fascists across the world? Yet the brief examples I provide above involve outsiders: neo-Fascists seeking to distinguish themselves from Nazis and anti-Fascists looking to identify the enemy. Predappiesi themselves are remarkably reticent in applying this label.

That is not because of a shortage of candidates. The most obvious candidates are the visitors themselves, many of whom would quite happily self-describe as Fascist. Predappiesi, however, very rarely refer to their visitors with any variant of political characterization. In line with the wider response to the ritual marches, the most commonly used term for these visitors is *nostalgici*, "nostalgics." This resembles Predappiesi descriptions of the marches themselves as "folkloric," "traditional," or "carnivalesque" and suggests that the visitors are more like a troop of historical reenactors than a political movement. As with the Crocean argument that Fascism was merely an interruption in the otherwise great history of Italy, the implication of calling the visitors nostalgic is that the object they venerate is dead and gone, a piece of history rather than a living political movement.

That is not to say that all the visitors are perceived in the same way. Massimo, the restaurateur described in chapter 3, for example, distinguishes between "historic" and "nostalgic" tourists. The former come because they are in the area, and Mussolini's grave is simply a tourist destination to them like any other ("Like I'd go to Jim Morrison's grave, wherever that is"). They come with their families, and if they stop at his restaurant they ask polite questions about the local area and leave again without further ado. The "nostalgic" tourists are those who come in uniforms, who come for the organized marches, and who tend to appear as large groups of men on buses. If Massimo does not attempt to stop them, they will perform Roman salutes in his restaurant after visiting the tomb, and of this group he is rather wary (though not necessarily unwilling to serve them, as we have seen). At no point does he use the word *Fascist* or any variant thereof to describe them. Massimo does not identify "nostalgics" with Fascists; he distinguishes them from "historical" tourists on the basis of the kind of feeling they have about Italy's Fascist period and the intensity of such feelings. Both groups are defined by their feelings about Fascism as a thing of the past, rather than either being isomorphic with it.

There are local candidates, too. We have met Sergio on a couple of occasions, the former prisoner of war and founder of the local chapter of the MSI, the postwar reincarnation of the Fascist Party. I have heard him called an "old Fascist" on occasion but invariably in a jocular tone and in contexts—discussions of the past—that suggest the label refers more to his history as a soldier and his recalcitrance after the war rather than any present quality in him. He is a genteel and extremely elderly man and is treated with the respect accorded to age. Nothing about his politics excludes him from sociality with others in the town, and we have seen how he himself keeps a trove of partisan songs dedicated to Mayor Ferlini. Some of his stories appear with attribution in *La fôja de farfaraz*, despite the left-wing politics of its authors.

Other obvious candidates are the owners of the three main souvenir shops. Here the label *Fascist* is used more frequently, at least in one case. But even in these cases, waters may be muddied. The most obvious question—often raised by Predappiesi—is whether it is ideology or money (or some combination of the two) that motivates the shop owners.

Two of these proprietors are from Predappio, one of them now deceased. This latter is one whom a number of Predappiesi would willingly call Fascist: he effectively began the souvenir trade by selling postcards and relics near the cemetery on the days of the anniversary marches. "He was always a Fascist," Chiara, a council employee tells me, "even before, even when he wasn't selling gadgets [another common euphemism for Fascist paraphernalia]." Her father, a retired lorry driver, disagrees immediately: "No, I think it's for the money. It's not for the politics, it's the money." Angela, the café owner, says that when this proprietor opened the first souvenir shop, people in the town joked that he would be selling Che Guevara T-shirts if Predappio had been lucky enough to be Che's birthplace. But Angela also adds Chiara's point: "He was always a Fascist, though."

Federica, a retired schoolteacher who has taught most of the town's inhabitants, is similarly somewhat equivocal: "Let's say that this guy was the most involved from the beginning, from the point of view of politics. But even he didn't only do this; he did other, ordinary [*sic*] things, too [he owned a hardware store]. And I know his family, they are actually really good people. His wife bends over backward to help. When I needed a flag in school, she would always find one for me, and give me a good price. But it would really bother me every time I went to the shop and had to see all those other things."

The second proprietor from Predappio, still living, is one about whom Predappiesi are much more cynical. "He was in a totally different business," recounts Federica, "selling chickens, owning poultry houses. But then he went bankrupt, found himself without work, and had the idea to take advantage of this situation and open the shop. So he reinvented himself selling Mussolini souvenirs, but without, I think, any specific political inclination. I mean, it was a way to survive."

Angela is less generous, and makes no mention of bankruptcy: "He had this poultry farm, and he made so much money, because it was a huge business, and his brother had an amusement arcade in Predappio. So, when he got old and closed this down, the other one decided to open this shop. He was, how would you say, a 'busy bee.' He knows where the money is. But there is no ideology there. If tomorrow someone else is popular, he will change his whole business."

Chiara is similarly convinced: "There's definitely more self-interest than ideology in his shop. He saw the business; he did it for the money. I know the family, they have never been Fascists, and he was never involved in politics his whole life before this."

Though it is not the largest, this second shop is in some ways the most conspicuous, at least for pedestrians, because it sits in the middle of Predappio's main street, and the merchandise spills out onto the pavement outside. The owner, a short, gray-haired man with a handlebar mustache, is often at work behind the counter or tidying up the displays, and his compatriots usually greet him politely as they pass. Even Giorgio, the erstwhile left-wing mayor, says hello.

The third proprietor is not from Predappio, as Predappiesi will happily tell you, and therefore not seen as their responsibility. He is the most widely known of the three outside of Predappio—even though his shop is the smallest and the least noticeable—because he is also the owner of the Villa Carpena, the "museum" I described in chapter 4. His pecuniary motivations are taken for granted by most Predappiesi, and there is a degree of resentment at the fact that an outsider is profiting from the town's heritage.

Self-interest and ideological conviction need not be mutually exclusive, and my point here is not about whether or not these men are, in fact, really Fascists. It is that Predappiesi frequently deploy monetary self-interest *as if it were* mutually exclusive with political beliefs. When Predappiesi speculate about the self-interest of these men, they are not doing so in order to add greed to the men's charge sheets. Predappiesi do so in order to dismiss these men, with a snicker or a guffaw and a wave of the hand. There is nothing really special about them, is the implication; they are simply businessmen, unscrupulous perhaps, but this is not an unusual assumption for Italians to make about businessmen in general. In other words, there is a degree of reluctance involved in attaching the label of *Fascist* even to those who might seem most obviously to merit it. But the way in which that reluctance is evidenced is by opposing something pragmatic or ordinary, such as "making a living," being a "busy bee," or knowing where the money is, to the high politics of Fascism.

One might imagine that this sort of distinction would at least lead one to a certain set of criteria with which to identify who is, in fact, a Fascist. If self-interest is a characteristic that excludes people from this set, then presumably there are nevertheless other, less self-interested, individuals who fit more comfortably within it.

The problem, however, is that self-interest is frequently perceived to be at the heart of apparently genuine political convictions more generally. This is a broader Italian phenomenon, but it takes on a specific character in Predappio, as I noted in chapter 2 of the fascination with stories of *voltagabbana*, or turncoats. The implication of such stories is that political affiliation usually runs only skin-deep and that beneath the color red or black is simple self-interest (hence the "poplar leaf" insult from which the title of *La fôja de farfaraz* is derived). There are a number of such stories that Predappiesi like to tell.

One concerns a *repubblichino* returning to Predappio after the Axis surrender and being stopped on the road outside the town by a band of anti-Fascists looking to exact punishment on any returning RSI soldiers they encountered. Among this band, the *repubblichino* was very surprised to find his former battalion sergeant, who had deserted from the army of the RSI only a month before the end of the war (Capacci, Pasini, and Giunchi 2014, 216–217). Another favorite is very similar: In the early 1920s, a local man refused to sign up to the PNF and was regularly beaten up by local Fascists as a result. Finally, he converted, and with a convert's zealotry he even went on to fight for the RSI after the fall of Mussolini in 1943. After the surrender in 1945, he went back to Predappio, and as in the previous story, was seized by a band of anti-Fascists in the town upon his return. Upon realizing that one of the men about to beat him for being a Fascist was one of the men who used to beat him for not being a Fascist, he said calmly to the group, "All of you can punch me as much as you want, except him. He's already had his turn." (217).

But as I also suggested in chapter 2, it is Mussolini himself who is perceived as a sort of "turncoat in chief," given his own switch from red to black between leaving the town as an "ordinary man" and returning as Italy's Duce. In other words, at the very heart of Predappiesi conceptions of Fascism is an even deeper skepticism about identifying it than that expressed by doubt over any particular characteristic. In these conceptions, there is a sense in which Fascism was never, in fact, anything more than a cloak for self-interest.

Eco describes *Fascism* as an all-purpose term. His point, broadly speaking, writing about both an Italian and an international context, is that anti-Fascism is a vital and important cause and that we know, in some sense, to what it is opposed. This is revealed not by some fact about Fascism, but by the ways in which we use the word *Fascism* in ordinary language. "Who are They?" Eco asks, posing the skeptical philosopher's question, and then gives us the ordinary language philosopher's answer: "They" are those whom we call Fascist.

But who are *we*? In Predappio, it is far from clear that a sense of the inde-finability of the word either stems from a feeling that people know a Fascist when they see one or serves the purpose of allowing them to pick out the family resemblances between different kinds of Fascist. Ironically, Predappi-esi ordinary language about Fascism instead looks like that of the skeptical philosopher. Either it questions the application of the term based on a partic-ular characteristic or set of characteristics ("he's not Fascist, he's just self-interested," "they're not Fascists, they're just nostalgic clowns"), or, as in the stories of Mussolini and other turncoats, it implies an even more profound skepticism: if a man wears a Fascist uniform, serves the Fascist regime, holds a Fascist Party membership card, and yet later is to be found proclaiming his anti-Fascism and beating returning soldiers, what hope is there of ever answer-ing Orwell's question? If Mussolini himself is thought to have founded Fas-cism in part because the French bribed him into supporting the Entente in the First World War, then what does it even mean to be a Fascist?

My argument here is that the "underlying feelings," as Eco puts it, revealed by Predappiesi ordinary language about Fascism revolve not around some unspo-ken notion of "Ur-Fascism" revealed by a we-know-it-when-we-see-it mental-ity. Instead, they revolve around a deep-seated and profound skepticism about whether or not anyone is really identifiable as a Fascist (see Heywood 2024b). Yet the ordinary skepticism produced as a result is not simply ordinary in the sense of being common and everyday in the town but also ordinary in that its effect is to scale Fascism down to the color of a shirt one wears for the convenience and benefits it confers. In this vision, the high politics of Fascism and of accusations of Fascism come down simply to where people think their interests lie.

As with the other instances of ordinariness, such scaling operations are not simple. While this way of speaking of Fascism may be ordinary in Predappio, it is not so ordinary elsewhere, and of this most Predappiesi are perfectly cogni-zant. As I noted at the outset of this chapter, outsiders who have heard of Pre-dappio rarely share Predappiesi skepticism about identifying Fascism—indeed, instead they often take the town itself, its inhabitants, and its appearance as em-blematic signs of the regime. Roman neo-Fascist restaurateurs provide cheap dinners to Predappiesi tourists, policemen forgive speeding tickets to Predappi-esi drivers, and army sergeant-majors hand out the best jobs to Predappiesi con-scripts. Meanwhile, others consign the whole town to the "toxic waste dump of history" for its associations with Fascism (Wu Ming 2017). Newspaper reports about the ritual marches in Predappio are much more likely to call the marchers "Fascists" than "nostalgics," and non-Predappiesi are usually shocked to discover that the town consistently elected left-wing mayors until 2019. The sorts of fine distinctions Predappiesi make to distinguish their visitors and themselves from Fascism are usually of little interest to outsiders.

Fascist Family Resemblances

There is one respect in which Predappiesi speak of political affiliation—and even occasionally of Fascism—in a manner somewhat similar to Eco's characterization. Interestingly, this respect involves relations of kinship—actual family resemblances, in other words.

A number of recent anthropological studies have pointed to the importance of kinship-related phenomena to economic and political life in a range of contexts (e.g., Bear 2007; Herzfeld 2007; McKinnon and Canell 2013; Yanagisako 2002). This runs counter to classic anthropological arguments that divided non-modern societies from modern ones on the basis that only the former assimilate their political systems and their lineage systems. It also runs counter to what some of this literature describes as a "taboo" in "modern societies" on blurring these boundaries between domains, even if, as Sian Lazar points out, "they are in fact constantly experienced and held together in . . . everyday practices" (Lazar 2018, 259).

Lazar's is one of the most powerful and convincing recent calls for us to appreciate the interconnected nature of kinship and politics (2018; see also 2017). Her work on trade unions in Argentina shows how a range of kinship-related practices and metaphors such as "blood," consubstantiality, sociality, and care are important in creating something that looks very much like a kin-group in trade union life. Though she retains something like the distinction between kinship and politics as a heuristic device of her analysis (2018, 259), her point is that in everyday life this distinction is very much blurred.

Interestingly for present purposes, one of the main targets of Lazar's argument is the assumption—not very common in contemporary anthropology but arguably more common beyond it—that politics is driven primarily by self-interest, rather than by sentiment, say. She is of course arguing, not that self-interest has no role to play in political life, but that in some contexts, some versions of "everyday life," it may be less important than other drivers of action.

Though Lazar points out that the assumption that self-interest determines politics is in part derived from notions of *Homo economicus* and the "rational actor," she makes relatively little of the fact that this is itself another instance of domain-blurring, this time from the economic into the political. This is worth remarking on in the case of Predappio because distinguishing between the domains of the economic and the political, self-interest and conviction, is part of what allows people to express skepticism about whether people are really Fascist or not. So, Lazar's point that we ought to be ethnographically sensitive to the relative importance of self-interest as a motivation for politics is borne out.

But what about kinship? Lazar makes a thoroughly convincing case for the blurring of kinship and politics in her own fieldwork context. But if one of the risks of utilitarian analyses of politics is that they presume a subsumption of the political into the economic, might there be contexts in which it may be similarly mistaken to assume that kinship and the political are exactly isomorphic? What if sometimes, in some versions of "everyday life," politics must be distilled from kinship, just as Lazar distills it from economics?

There are some respects in which kinship and politics are very clearly intertwined in Predappio. A number of Mussolini's descendants are famous in contemporary Italy, though none of them live in Predappio. Most well-known of all is Alessandra Mussolini, an erstwhile member of both houses of Italy's parliament and the European parliament, as well as a former actress and *Playboy* model. She has regularly defended her grandfather in public, as have other grandchildren such as the writer and television presenter Edda Negri Mussolini and the one-time candidate for mayor of Rome Guido Mussolini. The political affiliation of the family has never been in doubt. In a manner akin to Lazar's description of how one is "born," not made, a Peronist in Argentina, Benito Mussolini wrote of his son Bruno after his death in a flying accident that he was "Fascista—nato e vissuto" (born and lived a Fascist), and that could aptly describe Benito's more distant descendants as well. Though they do not live in Predappio, they do sometimes attend the ritual marches, and they retain control over the family crypt.

This fact led to public spat between the family and Mayor Giorgio Frassineti in 2017, over a TV interview he conducted alongside Miro Gori, the local head of ANPI, the partisans' organization, inside the crypt itself. Alessandra Mussolini declared the crypt to have been "violated," and the family closed it to visitors, in a gesture that most thought was intended to punish Predappio by depriving it of its main source of tourist income. Alessandra Mussolini ceremonially reopened the tomb in 2019 while campaigning for the right-wing candidate to replace Giorgio as mayor, a candidate whose victory made him the first right-wing mayor of Predappio since the end of the Second World War. It would be a mistake, though, to think that politics precluded any kind of relationship between Predappio's former left-wing local administrations and the Mussolini family; before the spat, in 2016, Giorgio got into hot water with ANPI, this time by appearing as a speaker at a book symposium for Edda Negri Mussolini's biography of her grandmother, Rachele Mussolini.

Nobody seriously doubts the political affiliation of anybody whose surname is Mussolini (although the word *Fascist* is still used relatively sparingly in Predappio even with reference to the family). The Mussolini family is an extreme case, but some version of the notion that one is "born" into one's politics is more broadly common in Predappio (and elsewhere in Italy). Relatives of Mussolini's widow, Rachele, for instance, who do live in the town, are known for their continued loyalty to their affinal kin. More generally, people in Predappio are for the most part aware of the political affiliations of any particular family. There is a "left-wing" bar (the former working men's club, or Casa del Popolo) and there is a "right-wing" bar, and most people know in which bar any particular family belongs. This idea of politics as inheritance was particularly brought home to me on one occasion when I first met Giovanni, a retired man with a large collection of Fascist memorabilia who also acted as a general factotum for a prominent local right-wing politician. As we were looking through his photos of Predappio in the 1930s, I happened to mention that I had affinal relatives of my own in the town and gave him their name. "Ah!" he said, looking sharply at me, "but they're of the left!" Then, smiling, he added, "But it's not your fault." As in Lazar's account, kinship seems thus to play a significant role in political life.

Yet there is a sense in which things are also more complicated, one hinted at in Giovanni's comment that my family's politics were "not your fault." To return to the Mussolini family, for example, Edda Negri Mussolini and her sister led the ritual march on the anniversary of their grandfather's death in April 2017. Watching them with Predappiesi friends from a nearby bar, I was struck by how much of the conversation among locals here and afterward was focused on kinship—indeed on literal family resemblances—*instead of* politics.

Edda and her sister Silvia bear a remarkably striking resemblance to their grandfather. They share the same round face and prominent nose, and their eyes are unmistakably alike. It is impossible not to notice the similarities once you know who they are. It was upon these family resemblances, rather than metaphorical political family resemblances, that many Predappiesi I knew chose to focus.

"Don't you think it's incredible how much they look like him?," remarked Marco, as we watched the marchers coalesce around the sisters. "Look at the shape of the head and the eyes! It's like looking at a picture from a history book. Imagine growing up with that!"

"Ah, it must have been hard," responded his partner, Eleonora. "Poor things. They had nothing to do with any of that, they weren't even born, but what can you do about it? It's their blood."

As they were having this conversation, we were watching the sisters lead a parade of thousands wearing Fascist uniforms and holding up slogans in praise

of their grandfather and his politics. Yet the only hint of politics in this exchange is Eleonora's comment that the sisters "had nothing to do with any of
that," *that* presumably being the many things that people find objectionable
about Fascism. The sentiment of sympathy ("poor things") was often expressed
in Predappio toward members of the Mussolini family on the basis that they
had inherited a legacy over which they had no real control, a situation with
which Predappiesi are more than familiar.

In other words, there is a sense here in which literal family resemblances
and kinship phenomena such as "blood" actually serve as political alibis of a
sort, substitutes, like self-interest, for "true" politics. The implication of this
view is that people such as Edda Negri Mussolini and her sister have no real
choice about their affiliations, thus placing such affiliations beyond the question of political conviction. If it is choice inspired by self-interest that puts the
shop owners out of the realm of politics and into that of economics, here it is
lack of choice determined by "blood" that puts the Mussolinis out of the realm
of politics and into that of kinship.

This sort of idea is also replicated on a smaller scale in cases much less extreme than that of the Mussolinis. It is there, for instance, in Giovanni's remark that my affinal kin's political affiliations were not my fault. He was not
suggesting that I might differ in my own politics from my kin network. Indeed, he assumed that I did not and went on to make frequent jokes about
"Communists like you" throughout our acquaintance. He was suggesting instead to an outsider—and a foreigner—that he would not blame me for my
politics precisely *because* he knew of my family connections.

Not everyone follows their family's politics. Angela, for example, relates
having blazing rows with her father when she was young and now believes
her left-wing politics are in part a reaction to her father's right-wing beliefs.
Chiara and her father—both of whom we met earlier commenting on the shop
owners—are less extreme in their political divergences, but they do have differences. She is quite forthright in her left-wing politics, whereas he is more
quietly circumspect but certainly more conservative in his views; whereas Chiara abhors the souvenir shops, for example, her father has a more live-and-let-
live attitude. He is much more comfortable attributing pecuniary motivations
to all the owners, whereas Chiara is confident in her claim that at least one of
them really is a Fascist. Interestingly, given her own differences with her father,
Chiara cites her knowledge that the family of one owner has never been Fascist as evidence for the fact that he himself cannot be. If this were always true,
then Mussolini would have remained a socialist, like his own father.

My point in this section has been that though Predappiesi seem to adopt a
form of Eco's you-know-it-when-you-see-it attitude to Fascism in this partic-

ular sense, the family resemblances they pick out to identify a shared politics often do not, in fact, have anything to do with politics at all in the sense of ideological conviction. They are literal family resemblances, or shared surnames, as in the case of the Mussolinis. While to some extent this makes sense as an instance of Lazar's description of a form of politics underlain by kinship-related phenomena, there is also something slightly distinct about this case. Predappiesi deploy kinship-based concepts precisely because their understanding of politics is *not* largely kinship-based, and talking about kinship-based political resemblances can be a way of avoiding talking about actual shared political convictions. To speak of affinal or consanguineal resemblances and loyalties is another way of rendering ordinary the continuing presence of Fascist politics.

Predappio has long been synonymous with Fascism as far as most outsiders are concerned. From the mass production of picture postcards of its construction under the regime, to the photographs of men wearing black that adorn the pages of contemporary newspapers every October, it is indissolubly linked in a wider public imaginary with its most famous son and the movement he created. Yet Predappiesi themselves go to great lengths to scale apparent Fascism down to more ordinary motivations: basic self-interest and family loyalty. Thus, ordinary language about Fascism in Predappio in fact looks rather skeptical, prone as it is to doubt about the category's applicability. As I have noted before, this is a very particular vision of ordinariness, as any will be, but it is not hard to imagine why Predappiesi might see pecuniary motivation or kinship allegiances as more ordinary than Fascist political convictions.

But what is it that these ways of talking about Fascism scale down from, as it were? What constitutes the domain of Fascist politics, to which that of kinship or economics may be counterposed? So far in this book, my concern has been largely with establishing the various ways in which people produce a sense of ordinariness in Predappio. The next and final chapter will aim to describe some of the controversies, local and national, that erupted over an initiative that put Predappio squarely back in the headlines of global news: a proposal to install a museum of Fascism in the ruins of the old Fascist Party Headquarters.

CHAPTER 6

Recycling the Past and the "Museum of Fascism"

In March 2016, the word *Fascism* seemed suddenly to be ubiquitous. Donald Trump had just won a series of Republican primary elections on Super Tuesday, and American media were awash with comparisons to Hitler and Mussolini. *Time* magazine ran a piece noting that even Mike Godwin—inventor of the eponymous "Godwin's Law," whereby prolonged internet arguments inevitably devolve into comparisons with Fascism—was encouraging such comparisons (Hoffman 2017).

In Italy, the far-right Lega Nord, led by former journalist Matteo Salvini, was back from near political oblivion earlier in the decade and polling at around 17 percent, a figure that would go on to double by the elections that would bring the party to power in 2018.

And in Predappio, March 2016 witnessed a historic transfer: the former Casa del Fascio e dell'Ospitalità, property of the Italian state since its expropriation from the Fascist Party after the end of the war and left to ruin, was officially handed over to the *comune*. As Simona Storchi has demonstrated, successive administrations in Predappio had made numerous attempts to buy or lease the Casa del Fascio since the war, none of them successful (2019). Seventy years later, the most prominent Fascist edifice in Predappio finally belonged to the town itself.

The transfer was the first significant moment in an ongoing process, the eventual aim of which was to transform the derelict Casa del Fascio into a "documentation center" on Fascism, a place where tourists and scholars from around the world could come to learn about the regime and its history. I was able to observe much of this process at close quarters, as Carlo (the project's technical director) and Giorgio (the mayor) sought to bring it to fruition.

Many of the difficulties the project encountered stemmed from widespread public and intellectual distrust in Italy of the idea that Predappio could be a suitable location for any proper historicization of the Fascist period. For years, Italian and international press coverage of Predappio had consisted of diatribes of an increasingly acerbic nature regarding the Casa del Fascio project, the culmination of which was a series of blog entries written by Roberto Bui, a member of a world-famous Bolognese Marxist collective called Wu Ming (who also write popular novels under the pseudonym of Luther Blisset), in which he labeled Predappio a "toxic waste dump" (2017) and attacked Giorgio for, among other things, his attendance at the event with Mussolini's granddaughter I mentioned in the last chapter. Giorgio responded in a Facebook post by suggesting that "Signor Wu Minchia [a rude Italian word for penis]" should have better things to do with his time than follow the mayor of Predappio around, and, as a counterpoint, he framed a copy of an interview the *Washington Post* did with him on the Casa del Fascio project to hang in his office.

Well-known public intellectuals in Italy such as Serge Noiret (a historian at the European University Institute in Florence), Sergio Luzzatto (historian and author of a popular book on the fate of Mussolini's body), and Carlo Ginzburg all weighed in on the controversy about the Casa del Fascio (Noiret 2016; Luzzatto and Ginzburg 2016; see also Fuller 2018); signatures in support or against the project were collected from academic history departments across the world; and the debates prompted an Italian member of parliament to put forward a law that would ban the overt display of Fascist symbols. In the wider region, these arguments also took place beyond the sphere of blogs and newspaper articles. As I noted in chapter 3, many of Carlo's old comrades from the regional sections of Lotta Continua and other left-wing groups opposed the project, leading to arguments, tensions, and the severing of long-standing friendships and relationships.

One evening around the height of the controversy surrounding the Casa del Fascio, I drove up the hill from New Predappio to Predappio Alta, its older twin, to have dinner at an osteria in the town square. The restaurant was one of Giorgio's favorites, owned by friends of his, and so I was unsurprised to see him appear around nine for a late-night digestif. I was surprised, though, by how exhausted and worn-out he looked, more so than I had ever seen him. One of the first things he said after sitting down with me was how much he was looking forward to giving up the mayoralty in two years' time, when his second mandate was due to expire.

Before this, however, and as soon as Giorgio appeared in the square, a local man at a table adjacent to mine rose and advanced on Giorgio, haranguing him loudly and aggressively and threatening to physically attack him, before striding off, still hurling insults over his shoulder. In several years of witnessing neo-Fascist marches in Predappio, sometimes taking place on the same day as the ANPI celebrations of its liberation, this was the closest thing to physical violence I had yet seen occur in the town.

The man's anger, however, and Giorgio's exhaustion, had nothing to do with the Casa del Fascio project, which, as I will describe in this chapter, Predappiesi largely ignored. While intellectuals, politicians, commentators in the regional, national, and international press, and outsiders of all varieties were debating the rights and wrongs of the Casa del Fascio project, the problem that consumed Predappio politically—to an extent that it produced several other such near-violent altercations—was the question of how they would dispose of their rubbish.

The Politics of Scale

At the end of the previous chapter, I promised that I would fill out my description of what politics means in Predappio. In that chapter, we met some things politics often does not mean: it is not, or at least is not always, isomorphic with either kinship or economics, insofar as we met examples of Predappiesi deploying idioms of both relatedness and of self-interest in an effort to detach people from the politics of Fascism. I am also conscious that in describing throughout this book the various ways in which Predappiesi seek to scale themselves down and away from debates about their Fascist heritage, I may leave readers with the impression that these practices of scaling are a sort of "anti-politics machine" (Ferguson 1990), a way to depoliticize Predappio, a place that is nothing if not political to most outsiders.

That is not the case, as I will describe in this chapter. Predappiesi are capable of intense politicization. However, the issues that become political—that is, that become the subject of public debate, argumentation, and even near-violence— are not those an outsider would necessarily expect. Instead, as should come as no surprise by this point, they are issues—such as rubbish collection and recycling, as we will see in this chapter—that scale differently from that of Fascism and its legacies.

A range of recent work in the anthropology of politics has made important contributions to our understanding of the complex relationship between
politics and scale-making. For example, building in part on feminist scholarship (e.g., Gal 2002; Benhabib 1998), Esra Özyürek has pointed to the ways in
which the line between the public and private spheres is shifting and blurring
in contemporary neoliberal Turkey, noting that familiar ways of hierarchically
scaling the public and the private so that the former encompasses the latter
are not sufficient to capture this phenomenon (2006). Similarly, James Ferguson, in line with earlier work by Timothy Mitchell (e.g., 1991), has troubled
our assumptions about the scaled relationship between civil society and the
nation-state in Africa by showing how many actors and institutions exist across
such a simplistic divide and cannot be captured by a simple "above versus below" conceptual topography (2006). Other work, both new and old, has also
shown the labor that goes into making politics look either local or global (e.g.,
Brenner 2009; Latour 2005; Smith 1992). Zoltan Glück, for example, describes
how the Occupy Wall Street movement worked hard to produce itself as local, in contrast to the global investment banks metonymized in Wall Street
(2013). One of the important things that all this work demonstrates is that the
scaling of political questions is itself a political question: there is nothing intrinsic to certain phenomena that make them "public" or "private," "local" or
"global," and work must be done by actors involved to produce a sense of such
scales.

In similar fashion, in this chapter I aim to interrogate the relation between
politics and scale in Predappio. In particular, I share the interest of such work
in pointing to the ways in which scales are constructed and sustained by participants involved in political contexts, rather than just being there (a point
made in depth by Summerson Carr and Lempert 2016 and earlier by Latour
2005; Candea 2012): that there is, in other words, a politics to scale. There are
also many respects in which the relationship between debates over the Casa
del Fascio project and those I will describe over rubbish and recycling in Predappio could map on to the scales of local versus global, civil society versus
state, and private versus public, as we will see.

However, here I want to pick at the threads of a different scalar relationship. Ferguson notes in passing that the imagined topography of state versus
civil society is one that undergirds many of our own preferred anthropological visions of political struggle, "as coming 'from below' (as we say), as
'grounded' in rooted and authentic 'lives,' 'experiences,' and 'communities'"
(2006, 48). It is to the construction of this (part anthropological and part ethnographic) distinction between the everyday, experiential, community-based

politics of where and how often to dispose of your rubbish, on the one hand, and the highly ideologized and often rather abstract political debates about Fascist heritage, on the other hand, that I turn in this chapter.

The Chernobyl of History

It is difficult to date with precision the origins of the idea to turn the Casa del Fascio into something like a museum, or "documentation center," of Fascism. As Storchi shows, the idea of doing something with the biggest derelict building in the town has certainly been around for some time (2019), and one of Giorgio's predecessors has claimed credit for the original plan to me. What is certainly not in doubt, though, is that Giorgio's energy and dedication to the project brought it closer to fruition than it had ever come before, winning him the public backing of the Italian national government, a Holocaust Memorial Award from Austria, and a meeting with and endorsement from then Italian prime minister Matteo Renzi.

A short, barrel-chested man with a round head and a neat beard, Giorgio was a geology teacher and local councillor before his first election to the mayoralty in 2009, on the ticket of the Democratic Party, formerly the Italian Communist Party and at the time the main center-left Italian political party. He smokes incessantly—mainly very slim cigarettes but occasionally an e-cigarette—and likes a drink and good food. He is charismatic, and it is easy to see how he won two local elections handily and became a favorite go-to source of interviews for the national and international press (figure 6.1).[1]

Giorgio's charisma sets him apart from his predecessors and is in part responsible for the amount of publicity the Casa del Fascio project has received over the years. He liked to couch his arguments in favor of the project in metaphors that he returned to time and time again in public speeches. The one I have heard him use most often is that Fascism is a virus (akin to Croce's characterization of it as a moral sickness), and the only antidote to a virus is vaccination. "Culture" is what Giorgio argued constitutes vaccination, and he saw the Casa del Fascio documentation center as a place for people from around the world to come and learn from the mistakes of the past. But Giorgio laments his own lack of culture, with perhaps a touch of false modesty. He would regularly complain that he was just a poor geologist forced, by virtue of the office he held, to make pronouncements about complex historical questions. Yet he is clearly well read. He once said to me that if he encountered another book that cited Walter Benjamin's famous image of the angel of history, he would throw it in the trash: "We are not rubble, you know, we

FIGURE 6.1.   Giorgio interviewed by a Danish television crew outside of the Casa del Fascio. Photo by author.

also built things. And why does he always walk backward, like a shrimp? Look ahead, for God's sake!"

Giorgio dates the origins of his own interest in the Casa del Fascio project to the time he was running for his first mandate:

> It's the most massive, the most representative and symbolic place in all Predappio, and it's in a central position, right in the main square. But it's completely abandoned, left to itself. So, what do we do with it? At first there was an idea to turn it into a museum of architecture and link it up to the University [of Bologna] faculty of architecture. But this was 2008, 2009, there was the crisis, and there was very little money around. So then I met Carlo, but even before that, I had this great idea: Why should I have to swallow just a little Fascism, when I could eat the whole lot?

Giorgio and his fondness for publicity thus overturned a decades-old tacit rule in Predappiesi administration: stay away from talk about Fascism. Indeed, he did the opposite; as his remark about "eating the whole lot" of Fascism instead of "swallowing just a little" suggests, his strategy was effectively to try to turn Predappio's greatest liability into a strength. Despite his ubiquity in Italian public discourse about Fascism however, Giorgio himself still evinced some equivocation over this status. He regularly framed his public discourse on Fascism as a duty, imposed on him by his office rather than assumed out of choice, and would complain that the mayor of any other *comune* in Italy of the same proportions would never be subject to the same level of press scrutiny or be expected to be an expert on complex historical questions. At the same time, his enjoyment of the attention was palpable; he would pore over newspaper coverage of his speeches and often send to me anything in the press that touched on him.

Carlo also came to the project by making his voice heard on the uncomfortable subject of Fascism. In the early 2000s, he had been working for some time as a sort of cultural project manager, setting up and curating exhibitions and projects in empty spaces. He had come to Giorgio's attention when Carlo wrote a newspaper article that was deeply critical of a project to install a sort of museum in the Rocca delle Caminate, Mussolini's summer residence. The idea at the time was that the Rocca would be turned into a sort of upscale wine bar, restaurant, and guest house, complete with a small museum to memorialize famous figures from the Romagna (including Mussolini). Carlo thought this a ridiculous plan, almost guaranteed to end up attracting exactly the sort of tourists he wanted to see fewer of coming to Predappio. He suggested instead that it ought to be turned into a natural history museum ("then if the nostalgics come, all they have to look at is plants"). This plan, too, came to nothing, and as we have seen, the Rocca is now supposed to be a small business hub but is in fact largely empty, despite the money spent on its renovation.

Carlo's intervention in the Rocca debate attracted Giorgio's attention, and he asked Carlo to draw up a plan for the Casa del Fascio that Giorgio could use in his 2014 electoral campaign. In 2015, Carlo was made the project's technical director, and the town council unanimously approved his plan. An academic historian affiliated with the University of Siena was drafted as the project's scientific director, but Carlo and Giorgio remained the main driving forces throughout the project's life span.

Almost as soon as the plans for the project were publicized, public polemics began. "As soon as it became public knowledge, pandemonium broke out," recalls Giorgio.

And why is this? Why this pandemonium? This is exactly why the project is necessary! If this history was all settled, then nobody would have gotten so upset, see? This is exactly why our project was needed, because there's nothing like it in Italy. All there is is this swampy world of historians who sit in their chairs and fiddle about Mussolini, but they never say anything useful. So, we said, "We're going to rub this in your faces, in the faces of all

Italians." Because . . . look at what's happening in Europe right now, look at the rise of neo-Fascism: if you know about this stuff, then you can fight it, but if you try and hide or suppress it then you'll never fight it.

In line with his favorite analogy of virus and vaccination, Giorgio's justifications for the project often relied on this idea that knowledge of Fascism would aid in the fight against it. Carlo took a similar position: "Giorgio is right when he calls Predappio the Chernobyl of history. Nobody wants to touch it, nobody wants to do anything about it, so you just leave it abandoned to its fate with the shops and the marchers. We want to change that."

Objections, however, came thick and fast and on a range of different grounds.[2] A number of public figures and historians were against the very premise of the idea of a museum of Fascism, suggesting alternative topics instead, such as the Holocaust or the Resistance; others argued that Italy was far from ready for a historicization of Fascism, as it had failed to reconcile itself to its own history, with Germany often cast as an example of success in this endeavor (e.g., Bernabei 2014; Foa 2016). Still more disliked what they saw in the plans for the project, particularly the lack of focus on anti-Fascism and an apparent emphasis on the consent with which Mussolini governed for the majority of his time in power (e.g., Fondazione Alfred Lewin 2016).

The majority of the objections, however, and the ones that most infuriated Carlo and Giorgio, were the ones that questioned Predappio itself as a location for the project. A great number of commentators worried about the likelihood that the Casa del Fascio would simply become another pilgrimage site for neo-Fascist tourists. Some were also concerned about how such a museum could do its job properly when a hundred yards down the road were souvenir shops selling Fascist bric-a-brac (e.g., Schwarz 2016). "What would a teacher tell their schoolchildren," ran a common line of reasoning, "if, after visiting the museum they want to go into the shops to buy some memorabilia?" (see, e.g., Fondazione Alfred Lewin 2016). Still other commentators simply asserted that Predappio was too small to handle a project of this size, and that if there were going to be a "museum of Fascism" in Italy it ought to be in a large urban center such as Rome or Milan (e.g., Luzzatto and Ginzburg 2016). These sorts of comments about Predappio as a location for the project would enrage Carlo and Giorgio, who would point out, first of all, that this was their idea, that nobody else had proposed such a project, and so where exactly should it be sited if not in the place they wanted it to be; and, second, that the whole point of the project was to change the broader public image of Predappio and that only by achieving this would you drive the shop owners out of business and the neo-Fascist tourists away.

Perhaps the most damning public intervention in these debates were three blog entries written by Wu Ming 1, otherwise known as Roberto Bui, a short man with a shaved head with whom I had lunch in nearby Bologna a month or so before the entries were published.

When we met, Bui was deeply cynical about the motivations behind the project:

> The mayor doesn't want to eliminate neo-Fascist tourism. . . . He wants to keep it, but to offer another kind of merchandise, and this kind of merchandise will be the museum. So, then he can say, "See, there aren't just neo-Fascists here, there are also people with a real, serious desire for knowledge of that period." But in reality, it wouldn't replace neo-Fascist tourism, it would simply be an addition. It would be an integration of neo-Fascist tourism within this toxic frame. Because it's not just a matter of Il Duce's tomb at San Cassiano: the whole town is Il Duce's tomb. From a symbolic point of view, the whole town is Il Duce. . . . There's no other reason that it's famous.

Later, couching his position on the museum more succinctly, he put it this way: "There will always be that gross stuff [neo-Fascist tourism in Predappio], and what we must absolutely not do is try to plant a daisy on a pile of shit."

When I noted the argument that Carlo would make to such claims about Predappio—that doing something is better than doing nothing, as doing nothing will simply leave Predappiesi in the position they have always been in—Bui was dismissive: "This can't be at the expense of everyone else. Because this is a national project, which will probably receive millions of euros from the government, so this can't just be about Predappiesi. It concerns all Italians, and indeed not only Italians. The risks of this operation go far beyond Predappio: so, on one side of the scale you have six thousand villagers, and on the other side you have the whole country. I mean, really."

Bui's distaste for Predappio emerges even more clearly in the Wu Ming blog entries titled "Predappio: Toxic Waste Blues": "Days later, I . . . still feel the aftereffects of the nausea [of his visit to Predappio]," it begins (2017). Much of the three blog entries is taken up by a forensic demolition of the Casa del Fascio project as poorly planned, motivated by the self-interest of Giorgio (who is painted as a duplicitous character who says one thing to the left-wing press and another thing to the right-wing press), and above all, impossible to execute in the "toxic frame" of Predappio.

A relatively small proportion of the blogs is dedicated to Predappio itself, but what there is is as caustic as Bui's remarks to me about Predappio (all translation my own): "By dint of all the talk about it, Predappio seems bigger than it actually is, and much more glamorous than it actually is. When you get there, it shrivels up, and isn't glamorous at all . . . sad little bars with a rarefied, aged clientele bent over their scratch cards. . . . The architecture of the twenties, designed largely by Florestano di Fausto, seems disproportionate to the town— it appears like a child in a man's boots—and the buildings are less opulent and sparkling than they appear in the photos" (Wu Ming 2017).

Bui also reiterates the sentiment he had expressed to me earlier about the relative importance of Predappio in contrast to the national problem of neo-Fascism: "The problem of neo-Fascism, of which the situation in Predappio is an epiphenomenon, has been replaced by the lesser problem of what to do in Predappio and for the Predappiesi. A dilemma that is mainly that of Frassineti and his constituents—'How to break free from black [neo-Fascist] businesses without losing the money they bring to the town?'—was presented as an urgent problem for all of us, to be addressed as soon as possible with public injections of millions of euros" (Wu Ming 2017).

What I wish to emphasize here is the fact that many of these arguments, both for and against the Casa del Fascio project, turn on questions of political scale. For example, much of Giorgio's public discourse around the project centers on its potential ability to speak to a "European" problem and to draw in visitors from across the continent. His visions of its success conjured up pictures of schoolchildren from Britain, France, and Germany coming to Predappio to learn the facts about Fascism. He delighted in pointing to his European connections—in addition to the Austrian Holocaust Memorial Prize, he had forged links with mayors of towns with troubled heritage across the continent, he had aligned the Casa del Fascio project with continental memory associations such as EUROM (the European Observatory on Memories) and European Cultural Route ATRIUM (Architecture of Totalitarian Regimes of the 20th Century in Europe's Urban Memory), and he sought European funding for the project. He enjoyed reeling off a list of countries whose newspapers or television stations had interviewed him. The documentation center was deliberately planned to speak to European issues.

Bui is surely right to point to a degree of interested motivation here. Emilia-Romagna—in particular its interior—is starved of income from tourism in comparison to its proximate neighbors, well-known hot spots such as Tuscany and Umbria. The border with Tuscany is only a little way down the road from Predappio—and was even closer before Mussolini shifted it westward—and much of the landscape of this area is characteristically Tuscan. Yet very few tourists pass through the area, and Giorgio was certainly on the lookout for ways in which to increase the flow (putting a lot of energy into initiatives to promote local producers of Sangiovese wine, for example).

My interest is less in questions of motive, though, and more about the scalar imaginary at work here. I have no doubt that Giorgio really did believe in the possibility of using Predappio's history to "scale up" the town to regional and international relevance. His own capacity to garner the attention of the international press, such as the *Washington Post*, was one of his proudest achievements. He stands apart from any of his mayoral predecessors because of his willingness to, as he puts it, "eat the whole lot" of Fascism: to use what previous administrations considered Predappio's greatest weakness as its strength, to employ—rather than downplay—its Fascist heritage as a scaling device to magnify Predappio's significance far beyond the boundaries of the town itself.

Questions of scale also intruded into other objections to the Casa del Fascio project. In 2017, for example, a collection of regional cultural and political associations issued a damning press release criticizing the management of the project for failing to consult and dialogue with them over the plans for the documentation center. In this failure, "instead of being a resource for the cultural and social development of the Forlì and Romagna areas, an opportunity for Italian and foreign students and researchers, [the project] risks being a sensational own goal, served on a plate of silver to nostalgic and 'curious' tourism" (Istituto storico della Resistenza e dell'Età contemporanea di Forlì-Cesena et al. 2017).

The objection here introduces another layer of scale in between the town of Predappio and the European and international arena: the "territory," as the release puts it, in which Predappio resides. I know that a number of the authors behind this release had serious intellectual and political qualms about the Casa del Fascio project; however, there is also a disagreement about how Predappio should scale up at work here. Because of Italy's centralized and integrated political system, regional branches of national associations (such as ANPI, the local chapter of which was a signatory of the press release above) have a considerable degree of clout within their particular area. So, for a town or *comune* to leapfrog over them directly onto the national and European stage, as Giorgio did with Predappio, was bound to result in a degree of ill feeling.

Bui's logic, too, has a significant scalar dimension, like that of other opponents of the project. He takes some pains, in fact, literally to minimize Predappio—hence the contrast between its discursive and actual size in his introduction to his blogs and the image of it as a "child in a man's boots," its monumentalist architecture disproportionate to its size. The question of scale is also quite explicit whenever he addresses the issue of balance: neo-Fascism is not "just" a Predappiesi problem; it is, as he put it to me, a national problem, indeed an international one. So whatever claim Predappiesi (or Giorgio, at least) may have to a resolution for their problematic heritage is far outweighed by the Italian—

indeed global—problem of the rise of the far right and the need to combat it. This scalar imaginary is mirrored in claims by other opponents of the project that if there is going to be a museum of Fascism in Italy, it ought to be in an urban center such as Rome or Milan. Yet unlike these other opponents, Bui's problem with Predappio as a site for a documentation center is not just a matter of size; it is, as he puts it, about the "frame." For Bui, as for others whom we met in the last chapter, Predappio is an index or a metonym for Fascism and Mussolini: "the whole town is Il Duce's tomb."

There is, in other words, a normative dimension to both Bui's and Giorgio's scalar visions. Both in fact agree that Predappio represents something "more" than itself, though they disagree about exactly what that is: for Giorgio it is Fascism as history, whereas for Bui it is Mussolini himself and the neo-Fascist personality cult that equates a man with a political movement (Ginzburg 2016). But while Giorgio seeks recognition for that "more" and aims to use it to earn Predappio a place on the international stage, Bui seeks to diminish it. Like others I discussed in the last chapter, his antipathy to Predappio and his attacks on it as a "toxic waste dump," as "smaller" than its place in national discourse, as a "child in a man's boots," or simply "a pile of shit," are attacks on Predappio as a stand-in for neo-Fascism. To diminish Predappio is to diminish neo-Fascism.

However, the scale at work in these debates is not just that of comparative size (Predappio the *comune* versus Europe or the global problem of neo-Fascism). At stake, too, across many of these arguments is the relationship between the abstract and the concrete, the rarefied air of academic debates about the history of Fascism and the reality of life in Predappio. Carlo and Giorgio, for instance, would regularly point out that their critics in cultural associations of the region never actually came to Predappio, never experienced what it was really like, except perhaps to come to the anti-Fascist tagliatelle dinner on October 28 (hence their characterization as "colonialists" by one local council member—unable to understand the daily struggle of living with Fascist heritage). Giorgio would also often speak with derision of academic historians "fiddling," as he put it to me, about Mussolini, instead of coming up with concrete solutions. Part of his justification for the Casa del Fascio project rested precisely on this distinction between the academic debates and reality; Predappio, according to Giorgio, could give concrete form to the history of Fascism, given that in many ways and to many people Predappio *is* Fascism in (literally) concrete form. Carlo would often argue in a similar fashion that the Casa del Fascio project would help solve an eminently practical set of problems for Predappiesi centered around the ritual marches: traffic congestion, the town's public image, offensive behavior in the cemetery.

Yet the project's opponents also drew on precisely the same distinction between the abstract and the pragmatic, positioning themselves, too, on the side of the everyday and the real. Bui's blog is littered with references to the "concreteness" of neo-Fascism, in contrast to the "wishful thinking" of the Casa del Fascio project, an irresponsible gamble on the part of academics who fail to understand the "concrete, corporeal" reality of neo-Fascism in Predappio. He himself makes a clear effort to be "concrete" about Predappio, visiting it in preparation for writing his blog entries. In dialogue with an Italian historian, he contrasts the abstraction of the Casa del Fascio plans with the "individual stories" and "the concreteness of people's lives" on which work on Fascism should really be focused but which is often neglected by "scholastics" and "academics" (Wu Ming 2017).

Both sides of these arguments, in other words, invoke the scale of the abstract and the concrete, the academic and the everyday, and both sides claim for themselves the same dimension of it. Nobody, it seems, wants to be on the side of abstraction (or academics), despite the fact that there is arguably much that is abstract on either side, as each was wont to point out of the other. While Bui clearly did visit Predappio, little of his writing concerns life in Predappio itself. He describes visiting two of the souvenir shops and the local cemetery, but beyond these brief narratives Predappio largely appears as a cipher, and no individual Predappiesi appear, except for a thinly characterized assistant in a souvenir shop. Similarly, in his public speeches and interviews on the Casa del Fascio project, I rarely if ever heard Giorgio invoke the town in any clearly concrete sense. As I have noted, his riposte to those who criticized the choice of Predappio as a site for the project was usually simply to say that it was his idea and so where else should it be sited; he might—depending on his audience—sometimes add that siting the project in Predappio would lead to new forms of tourism that would in turn eventually put its souvenir shops out of business, but this was clearly to be seen as a possible happy by-product, rather than a key rationale. What was important about Predappio was resignifying its existing symbolic status in such a way as to allow it to speak to an international audience beyond that of neo-Fascism.

I mean none of this as criticism. Bui's intention in his blog entries was clearly not to write an ethnography of everyday life in Predappio, and Giorgio's aims for Predappio obliged him, to a large extent, to speak in a language that would make him and his *comune* of six thousand people look relevant to national and international pundits and funders. My point is merely that the scale of concreteness and everyday life versus abstraction and wishful thinking is very much what is at stake in these arguments, not a premise for them.

Perhaps unsurprisingly, though, it was not just participants in these public debates who contested the meanings of concreteness and abstraction; it was also Predappiesi themselves. In contrast to the arguments of both Giorgio and his opponents, the concrete and the everyday that Predappiesi invoke have nothing to do with Fascism. They are an escape from Fascism. That they are not also an escape from politics per se is what I will endeavor to make clear below.

"Are You Going to Rifle Through My Sanitary Napkins?"

In 2017, in the midst of the most heated period of debates about what to do with the Casa del Fascio, at almost exactly the same time as Bui's blog about Predappio as a "toxic waste dump" was published, the majority of Predappiesi were wholly occupied by a rather different political firestorm. As I sought to gauge local reactions to the plan to put Predappio at the center of global debates on neo-Fascism, I soon discovered that conversations that I might try to begin on the subject of the Casa del Fascio would very swiftly segue back to what most Predappiesi really wanted to talk about: recycling.

My account above of the debates over the Casa del Fascio project has its own scale. Wu Ming and many of the other critics I have noted are internationally renowned commentators, and I have described Giorgio's defenses of the project to the outside world, as it were. What, one might ask, did Predappiesi themselves think?

That is exactly one of the questions I sought to answer when I came to Predappio. I had arrived in the town the year before, with the aim of investigating how Predappio's complex and contested heritage made itself felt in everyday life in the town. Now, thanks to the plans for the Casa del Fascio project, debates about that heritage had spilled out onto the global stage. Colleagues back in the United Kingdom, or across the ocean in the United States, were following these debates, had been asked to sign petitions for and against the project, and were keen to hear what I thought Predappiesi themselves felt about these plans. Yet in the town itself, despite its name ringing in the ears of readers of the *Washington Post* and the *New Yorker*, despite the recent visit by Bui and his controversial blog, very few people wanted to talk about the Casa del Fascio project; what most people wanted to talk about was their rubbish.

As ethnographers sometimes do, I dealt with this problem at first by simply butting my head against it. I would persist in raising the topic of the Casa del Fascio project at every opportunity, seeking in vain for some flutter of interest or excitement on the part of a friend or interlocutor. With Carlo and Giorgio, I could speak about it endlessly, but conversation on the topic with anyone else in town would be exhausted in a matter of minutes. Some people might nod and say it would be good thing to rescue the old building, though they would doubt the likelihood of the project coming to fruition. Others would wonder about where all the money would come from. Others still might have some opinions on what sort of content the museum should include. But nobody I met had opinions on the sorts of questions that Giorgio and the project's critics raised, such as how the town's heritage might speak to global concerns regarding the rise of the far right. And soon enough any conversation about the local administration would turn away from the Casa del Fascio and back to what my friends felt was a much more pressing issue: recycling.

Recycling in Italy is a complex and controversial topic, and in some areas, thanks to the involvement of the Mafia, a matter of life and death (see e.g., De Rosa 2018). This is not the case in Predappio, though, as we will see, that did not prevent tensions on the subject from reaching a fever pitch and near-violence.

The controversy in Predappio concerned the introduction of a new waste disposal system in the town and in another twelve neighboring *comuni*. Prior to 2017, Predappiesi, like many other Italians across the country, disposed of their waste by dumping it in large communal containers positioned throughout the town. There were specific containers for certain sorts of recyclables—glass, paper, and plastic—but nothing beyond conscience obligated villagers to make use of these particular bins, and many residents simply disposed of their waste in the nearest bin of whichever variety.

In 2017, thirteen *comuni* in Emilia-Romagna, including Predappio, banded together to create their own autonomous waste disposal company, called Alea. The foundation of Alea would herald the arrival of what is called "differentiated" or "door-to-door" waste disposal, in which each household is allocated its own separate bins for different sorts of waste—in Predappio's case, of no fewer than five different types—that would then be collected directly from the household by Alea on a regular schedule. Tariffs for waste disposal would be calculated on a household basis, depending in part on exactly how much nonrecyclable waste the household produced. The aim of the project was to increase the amount of differentiated waste to 74 percent, to reduce the amount of nonrecyclable waste produced by more than 400 pounds per inhabitant per year, and to pay less than the *comuni* were paying to the contractor they had employed up until then. The result, however, was furor and engagement on a scale I never encountered in relation to the Casa del Fascio project.

Take two contrasting examples of public politics in Predappio that year. The first was the official presentation of the Casa del Fascio project in Predappio in December, marked by the opening of an exhibition of the plans for the project in Mussolini's birth house and a public discussion in the town cinema. The event had been heavily billed in local press for some time and followed hot on the heels of the national presentation of the project in Rome. On the morning of the event, I drove to pick up one of the historians on the project's advisory committee from the local railway station in Forlì. Driving back carefully through the winter snow, I listened as he insisted on the importance of local support for the project and that it would be this that would decide its success. We arrived in Predappio in time for lunch at the town's oldest osteria, with Giorgio, Carlo, and a number of other participants in the project. As Giorgio sought to get through to the local president of ANPI on the phone, we ate beneath displays of wine bottles with Mussolini's face printed on the labels. After lunch we walked over to the birth house, which was surrounded by members of the press, with telephoto lenses and TV cameras in tow, and Giorgio donned his mayoral sash to open the exhibition officially. His speech, as usual, was calibrated for the ears of the national and international media: Predappio, he said, was the shame of Italy, a symbol of Italy's collective failure to confront its past. The Casa del Fascio project was the only antidote. As we stood in the cold listening to words we had often heard before from Giorgio, the historian I had brought from Forlì leaned across to another technician on the project and asked how many people from the town he thought had come. "Two or three, maybe" came the reply, with a sigh.

Meanwhile, earlier that year on a Wednesday evening in August, more than two hundred Predappiesi filled the same cinema that would go on to host the panel discussion on the Casa del Fascio in December. It was rubbish, rather than Fascism, however that brought people together that night. Giorgio and the then-director of Alea had invited Predappiesi to the cinema in order to respond to a growing chorus of opposition to the plan for door-to-door recycling. Giorgio, who as mayor had signed Predappio up for the Alea initiative, was very much in favor of the new recycling system. A significant constituency of his electorate, however, were not, and it swiftly became clear that Predappiesi had not come to the cinema that night to listen. Within moments of the Alea director beginning to speak, an elderly man stood up and threatened to punch him. Shortly afterward, as Giorgio was trying to explain the rationale behind the project, a woman of eighty shouted that she considered him a *delinquente* (literally a "delinquent," but commonly used in Italy as a pejorative term for someone who behaves badly or criminally), despite knowing him since he was a young boy. Soon the meeting became so raucous, with accusations and insults hurled at Giorgio and the director from the audience, that it had to be closed, and even then the crowd surrounded Giorgio and the director outside the cinema, threatening violence.

Angela, the café owner and a nearby neighbor of mine, was one of the organizers of the vocal opposition movement against Giorgio and Alea that grew steadily over the course of 2017. We sat in her kitchen one Saturday afternoon in August, drinking coffee and discussing the latest town gossip. It was, as usual for this period, recycling that dominated conversation: "I am ignorant, Paolo, I went to a hospitality industry high school, I'm not an engineer or an accountant. Neither are my friends. But we have studied, and we have read up—and now we know they have lied to us."

Angela and others had by this point gathered together more than 1,300 signatures to a petition demanding a number of reforms to the Alea proposal, a petition they delivered to Giorgio in person. They had a range of objections to the project. They argued, for instance, that it had been brought in with no consultation. According to Angela, Predappiesi simply woke up one day to find different bins outside their doors, along with a note demanding payment for the bins and explaining that the new system would come into force soon. They also criticized the way in which Alea was set up, arguing that if cost savings were really a motivation for the new system, then a request for bids on a contract for waste disposal should have been put out, rather than simply awarding the contract directly to a new entity with no experience in the business. The protestors also objected to the new charging system, one that would penalize most those who generated the most amount of nonrecyclable waste. This, they argued, would unfairly discriminate against poor households of large families. Angela and others pointed out with some venom that Giorgio could afford to eat out for dinner at restaurants all the time, and so he would not have to pay as much as they would.

Many of their most vehement objections were eminently practical and extremely specific. For instance, some of the bins provided to householders were large and heavy even when empty. Predappio has a substantial population of elderly residents, many of whom live, like Valentina and her sister, in flats in one of Predappio's many apartment blocks, few if any of which are equipped with elevators. How, Angela and others asked, were octogenarians supposed to carry a different bin up and down flights of stairs on an almost daily basis? Giorgio's suggestion that the local scout troop would help was met with derision. A similar objection was made on the behalf of rural farmers living out in the countryside around the town. Many of their farms are set far back from the road. Were they to be expected to ferry their bins to and from the roadside in their cars every day? Questions were asked about what would happen if someone had an accident while moving one of these bins or if bins in the road caused a car crash: Who would be liable, Alea or the household? Some residents were incensed at the cost of disposing of diapers. One of the most talked-about objections, which surfaced in the August meeting at the cinema and was much reported on in the press, was to the idea that Alea could inspect people's rubbish to ensure that they were correctly distributing their waste. "What," Angela is proud to have asked indignantly at the meeting at the cinema, "are you going to rifle through my sanitary napkins? What if I've thrown away a vibrator?"

Over a period of months—the same months in which national and international furor over the Casa del Fascio project was at its peak—Predappio was consumed by these questions. It was anger over the Alea project that led the man I described at the outset of this chapter to physically threaten Giorgio at the restaurant at Predappio Alta. Many people I knew attributed the subsequent election victory of the first right-wing mayor in Predappio's postwar history to persistent anger at Giorgio over the rubbish issue: "He behaved like a *Ducetto* [a 'little Duce'], and we haven't forgotten that," Angela told me, years later. Giorgio, too, invoked Mussolini as we ate that night in Predappio Alta: "Mussolini is a curse, a bringer of bad luck [*porta sfortuna*]. That's why nothing ever changes in this place."

At the time I was rather baffled. In 2017, everybody in the world seemed to want to talk about Fascism, and indeed plenty of people wanted to talk about Fascism and Predappio, thanks to the Casa del Fascio project. There I was, in the heart of things, the birthplace of the founder of Fascism, the site of his grave and the center of the Italian neo-Fascist tourism industry, and the proposed locale for Italy's first and only museum of Fascism. But all anybody in Predappio wanted to talk about was rubbish.

After an initial and fruitless period of trying to elicit some interest in the Casa del Fascio from Predappiesi, it finally struck me that this imbalance was itself an interesting phenomenon, and I began to ask instead why people in Predappio could become so virulently politicized over the issue of recycling and yet appear entirely uninterested in their town's place in debates about the politics of Fascism. The response of Chiara, the council employee whom we met in chapter 5, was typical: "Listen, that stuff is not our lives. Let them come and have their Mussolini pantomime, who cares? This is our lives," she said, pointing to the array of shiny new plastic bins by her door. "How is my uncle going to carry those things down the stairs? What are my bills going to be like now? This is politics, local politics, for normal people."

In hindsight, this fits well with the pattern in Predappiesi attitudes to their heritage. Chiara's claims about the nature of politics sound as definitive as the anthropological assumptions James Ferguson notes about politics being "from below," "'grounded' in rooted and authentic 'lives,' 'experiences,' and 'communities'" (2006, 48). But both Chiara's and our own anthropological claims about the scale of politics are just as normative as the scalar claims of Giorgio and Bui we met earlier. Set against the backdrop of a contested and often violent history of political clashes over Fascism in Predappio, not to mention the town's regional, national, and international reputation—"the whole town is Il Duce's tomb," as Bui put it—all of which Chiara is well aware of, her claim looks in many ways aspirational, rather than simply descriptive: let rubbish disposal be politics, not Fascism; let us be "normal people." That is not to say that the concerns Predappiesi had about the recycling system were in any way performative or disingenuous, or a way to somehow distract attention from the debates over the Casa del Fascio. But assertions such as Chiara's about the nature of politics make sense only against the wider background of life in Predappio.

There is nothing per se that is everyday or ordinary about the politics of rubbish and recycling in Predappio. Such politics take on the weight of ordinariness, of "reality," "experience," and "life," only in contrast to the politics of Fascism that Predappiesi work so hard to avoid. Fascism can be just as everyday as recycling, as the arguments of Bui and Giorgio suggest, albeit in very different ways, and as some historians of Fascism have argued (Arthurs, Ebner, and Ferris 2017; Bosworth 2005; Passerini 1987). Indeed, to an outside observer, life in Predappio *is* "everyday Fascism," given how suffused simple and ordinary activities are by the symbols and remnants of the regime and its contemporary admirers. As I hope is clear by now, however, the everyday that Predappiesi valorize and strive to give form to has nothing to do with Fascism and indeed is given meaning precisely in opposition to Fascism ("that stuff is not our lives"). It is a very particular vision of everydayness: in some ways, it looks like social scientific versions of the idea of the everyday (one would not have to look far in the literature to find an analytical claim comparable to Chiara's about the "realness" of local political issues such as recycling); yet its distinctive character emerges from the way it is invariably opposed to the politics of Fascism that most people associate with Predappio.

At stake across debates about the politics of both recycling and Fascist heritage are a set of scalar questions that are as political as the debates themselves but that have little or nothing intrinsically to do with either issue: Who is more real, more concrete, more grounded, more ordinary than whom? Such questions are not confined to the context of Predappio. These sorts of scalar notions, as Ferguson implies, are often invoked and deployed in anthropological arguments, with little by way of interrogation as to their specific meaning or their potentially contested status in any given political context. We ignore the politics of our own scaling practices when we think it enough to attach one of these adjectives to a concept in order to win an argument.

Predappiesi lost their specific political argument about recycling. The Alea door-to-door system persists, despite ongoing grumbling, and in fact the town was recently praised for achieving a higher level of waste differentiation than many of its neighbors. But in many ways Predappiesi won their broader argument about what should and should not constitute "the everyday" in the town and its politics. In May 2019, for the first time in its postwar history, Predappio elected a right-wing mayor, Roberto Canali. Within six months, he had unceremoniously fired the administrators and technicians involved in the Casa del Fascio project, citing concerns over its architectural plans. Carlo was heartbroken, and Giorgio was resigned. The project's future is now uncertain. Most Predappiesi that I know barely batted an eyelid at the news. The Casa del Fascio will probably remain desolate and empty for decades more to come, looming over the town square, pointedly ignored by all but the black-shirted tourists and the pigeons.

Conclusion
Anthropology after Fascism

As the liberalism that both populist politics and anthropology often target seems of late to buckle under the strain of attack, it has become impossible to ignore the fact that both share several features. Both populist politics and anthropology despise and critique the liberal emphasis on the individual untethered from relations, but they have more than this foe in common. They both emerge from a strain of Romantic, counter-Enlightenment thought, exemplified by figures such as Johann Herder, that place both moral and explanatory weight on communitarian units such as "nations" and "cultures" (Holmes 2000, 2019; Berlin 1976, 1999; Wolf 1999; Wolin 2006); and they both understand themselves to be speaking for ordinary people, not elites, and to be firmly grounded in the pragmatics of everyday life, not in theory, metaphysics, or political principle.

I am not the first to point this out. Douglas Holmes has recently highlighted what he calls "the anthropology operating within Fascism" in analyses of a series of interviews he conducted with figures from the European far right in the early 1990s (2019, 83; emphasis removed). A particular exchange with Jean-Marie le Pen, then-leader of the French Front National, and the analysis that follows are worth quoting in full:

Le Pen: . . . You must know that in real life, these things [immigration, crime, and corruption] create a lot of suffering for citizens, especially the underprivileged. The problems of housing, family life, education, and unemployment are felt very harshly by people. They feel real anxiety for the future. Thus, these people believe our views to be right because they accurately reflect the dilemmas of real life. . . . Men perceive reality in two ways: either directly through lived experience of unemployment, poor housing, etcetera, or indirectly, thanks to the media. But when the lived facts become overwhelming, far beyond what is told in the media, you don't need the media anymore.

Holmes: The message of your presentations is that politics is not merely an intellectual discourse but an instinctual engagement.

Le Pen: Of course! Absolutely true! Human beings communicate not just by their intellects alone but also by their physical sensibilities, their emotions, and their gestures. Probably the worst sin of our time is to overvalue "intellectualism" and to limit humankind to their intelligence alone.

Accusations of racism and Fascism, he insists, are mere "devices" to silence him. He appeals to the listener to escape rarefied ideological engagements and, instead, to reenter the sublime certainties of lived experience. He draws the listener into an intimate relationship in which kinship is conferred—not through rational disputation but through enthrallments that can be read in daily life. He postures as if to say: "Look at me: I am just like you, I believe what you believe, I feel what you feel. These things do not make you a racist; how can they make me one?" (Holmes 2019, 72–73)

Holmes presumably poses the final rhetorical question to an "ordinary person," but given what is said in the interview about "sensibilities," "emotions," "lived experience," and the overvaluation of "intellectualism" by modern society, it is even more aptly posed to the anthropologist.

Confronting this resemblance may be painful, but it is necessary, for it obliges anthropologists to recognize that they do not have exclusive rights over all their theoretical predilections. Just because Fascism possesses its own anthropology does not mean anthropology therefore possesses its own Fascism. But fetishizing ordinariness and ordinary people, while clearly far from being a sufficient condition for Fascism, is at least arguably a necessary one, and the overlap with anthropology points to elective affinities (or family resemblances) that demand consideration.

The anthropological impulse, methodological and theoretical, to privilege the everyday and the ordinary is clearly motivated by a range of different sensibilities. Perhaps key among those, as Joel Robbins has suggested (n.d., 23), is the (ironically, fundamentally liberal) belief in the *summum malum* of cruelty, especially on the part of the powerful toward the powerless (Shklar 1989). We may in general be pluralists when it comes to the good, but we are also often monists when it comes to the bad. Fascism, on the other hand, when not directly enjoying cruelty as an expression of strength, is certainly happy to employ it in the service of other ends.

The problem is, as I hope to have shown in this book, that it is more than possible to be both ordinary and powerful. Ordinariness indeed possesses a very great deal of power, of seductive and affective charge, especially when located on a moralized and naturalized scale in opposition to other qualities of which we are supposed to disapprove in proportion. Sometimes it takes a great deal of power, as I also hope to have shown in this book, to appear ordinary or everyday, to make these qualities come alive as virtues worth pursuing and embodying.

So while it might be vain, as well as unreasonable, to imagine that anthropology should abandon its built-in preference for the quotidian reality of everyday life, I hope this book at least serves as a cautionary tale for what can happen when that preference leads us implicitly to assume that the ordinary and the everyday are always "down," always weaker than whatever they are conjured up in opposition to.

Anthropologists, Predappiesi, and Fascists are not the only people to endow the ordinary and the everyday with special powers. The historian Claire Langhammer has noted the emergence of ordinariness as an important political category in postwar British politics (2018). The trope of "ordinary people" began to appear in films, on the radio, in churches, in the queen's Christmas Day message, in Enoch Powell's infamous "Rivers of Blood" speech, of course in psychoanalysis, and in sociological Mass-Observation studies. Indeed, a part of Langhammer's point is that although ordinariness in the Brexit era of British politics is said to be largely defined in opposition to "expertise" (see e.g., Mazzarella 2019), ordinariness as it emerged in the postwar era came with its own forms of expert knowledge: "lived experience and feeling were set against acquired knowledge and training in all manner of areas, including domestic and local issues, national politics and international relations" (2018, 190), as in contrast to the knowledge of scientists, politicians, and elites. Perhaps situated against this backdrop, the later Wittgenstein's philosophical focus on ordinariness (usually periodized as beginning in the 1930s) looks rather characteristic of its time.

Meanwhile, the vital role notions of ordinary or everyday life have played in twentieth-century French literature and theory has been documented in fantastic detail by Michael Sheringham, who traces the development of such notions from Charles Baudelaire through to anthropologist Marc Augé (2006).

Sheringham argues that the period 1960–1980, in particular, witnessed an explosion of intellectual, literary, and academic interest in the everyday and that—despite differences in the thought of figures such as Roland Barthes and Michel de Certeau—taken together, this interest was a distinctively French intellectual response to particular historical changes (rapid modernization, the events of May 1968, the fall of structuralism, and so on).

In France today, the political scientist Catherine Neveu has shown that invocations of ordinariness can serve both depoliticizing and politicizing ends, sometimes distinguishing "normal people" from the "dirtiness" of institutional politics and valorizing them for standing apart, and sometimes legitimizing contemporary forms of government focused on notions of participation and citizenship (2015).

In writing on contemporary meditation practices, Joanna Cook has described the ways in which ordinary life has come to take on particular salience in the field of metacognitive interventions, such as mindfulness, in mental health (2023). The aim of such practices is to invest everyday activities—for example, washing up—with heightened levels of awareness and attention with the idea that, by changing how one relates to ordinary life, one is able to effect much broader alterations to the ways in which one relates to one's mind, alterations that can help stave off psychological crises and improve resilience.

In all of these cases, what matters to people is not just something or some set of things that "are" (by nature or by virtue of an analyst's judgment) ordinary, but *the claim* that some things are ordinary. It matters that scales such as "ordinary life" or persons such as "ordinary people" exist and that they denote a specific kind of content, different in each case. In all these cases, the form of ordinary life has come to take on a life of its own, beyond the actual life it is intended to denote, and often it is valorized as a form precisely insofar as it can be perceived as ordinary.

As Neveu and Langhammer both note, analytical usage of ordinariness in the social sciences is often similarly implicitly (or explicitly) normative. In the discipline of history, there is of course a broad family of historical writing that includes the *Annales* school in France (e.g., Braudel 1981), *Alltagsgeschichte* in Germany (e.g., Lüdtke 1982), and the *microstoria* of Italian scholars such as Carlo Ginzburg (1980), in which the small-scale has come to matter as more exemplary of "real," "concrete" life than events or great men. None of these various movements are exactly identical with one another, but they all share a concern with scaling down historical narratives away from macrostructures and toward Braudel's "realm of routine" and "ordinary experience."

As emblematic of this tendency in recent anthropology, take the following section from Veena Das's recent *Textures of the Ordinary*, in which she quotes her own closing sentences from a previous book, *Life and Words*, in critique of French philosopher Pierre Hadot's vision of "spiritual exercises" (Hadot 1995):

> I conclude my book *Life and Words*, somewhat scandalously, with the following words:
>
> "My sense of indebtedness to the work of [Stanley] Cavell in these matters come from a confidence that perhaps Manjit did not utter anything we would recognize as philosophical in the kind of environments in which philosophy is done . . . but Cavell's work shows us that there is no real distance between the spiritual exercises she undertakes in her world and the spiritual exercises we can see in every word he has ever written. To hold these types of worlds together and to sense the connection of these lives has been my anthropological kind of devotion to the world." (Das 2007: 221).
>
> I say 'scandalously' because the kind of philosophical formation that Hadot is thinking of is about scaling heights, whereas I am trying to wrest the very expression of spiritual exercises away from the profundity of philosophy to the small disciplines that ordinary people perform in their everyday lives to hold life as the natural expression of ethics. (2020, 109–110)

Note the shifts of scale in the space of just a few sentences: first Cavell is praised for showing that "there is no real distance" between the spiritual exercises of philosophy and those of an "ordinary person"; then Hadot is attacked for "scaling heights" ("up" into philosophy and away from the ordinary, one assumes); then Das herself argues she is trying to wrest spiritual exercises "away from the profundity of philosophy to the small disciplines that ordinary people perform in their everyday lives." Despite the praise of Cavell and the claim in the quoted paragraph to be trying to "hold these types of worlds together," Das's scalar vision opposes ordinary life to what she elsewhere calls "the hallowed halls of philosophy," in spite of the fact, one might point out, that this vision itself is of course derived from the philosophy of Wittgenstein, Cavell, and Austin (2020, 96), who spent their careers in such hallowed halls.

I have written elsewhere of the paradoxes of this kind of theorizing, in which an antitheoretical or antiphilosophical argument is put forward in deeply theoretical and philosophical terms, as akin to the problem of Dumbo's feather: Dumbo, the eponymous hero of the classic Disney film, can fly because he has big ears, but because he dislikes his ears, he tells himself he can fly because he has a magic feather (Heywood 2018). In analogous fashion, this sort of vision of the ordinary has giant, Wittgenstein-shaped philosophical ears, but because it has been taught to see philosophy as a problem, it prefers to tell itself it has an ordinary magic feather. In fact, there is little that is ordinary about most anthropological talk about ordinary life.

Perhaps one of the most obvious instances of this point about the gap between the form or ideal of ordinary life and its reality in action is the inspiration for Das's argument, Wittgenstein himself, who spent much of the last twenty years of his life trying to persuade people not to do philosophy, while, in fact, doing philosophy. By this I mean not only that he sought to challenge the ideas most people had of what philosophy was (metaphysics, broadly speaking); he also ruined what might have been the brilliant academic careers of several of his students by using his influence over them to persuade them to pursue occupations he saw as more "ordinary," such as medicine or car mechanics (Monk 1991, 430, 618, 840). Wittgenstein himself was aware of the paradox involved in both senses. Intellectually speaking, for example, he wrote in an unpublished chapter of *Philosophical Grammar* that "all that philosophy can do is to destroy idols . . . and . . . that means not making any new ones—say out of 'the absence of idols'" (cited in Monk 1991, 760). Idolizing the absence of idols is in many ways an excellent description of some contemporary social scientific writing on ordinariness.

Wittgenstein was also eminently conscious of his own extraordinary position. For instance, his biographer Ray Monk cites him excusing the fact that he persisted with philosophy—while doing his best to oblige various students to abandon it—on the basis that he was special: "There is no oxygen in Cambridge, he told [Maurice] Drury [a brilliant student who Wittgenstein urged to get a job 'among the working class' (Monk 1991, 28)]. It didn't matter for him [Wittgenstein]—he manufactured his own. But for people dependent on the air around them, it was important to get away, into a healthier environment" (780). Yet Wittgenstein was clearly not himself entirely satisfied with this explanation, and throughout his life made repeated attempts to "ordinarify" himself.

In fact, in these repeated attempts, we can see a striking example of exactly the argument I have been making throughout this book. Wittgenstein, in many ways the father of much of our thinking on ordinariness, actually spent a lot of time engaged in precisely the activity I have described Predappiesi as engaged in: "doing being ordinary" or, as Monk puts it, "joining the ranks." As in the examples above, Wittgenstein often did things not simply because he was interested in the things themselves, but at least in part because he believed those things to be ordinary and ordinariness was what he was pursuing. He enlisted in the Austrian army as an ordinary soldier in the First World War and repeatedly resisted being commissioned as an officer, despite the fact he hated his fellow soldiers and the entire experience of military life (Monk 1991,

277). After the war, when he was a primary school teacher, he insisted on being posted to the most rural backwater he could find, and once again hated
the experience and despised his fellow villagers, leaving in disgrace after being physically violent to his young charges (473–475). And in the early 1930s,
he decided he would move to Soviet Russia with one of his students and become an ordinary working man on a collective farm. This last project came
to nothing partly because, as British Communist George Sacks recalled, "the
Russians told him his own work was a useful contribution and he ought to go
back to Cambridge" (821).

Monk sums up this last example of Wittgenstein's pursuit of ordinariness and
its failure as follows: "It is also, of course, one more manifestation of his peren-
nial desire to join the ranks. The Soviet authorities knew, just as the Austrian
authorities had in 1915, that he would be more use to them as an officer than
as a private; and Wittgenstein himself realized that he could not really tolerate
life among the 'petty dishonesty' of the ordinary soldiers. Yet he continued to
wish it could be otherwise" (1991, 828).[1]

At the very heart of our thinking on the ordinary, in other words, we find
a man who was anything but ordinary, just as Predappio is anything but ordinary, but who went to extraordinary lengths to try to make himself seem so,
just as Predappiesi do. And his attempts to do so only endowed his already
extraordinary aura with even greater mystique and authority for many of those
around him.

I hope that one insight for anthropology to have emerged from my description of the cultivation of ordinary life in Predappio is that if we are truly to
hold the worlds of philosophical concepts and ethnographic description of ordinary life together in some fashion, that must surely involve treating the
philosophical concept of ordinary life as a part of ordinary language like any
other part—asking what is at stake in all these various sorts of claims that some
thing or person is ordinary, and what forms of politics and ethics are con-
tained in the ways in which people moralize scales such as ordinary versus
abstract or ordinary life versus philosophy, instead of simply replicating them
ourselves.

As to Predappio itself, I have tried to shy away from pronouncing judgment
on the ways in which people there seek to manage their relationship to the trou-
bling heritage of their home. One can easily imagine a number of forms such
judgment might take. For instance, one might cast the cultivation of the everyday in Predappio as a sort of "weapon of the weak," a form of resistance to the
high-flown, abstract debates about Fascism in which Predappiesi are forcibly im-
plicated by the accident of Mussolini's birth in their town (e.g., Scott 1985). Such
an analytic perspective, however, would again simply replicate, rather than inter-

rogate, the scalar politics at work in opposing ordinary life to Fascism, which, as we have seen, has its own visions of ordinary life, too, and its own way of scaling them. Alternatively, one could imagine an argument that characterized people in Predappio's pursuit of ordinariness as a sort of "anti-politics machine," a way of depoliticizing their home and of neutralizing the really important questions of Italian attitudes to Fascist heritage that it poses (e.g., Ferguson 1990). Again, though, such an approach would not only assume that it is in "large" questions of Fascist heritage that politics really and properly resides—rather than in "small" and everyday questions such as what to do with one's recycling—but would also miss the moralizing politics of such scaling practices themselves. These dichotomous alternatives, in which the everyday is either a sanctified respite from or a problematic facet of the broader context in which it is situated, mirror the ambiguities of the everyday in scholarly discourse, as I noted in chapter 1, which appears in both senses in our usage of it. I have sought to avoid both of these alternatives.

Predappiesi themselves, of course, do not all share the same position on the question of how to deal with their heritage. Giorgio, for instance, sought in many ways to overturn decades of orthodoxy on this question by actively confronting this heritage and by seeking to transform it from a weakness into a strength. In his public speeches in favor of the Casa del Fascio project, he would lament what he called the *damnatio memoriae* into which Predappio had fallen thanks to its association with Mussolini, urging instead that people speak openly about Fascism and thereby learn of its perils. We have seen that some on the left in Italy doubted the sincerity of his anti-Fascist motivations, but what is not in doubt is that his approach would have been a radical departure from the norm in Predappio.

But we also saw in that chapter that Giorgio failed in his endeavors, or at least so it seems for now. The public justification his successor provided for calling a halt to the Casa del Fascio project relied on arguably minor quibbles with the architectural plan for the documentation center, a justification that some call into question and that has, reportedly, been refuted by the structural assessors on whose judgment it claims to rely (Consiglio Direttivo di Progetto Predappio 2019). Some people suggest the project was shut down to spite Giorgio; others that it was because the new mayor is right-wing and resented what anti-Fascist elements there were in the documentation center plans; others still point to the pecuniary interests of the souvenir shop owners and the pressure they may have exerted on the new administration (though it is unclear why their interest would lie in resisting the opening of a new tourist attraction in town).

Whatever his motivations, the mayor's decision led to no public outcry in town, no great lamentations at the loss of this unique opportunity, no protests, and no petitions, except from those involved in the Casa del Fascio project itself. From what I have observed since the decision was taken, most Predappiesi are quite happy to return to the status quo ante, to leave the Casa del Fascio to its pigeons and arguments about Fascism to their visitors in red or in black.

"Talking about such things [Fascism] is difficult, it's complicated," Antonio, an elderly vineyard owner, told me shortly before I left Predappio for the last time before the coronavirus pandemic. "It's better to talk about other things. Like wine," he added with a grin, "we all like wine." Or, as Wittgenstein put it less prosaically, "whereof one cannot speak, thereof one must be silent."

In this book, I have tried to narrate the gradual process, over the course of a century, by means of which the idea or form or category of ordinary life has come apart in Predappio from the actuality of ordinary life as it is lived there. The seeds of this process lie in the particular and somewhat contradictory moral valency ascribed to ordinariness in early Fascist thought and the ways in which that moral valency took on an especially heightened character in New Predappio, "the Land of Il Duce," built to exemplify both Mussolini's "ordinary" origins and his extraordinary character and feats. The fall of Fascism, the ongoing contestation of its legacy in postwar Italy, and the arrival and burial of Mussolini's remains all added further twists, for in their wake it must have seemed hard to believe that Predappio could ever be ordinary again, condemned instead to its island status as a metonym for something seen by most as extraordinary and indeed as extraordinarily evil. In response to this, the form of ordinary life pursued in contemporary Predappio is now characterized precisely by its distinction from the man who built it and from his own particular vision of ordinariness, despite the fact that life in Predappio is saturated by specters of Mussolini and despite the fact that the roots of this concern for ordinariness lie precisely in the ways in which ordinariness emerged as important in the Fascist political project.

Ordinariness and Fascism in contemporary Predappio are, therefore, both historically interwoven with each other and yet crucially distinct in important ways, not least because ordinariness in contemporary Predappio means having as little to do with Fascism as possible. In other words, this is a particular vision of ordinary life as a form, one that is a product of a specific set of historical, social, and cultural circumstances. This, I suggest, is an example of what we can learn from taking an ethnographic perspective not just on ordinary life as it is lived, but on the ways in which such specific visions of ordinariness play into people's understandings of how they should live.

In the social sciences, we sometimes fetishize the ordinary and the everyday, investing them as categories with special moral value. The fact that we are not the only ones to do so should cause us some hesitation. As I have sought to illustrate in closing here, Predappiesi, along with a great many other people, treat being ordinary as an important virtue, as the object of sustained work and attention. It matters to them and to many others like them to be *perceived* as ordinary, as if it were a more obviously laudable characteristic, such as being brave, kind, generous, or good.

Wittgenstein, whose ghost haunts this book as Mussolini's does Predappio, gave us an enormously influential analytical language with which to describe the simple facts of the way things are. Yet usually there is nothing simple about the way things are. What is really ordinary about life in Predappio: day-to-day existence in the shadow of Mussolini's grave and amid the sad remnants of his hateful regime, or the life many Predappiesi aspire to live, marked as ordinary precisely by its opposition to the way things are? What was really ordinary about Wittgenstein: the peculiar manners, temper, and philosophical genius that marked him out as far as others around him were concerned, or the times when he was a simple soldier, rural schoolteacher, or hospital porter? It is not reality but precisely the influence of language and practice—that of Wittgenstein and others—that endows a certain kind of answer to these questions with authority and credibility, that gives it life as "the ordinary," and not just life but a quite extraordinary allure and power, as many who have read Wittgenstein have felt, and just as many Italians in the 1920s and '30s no doubt felt looking at the straw bed in the unassuming house in Predappio in which young Mussolini was supposed to have slept. That power lived on beyond Mussolini's death and burial in the family tomb; it is part of what draws tens of thousands to his grave every year, and it haunts the streets of his hometown today.

Notes

Introduction

1. Valentina, like most of the other names in this book, with the exception of public figures, is a pseudonym.

2. The carabinieri are military police and constitute one of the main branches of Italian law enforcement.

3. See Ferrandiz 2022 for the comparable example of Franco's tomb in Spain.

1. Fascism and the Social Life of "Ordinary Life"

1. Archivio Luce Cinecittà, "La visita di Vittorio Emanuele III," uploaded June 15, 2012, YouTube video, https://www.youtube.com/watch?v=hXc26j6smrM.

4. Everyday Space and Walking in the Fascist City

1. Some of these are to be found in Zoli and Moressa (2007).

6. Recycling the Past and the "Museum of Fascism"

1. A successful documentary has even been made about him: Biografilm, *The Mayor: Me, Mussolini and the Museum*, https://www.biografilm.it/2020/selected-projects/.

2. Mirco Carrattieri makes this clear in a short summary (2018).

Conclusion

1. The one instance in which Wittgenstein appears to have found some happiness in his pursuit of being ordinary was during his time as a porter at Guy's Hospital in 1941–1942. Even then, however, he was soon drawn back to more cerebral pursuits, and he moved to Newcastle in 1943 to take part in a medical research project on "wound shock" and then back to Cambridge and philosophy in 1944.

References

Adler, Victor. 1954. *Briefwechsel mit August Bebel und Karl Kautsky*. Vienna: Wiener Volksbuchhandlung.

Allardyce, Gilbert. 1979. "What Fascism Is Not: Thoughts on the Deflation of a Concept." *American Historical Review* 84:367–388.

Ammerman, Nancy. 2007. *Everyday Religion: Observing Modern Religious Lives*. Oxford: Oxford University Press.

ANSA. 2022. "Predappio Politically Distant from Me, Says Meloni." *ANSA English*, October 31. https://www.ansa.it/english/news/politics/2022/10/31/predappio-politically-distant-from-me-says-meloni_d3cbdd19-0147-4052-b93b-d96cf23828c7.html.

Arthurs, Joshua. 2010. "Fascism as Heritage in Contemporary Italy." In *Italy Today: The Sick Man of Europe*, edited by A. Mammone and G. Vetri, 114–128. London: Routledge.

Arthurs, Joshua. 2012. *Excavating Modernity: The Roman Past in Fascist Italy*. Ithaca, NY: Cornell University Press.

Arthurs, Joshua, Michael Ebner, and Kate Ferris, eds. 2017. *The Politics of Everyday Life in Fascist Italy*. New York: Palgrave.

Augé, Marc. 1995. *Non-Places: Introduction to an Anthropology of Supermodernity*. London: Verso.

Austin, John Langshaw. 1946. "Symposium: Other Minds II." *Aristotelian Society Supplementary Volume* 20:148–187.

Bakhtin, Mikhail. 1984. *Rabelais and His World*. Bloomington: Indiana University Press.

Bataille, Georges. [1949] 1991. *The Accursed Share*, vol 1. New York: Zone Books.

Bear, Laura. 2007. *Lines of the Nation: Indian Railway Workers, Bureaucracy, and the Intimate Historical Self*. New York: Columbia University Press.

Benhabib, Seyla. 1998. "Models of Public Space: Hannah Arendt, the Liberal Tradition, and Jurgen Habermas." In *Feminism: The Public and the Private*, edited by J. Landes, 65–99. Oxford: Oxford University Press.

Ben-Yehoyada, Naor. 2017. *The Mediterranean Incarnate: Region Formation between Sicily and Tunisia since World War Two*. Chicago: University of Chicago Press.

Berezin, Mabel. 1997. *Making the Fascist Self: The Political Culture of Interwar Italy*. Ithaca, NY: Cornell University Press.

Berlin, Isaiah. 1976. *Vico and Herder: Two Studies in the History of Ideas*. London: Hogarth Press.

Berlin, Isaiah. 1999. *The Roots of Romanticism*. London: Pimlico.

Bernabei, Alfio. 2014. "Predappio, l'Italia, e il revisionismo storico." *Il Fatto Quotidiano*, July 19. https://www.ilfattoquotidiano.it/2014/07/19/predappio-litalia-e
-il-revisionismo-storico/1064792/.

Bosworth, Richard James Boon. 2002. *Mussolini*. London: Bloomsbury.

Bosworth, Richard James Boon. 2005. "Everyday Mussolinism: Friends, Family, Locality, and Violence in Fascist Italy." *Contemporary European History* 14:23–43.

Bourgois, Philippe. 2009. "The Moral Economies of Homeless Heroin Addicts: Confronting Ethnography, HIV Risk, and Everyday Violence in San Francisco Shooting Encampments." *Substance Use and Misuse* 33:2323–2351.

Boyte, Harry. 2004. *Everyday Politics: Reconnecting Citizens and Public Life*. Philadelphia: University of Pennsylvania Press.

Braudel, Fernand. 1981. *The Structures of Everyday Life*. London: Collins.

Brenner, Neil. 2009. "Open Questions on State Rescaling." *Cambridge Journal of Regions, Economy and Society* 2:123–139.

Candea, Matei. 2010. "'Our Division of the Universe': Making a Space for the Non-political in the Anthropology of Politics." *Current Anthropology* 52:309–334.

Candea, Matei. 2012. "Derrida en Corse? Hospitality as Scale-Free Abstraction." *Journal of the Royal Anthropological Institute* 18:34–48.

Candea, Matei. 2013. "Habituating Meerkats and Redescribing Animal Behaviour Science." *Theory, Culture, and Society* 30:105–128.

Capacci, Palmiro, Rolando Pasini, and Virna Giunchi. 2014. *La fòja de farfaraz: Predappio, cronache di una communitá viva e solidale*. Cesena, Italy: Il Ponte Vecchio.

Carrattieri, Mirco. 2018. "Predappio sì, Predappio no . . . il dibattito sulla ex Casa del Fascio e dell'ospitalità di Predappio dal 2104 al 2107." *E-Review*. https://e
-review.it/carrattieri-predappio-si-predappio-no.

Carter, Nick, and Simon Martin. 2017. "The Management and Memory of Fascist Monumental Art in Postwar and Contemporary Italy: The Case of Luigi Montanarini's *Apotheosis of Fascism*." *Journal of Modern Italian Studies* 22:338–364.

Cavell, Stanley. 1979. *The Claim of Reason: Wittgenstein, Skepticism, Morality, and Tragedy*. Oxford: Oxford University Press.

Cavell, Stanley. 1988. *In Quest of the Ordinary: Lines of Skepticism and Romanticism*. Chicago: University of Chicago Press.

de Certeau, Michel. 1984. *The Practice of Everyday Life*. Berkeley: University of California Press.

Clarke, Morgan. 2014. "Cough Sweets and Angels: The Ordinary Ethics of the Extraordinary in Sufi Practice in Lebanon." *Journal of the Royal Anthropological Institute* 20:407–425.

Comaroff, Jean. 2009. "Populism: The New Form of Radicalism?" Johannesburg Workshop in Theory and Criticism.

Consiglio Direttivo di Progetto Predappio, 2019. "L'incomprensibile scelta del sindaco di Predappio." Press release, November 24.

Cooper, Davina. 2014. *Everyday Utopias: The Conceptual Life of Promising Spaces*. Durham, NC: Duke University Press.

Crary, Alice, and Rupert Read. 2000. *The New Wittgenstein*. London: Routledge.

Crook, Stephen. 1998. "Minotaurs and Other Monsters: 'Everyday Life' in Recent Social Theory." *Sociology* 32:523–540.

D'Emilio, Franco, and Giancarlo Gatta. 2017. *Predappio al tempo del duce: il Fascismo nella collezione fotografica Franco Nanni*. Rome: Bradybus.

Das, Veena. 2007. *Life and Words: Violence and the Descent into the Ordinary*. Berkeley: University of California Press.

Das, Veena. 2012. Ordinary Ethics. In *A Companion to Moral Anthropology*, edited by D. Fassin, 133–149 Malden, MA: Wiley-Blackwell.

Das, Veena. 2020. *Textures of the Ordinary: Doing Anthropology after Wittgenstein*. New York: Fordham University Press.

De Felice, Renzo. 1965. *Mussolini il rivoluzionario 1883–1920*. Turin: Einaudi.

De Rosa, Salvatore Paolo. 2018. "A Political Geography of 'Waste Wars' in Campania (Italy): Competing Territorializations and Socio-environmental Conflicts." *Political Geography* 67:46–55.

Diggins, John P. 1966. "Flirtation with Fascism: American Pragmatic Liberals and Mussolini's Italy." *American Historical Review* 71:487–506.

Domenico, Roy. 1991. *Italian Fascists on Trial, 1943–1948*. Chapel Hill: University of North Carolina Press.

Duggan, Christopher. 2013. "The Propagation of the Cult of the Duce, 1925–1926." In *The Cult of the Duce: Mussolini and the Italians*, edited by S. Gundle, C. Duggan, and G. Pieri, 27–41. Manchester: Manchester University Press.

Eatwell, Roger. 1996. "On Defining the 'Fascist Minimum': The Centrality of Ideology." *Journal of Political Ideologies* 1:303–319.

Eatwell, Roger. 2017. "Populism and Fasciism." In *The Oxford Handbook of Populism*, edited by C. Kaltwasser, P. Taggart, P. Ostiguy, and P. Espejo, 363–383. Oxford: Oxford University Press.

Eco, Umberto. 1995. "Ur-Fascism." *New York Review of Books*, June 22.

Elliott, William Y. 1926. "Mussolini, Prophet of the Pragmatic Era in Politics." *Political Science Quarterly* 41:161–192.

Elliott, William Y. 1928. *The Pragmatic Revolt in Politics: Syndicalism, Fascism, and the Constitutional State*. New York: Macmillan.

Fadil, Nadia, and Mayanthi Fernando. 2015. "Rediscovering the 'Everyday' Muslim: Notes on an Anthropological Divide." *HAU: Journal of Ethnographic Theory* 5:59–88.

Faubion, James. 2001. "Towards an Anthropology of Ethics: Foucault and the Pedagogies of Autopoiesis." *Representations* 74:83–104.

Faubion, James. 2011. *An Anthropology of Ethics*. Cambridge: Cambridge University Press.

Ferrandiz, Francisco. 2022. "Francisco Franco Is Back: The Contested Reemergence of a Fascist Moral Exemplar." *Comparative Studies in Society and History* 64:208–237.

Ferguson, James. 1990. *The Anti-politics Machine: Development, Depoliticization, and Bureaucratic Power in Lesotho*. Minneapolis: University of Minnesota Press.

Ferguson, James. 2006. "Transnational Topographies of Power: Beyond 'the State' and 'Civil Society' in African Politics." In *Global Shadows: Africa in the Neoliberal World Order*. Durham, NC: Duke University Press.

Foa, Anna. 2016. "A meno che non diventi una chiamata di corresponsibilita' . . ." *Una Citta,* April. http://www.unacitta.it/it/intervista/2499-a-meno-che-non -diventi-una-chiamata-di-corresponsabilita.

Fondazione Alfred Lewin, 2016. "Un museo del Fascismo? La posizione della Fondazi-one Alfred Lewin." *Una Citta*, March. https://www.unacitta.it/it/articolo/1160 -un-museo-del-fascismo-la-posizione-della-fondazione-alfred-lewin.

Fuller, Mia. 2007. *Modern Abroad: Architecture, Cities, and Italian Imperialism.* London: Routledge.

Fuller, Mia. 2018. "Equivocal Mussolinis: What the Proposed Predappio Museum Can Learn from the *Piana del Orme* Collection." *Politika.* https://www.politika .io/fr/article/equivocal-mussolinis.

Gal, Susan. 2002. "A Semiotics of the Public/Private Distinction." *Divergences* 3:77–95.

Gatta, Giancarlo. 2018. *Predappio: Il racconto di un progetto compiuto 1813–1943.* Forli: Graficamente.

Geertz, Clifford. 1973. *The Interpretation of Cultures.* New York: Basic Books.

Gentile, Emilio. 1990. Fascism as Political Religion. *Journal of Contemporary History* 25:229–251.

Ginzburg, Carlo. 1980. *The Cheese and the Worms: The Cosmos of a Sixteenth-Century Miller.* Baltimore: Johns Hopkins University Press.

Glück, Zoltan. 2013. "Between Wall St and Zuccotti: Occupy and the Scale of Politics." *Cultural Anthropology Hot Spots*, February 14, 2013. https://culanth .org/fieldsights/between-wall-street-and-zuccotti-occupy-and-the-scale-of -politics.

Gramsci, Antonio. 1971. *Selections from the Prison Notebooks.* London: Lawrence & Wishart.

Gregor, Anthony James. 1974. *The Fascist Persuasion in Radical Politics.* Princeton, NJ: Princeton University Press.

Gregor, Anthony James. 1979a. *Young Mussolini and the Intellectual Origins of Fascism.* Berkeley: University of California Press.

Gregor, Anthony James. 1979b. *Italian Fascism and Developmental Dictatorship.* Princeton, NJ: Princeton University Press.

Gretel Cammelli, Maddalena. 2015. *Fascisti del terzo millenio: Per un'antropologia di CasaPound.* Rome: Ombre Court.

Gretel Cammelli, Maddalena. 2017. "Fascism as a Style of Life: Community Life and Violence in a Neofascist Movement in Italy." *Focaal* 79:89–101.

Griffin, Roger. 1991. *The Nature of Fascism.* London: Psychology Press.

Green, Dominic. 2016. "The Elusive Definition of 'Fascist.'" *The Atlantic*, December 18.

Hadot, Pierre. 1995. *Philosophy as a Way of Life.* Oxford: Blackwell.

Heller, Agnes. 1984. *Everyday Life.* London: Routledge.

Helmreich, Stefan. 2009. *Alien Oceans: Anthropological Voyages in Microbial Seas.* Berkeley: University of California Press.

Herzfeld, Michael. 1988. "The Poeticity of the Commonplace." In *Semiotic Theory and Practice*, vols. 1 and 2, edited by M. Herzfeld and L. Melazzo, 383–392. Palermo: De Gruyter Mouton.

Herzfeld, Michael. 2016 [1997]. *Cultural Intimacy: Social Poetics in the Nation-State.* New York: Routledge.

Herzfeld, Michael. 2007. "Global Kinship: Anthropology and the Politics of Knowing." *Anthropological Quarterly* 80:313–323.

Herzfeld, Michael. 2009. *Evicted from Eternity: The Restructuring of Modern Rome.* Chicago: University of Chicago Press.

Heywood, Paolo. 2018. "Making Difference: Queer Activism and Anthropological Theory." *Current Anthropology* 59:314–331.

Heywood, Paolo. 2019. "Fascism, Uncensored: Legalism and Neofascist Pilgrimage in Predappio, Italy." *Terrain* 72:86–103.

Heywood, Paolo. 2022. "Ordinary Exemplars: Cultivating the Everyday in the Birthplace of Fascism." *Comparative Studies in Society and History* 64:91–121.

Heywood, Paolo. 2023a. "Out of the Ordinary: Everyday Life and the 'Carnival of Mussolini.'" *American Anthropologist* 125: 493–504.

Heywood, Paolo. 2023b. "Are There Anthropological Problems?" In *Beyond Description: Anthropologies of Explanation*, edited by P. Heywood and M. Candea, 25–45. Ithaca, NY: Cornell University Press.

Heywood, Paolo. 2024a. "Making Fascism History in 'The Land of the Duce.'" In *New Anthropologies of Italy: Politics, History, and Culture*, edited by Paolo Heywood, 105–120. Oxford: Berghahn.

Heywood, Paolo. 2024b. "Fascism, Real or Stuffed: Ordinary Skepticism at Mussolini's grave." In *Freedoms of Speech: Anthropological Perspectives on Language, Ethics, and Power*, edited by M. Candea, T. Fedirko, P. Heywood, and F. Wright, 118-130. Toronto: University of Toronto Press.

Heywood, Paolo, and Matei Candea. 2023. *Beyond Description: Anthropologies of Explanation.* Ithaca, NY: Cornell University Press.

Highmore, Ben. 2002. *Everyday Life and Cultural Theory: An Introduction.* London: Routledge.

Hirschkind, Charles. 2006. *The Ethical Soundscape: Cassette Sermons and Islamic Counter-publics in Egypt.* New York: Columbia University Press.

Hoffman, Ashley. 2017. "Should You Call Someone Hitler? Here's What the Man behind Godwin's Law Thinks." *Time*, June 29. https://time.com/4837881/godwin-law-interview-2017/.

Hökerberg, Hakan. 2017. "The Monument to Victory in Balzano: Desacralisation of a Fascist Relic." *International Journal of Heritage Studies* 23:759–774.

Holmes, Douglas. 2000. *Integral Europe: Fast Capitalism, Multiculturalism, Neofascism.* Princeton, NJ: Princeton University Press.

Holmes, Douglas. 2019. "Fascism at Eye-Level: The Anthropological Conundrum." *Focaal* 84:62–90.

Humphrey, Caroline. 1997. "Exemplars and Rules: Aspects of the Discourse of Morality in Mongolia." In *The Ethnography of Moralities*, edited by S. Howell, 25–47. London: Routledge.

Istituto storico della Resistenza e dell'Età contemporanea di Forlì-Cesena; Fondazione Alfred Lewin, Forlì; Associazione Mazziniana Italiana, Forlì; ANPI, Forlì-Cesena; CGIL, Forlì; UDU; Associazione Luciano Lama. 2017. "Museo di Predappio: Un Progetto elaborato senza la partecipazione del

Territorio." Press release, November 15, 2017. https://www.4live.it/2017
/11/museo-predappio-un-progetto-elaborato-senza-la-partecipazione-del
-territorio/.

Jones, Donna V. 2010. *The Racial Discourses of Life Philosophy: Négritude, Vitalism, and Modernity.* New York: Columbia University Press.

Jonsson, Stefan. 2013. *Crowds and Democracy: The Idea and Image of the Masses from Revolution to Fascism.* New York: Columbia University Press.

Kallis, Aristotle. 2014. *The Third Rome, 1922–1943: The Making of the Fascist Capital.* London: Palgrave Macmillan.

Kallius, Annastiina. 2023. *Politics of Knowledge in Late 2010s Hungary: Ethnography of an Epistemic Collapse.* Doctoral dissertation, University of Helsinki.

La Repubblica. 2018. "Per il leader di Casapound a Predappio si sono visti 'pagliacci mascherati.'" *La Repubblica*, October 28.

Laidlaw, James. 2002. "For an Anthropology of Ethics and Freedom." *Journal of the Royal Anthropological Institute* 8:311–332.

Laidlaw, James. 2012. *The Subject of Virtue.* Cambridge: Cambridge University Press.

Laidlaw, James, and Jonathan Mair. 2019. "Imperfect Accomplishments: The Fo Guang Shan Short-Term Retreat and Ethical Pedagogy in Humanistic Buddhism." *Cultural Anthropology* 34:328–358.

Lambek, Michael. 2000. "The Anthropology of Religion and the Quarrel between Poetry and Philosophy." *Current Anthropology* 41:309–320.

Lambek, Michael, ed. 2010. *Ordinary Ethics: Anthropology, Language, and Action.* New York: Fordham University Press.

Lambek, Michael. 2015a. *The Ethical Condition: Essays on Action, Person, and Value.* Chicago: University of Chicago Press.

Lambek, Michael. 2015b. "On the Immanence of the Ethical: A Response to Lempert's 'No Ordinary Ethics.'" *Anthropological Theory* 15:128–132.

Langhammer, Clare. 2018. "Who the Hell Are Ordinary People? Ordinariness as a Category of Historical Analysis." *Transactions of the Royal Historical Society* 28:175–195.

Lash, Scott. 2006. "Life (Vitalism)." *Theory, Culture, and Society* 23:2–3.

Latour, Bruno. 2005. *Reassembling the Social: An Introduction to Actor Network Theory.* Oxford: Oxford University Press.

Lazar, Sian. 2017. *The Social Life of Politics: Ethics, Kinship, and Union Activism in Argentina.* Stanford, CA: Stanford University Press.

Lazar, Sian. 2018. "A 'Kinship Anthropology of Politics'? Interest, the Collective Self, and Kinship in Argentine Unions." *Journal of the Royal Anthropological Institute* 24:256–274.

Leach, Edmund. 1961. "Rethinking Anthropology." In *Rethinking Anthropology*, 1–28. London: Athlone Press.

Leach, Edmund. 1984. "Glimpses of the Unmentionable in the History of British Social Anthropology." *Annual Review of Anthropology* 13:1–23.

Le Bon, Gustav. 1896. *The Crowd: A Study of the Popular Mind.* New York: Macmillan.

Le Bon, Gustav. 1910. *La psychologie politique et la défense sociale.* Paris: Flammarion.

Le Bon, Gustav. 1914. *La vie des vérités.* Paris: Flammarion.

Lefebvre, Henri. [1947, 1961, 1981] 2014. *Critique of Everyday Life*. London: Verso.

Lempert, Michael. 2012. *Discipline and Debate: The Language of Violence in a Tibetan Buddhist Monastery*. Berkeley: University of California Press.

Lempert, Michael. 2013. "No Ordinary Ethics." *Anthropological Theory* 13:370–393.

Lempert, Michael, and Michael Silverstein. 2012. *Creatures of Politics: Media, Message, and the American Presidency*. Bloomington: Indiana University Press.

Lichtenberg, Judith. 1994. "Moral Certainty." *Philosophy* 69:181–204.

LoPerfido, Giacomo. 2018. "What Can Anthropology Say about Populism?" *Anthropology News*, November 8. https://anthrosource.onlinelibrary.wiley.com /doi/epdf/10.1111/AN.801.

Lukács, Georg. [1911] 1994. *Soul and Form*. London: Merlin Press.

Lüdtke, Alf. 1982. "The Historiography of Everyday Life." In *Culture, Ideology, and Politics*, edited by R. Samuel and G. Stedman-Jones, 38–54. London: Routledge.

Luzzatto, Sergio. 2014. *The Body of Il Duce: Mussolini's Corpse and the Fortunes of Italy*. London: Henry Holt and Company.

Luzzatto, Sergio, and Carlo Ginzburg. 2016. "Predappio no, Predappio sì." *Il Sole 24 Ore*, March 6.

Macdonald, Sharon. 2006. "Undesirable Heritage: Fascist Material Culture and Historical Consciousness in Nuremberg." *International Journal of Heritage Studies* 12:9–28.

Macdonald, Sharon. 2009. *Difficult Heritage: Negotiating the Nazi Past in Nuremberg and Beyond*. London: Routledge.

Mack Smith, Denis. 1981. *Mussolini*. New York: Alfred Knopf.

Maestri, Gabriele. 2017. "Quando il problema non è il (solo) fascio." *I simboli della discordia*, June 13. http://www.isimbolidelladiscordia.it/2017/06/quando-il -problema-non-e-il-solo-fascio.html.

Mahmood, Saba. 2005. *Politics of Piety: The Islamic Revival and the Feminist Subject*. Princeton, NJ: Princeton University Press.

Malinowski, Bronislaw. 1922. *Argonauts of the Western Pacific*. London: Routledge.

Malone, Hannah. 2017. "Legacies of Fascism: Architecture, Heritage and Memory in Contemporary Italy." *Modern Italy* 22:445–470.

Markie, Peter. 1986. *Descartes's Gambit*. Ithaca, NY: Cornell University Press.

Mattingly, Cheryl. 2013. "Moral Selves and Moral Scenes: Narrative Experiments in Everyday Life." *Ethnos* 78:301–327.

Maulsby, Lucy. 2014a. *Fascism, Architecture, and the Claiming of Modern Milan, 1922–1943*. Toronto: University of Toronto Press.

Maulsby, Lucy. 2014b. "Drinking from the River Lethe: Case del fascio and the legacy of Fascism in Postwar Italy." *Future Anterior* 11:18–39.

Mazzarella, William. 2019. "The Anthropology of Populism: Beyond the Liberal Settlement." *Annual Review of Anthropology* 48:45–60.

McDonough, Richard. 2004. "Wittgenstein, German Organicism, Chaos, and the Center of Life." *Journal of the History of Philosophy* 42:297–326.

McKinnon, Susan, and Fenella Cannell, eds. 2013. *Vital Relations: Modernity and the Persistent Life of Kinship*. Santa Fe, NM: School for Advanced Research Press.

Megaro, Gaudens. 1938. *Mussolini in the Making*. Woking, UK: Allen & Unwin.

Meisel, James. 1950. "A Premature Fascist? Sorel and Mussolini." *Western Political Quarterly* 3:14–27.

Miltiadis, Elena. 2022. "Displacing Displacement: Narratives for a Haunting History." *Journal of Modern Italian Studies* 28:451–465.

Mitterhofer, Johanna. 2013. "Competing Narratives on the Future of Contested Heritage: A Case Study of Fascist Monuments in Contemporary South Tyrol, Italy." *Heritage & Society* 6:46–61.

Mitchell, Timothy. 1991. "The Limits of the State: Beyond Statist Approaches and Their Critics." *American Political Science Review* 85:77–96.

Monk, Ray. 1991. *Ludwig Wittgenstein: The Duty of Genius*. London: Vintage.

Moody, Katharine, and Steven Shakespeare. 2012. *Intensities: Philosophy, Religion, and the Affirmation of Life*. Farnham, UK: Ashgate.

Moretti, Franco. 1985. The Comfort of Civilization. *Representations* 12:115–139.

Moretti, Franco. 2013. *The Bourgeois: Between History and Literature*. London: Verso.

Mudde, Cas. 2007. *Populist Radical Right Parties in Europe*. Cambridge: Cambridge University Press.

Mudde, Cas, and Cristobal Kaltwasser. 2017. *Populism: A Very Short Introduction*. Oxford: Oxford University Press.

Needham, Rodney. 1975. "Polythetic Classification: Convergence and Consequences." *Man* 10:349–369.

Neveu, Catherine. 2015. "Of Ordinariness and Citizenship Processes." *Citizenship Studies* 19:141–154.

Noiret, Serge. 2016. "Il Mausoleo della memoria." *Il Manifesto*, February 25. https://ilmanifesto.it/il-mausoleo-della-memoria/.

New Republic. 1927. "An Apology for Fascism." *New Republic*, January 12.

Nolte, Ernst. 1965. *The Three Faces of Fascism: Action Française, Italian Fascism, National Socialism*. Munich: Piper & Co.

Nye, Robert. 1973. "Two Paths to a Psychology of Social Action: Gustave Le Bon and Georges Sorel." *Journal of Modern History* 45:411–438.

O'Hare McCormick, Anne. 1926. "Behind Fascism Stands a Philosophy." *New York Times Magazine*, September 26.

Orwell, George. 1944. "What Is Fascism?" *Tribune* (London). https://www.orwell.ru/library/articles/As_I_Please/english/efasc#:~:text=By%20%27Fascism%27%20they%20mean%2C,a%20synonym%20for%20%27Fascist%27.

Özyürek, Esra. 2006. *Nostalgia for the Modern: State Secularism and Everyday Politics in Turkey*. Durham, NC: Duke University Press.

Parlato, Giuseppe. 2006. *Fascisti senza Mussolini: le origini del neofascismo in Italia, 1943–1948*. Milan: Il Mulino.

Parlato, Giuseppe. 2017. "Delegitimation and Anticommunism in Italian Neofascism." *Journal of Modern Italian Studies* 22:43–56.

Passerini, Luisa. 1987. *Fascism in Popular Memory: The Cultural Experience of the Turin Working Class*. Cambridge: Cambridge University Press.

Passmore, Kevin. 2017. "Is This Fascism?" *Slate*, January 20. https://slate.com/human-interest/2017/01/define-fascism-why-nailing-down-a-comprehensive-theory-of-fascism-has-been-so-historically-difficult.html.

Paxton, Robert O. 2004. *The Anatomy of Fascism*. London: Penguin.

Payne, Stephen. 1995. *A History of Fascism, 1914–1945*. Madison: University of Wisconsin Press.

Pleasants, Nigel. 2007. "Wittgenstein, Ethics, and Basic Moral Certainty." *Inquiry* 51:241–267.

Pleasants, Nigel. 2009. "Wittgenstein and Basic Moral Certainty." *Philosophia* 37:669–679.

Poulantzas, Nicholas. 1974. *Fascism and Dictatorship: The Third International and the Problem of Fascism*. London: Verso.

Probyn, Elspeth. 2004. "Everyday Shame." *Cultural Studies* 18:328–349.

Putnam, Hilary, and Ruth A. Putnam. 2017. *Pragmatism as a Way of Life: The Lasting Legacy of William James and John Dewey*. Cambridge, MA: Harvard University Press.

Proli, Mario. 2013. "Politica e società nella media valle del rabbi da fine ottocento al fascismo." In *Studi su Predappio*, 177–203. Stilgraf: Cesena.

Reed, Adam. 2002. "City of Details: Interpreting the Personality of London." *Journal of the Royal Anthropological Institute* 8:127–141.

Reich, Wilhelm. 1933. *The Mass Psychology of Fascism*. London: Souvenir Press.

Robbins, Joel. 2016. "What Is the Matter with Transcendence? On the Place of Religion in the Anthropology of Ethics." *Journal of the Royal Anthropological Institute* 22:767–808.

Robbins, Joel. 2018. "Where in the World Are Values?" In *Recovering the Human Subject: Freedom, Creativity and Decision*, edited by J. Laidlaw, B. Bodenhorn, and M. Holbraad, 174–192. Cambridge: Cambridge University Press.

Robbins, Joel. n.d. "The Anthropology of Pluralism and the Pluralism of Anthropology." Unpublished paper.

Rosaldo, Renato. 1997. "A Note on Geertz as a Cultural Essayist." *Representations* 59:30–34.

Sacks, Harvey. 1985. "On Doing Being Ordinary." In *Structures of Social Action: Studies in Conversation Analysis*, edited by J. Maxwell Atkinson and J. Heritage, 413–429. Cambridge: Cambridge University Press.

Sahlins, Marshall. 1976. *Islands of History*. Chicago: University of Chicago Press.

Sayeau, Michael. 2016. *Against the Event: The Everyday and the Evolution of the Modernist Narrative*. Oxford: Oxford University Press.

Scott, James. 1985. *Weapons of the Weak: Everyday Forms of Peasant Resistance*. New Haven, CT: Yale University Press.

Schielke, Samuli. 2009. "Being Good in Ramadan: Ambivalence, Fragmentation, and the Moral Self in the Lives of Young Egyptians." *Journal of the Royal Anthropological Institute* 15:s24–s40.

Schwarz, Guri. 2016. "Sì a un museo di nazionale del fascismo, ma decisamente non a Predappio." *Gli Stati Generali*, April 7. https://www.glistatigenerali.com/musei-mostre_storia-cultura/si-a-un-museo-nazionale-del-fascismo-ma-decisamente-non-a-predappio/.

Serenelli, Sofia. 2013. "A Town for the Cult of the Duce: Predappio as a Site of Pilgrimage." In *The Cult of the Duce: Mussolini and the Italians*, edited by S. Gundle, C. Duggan, and G. Pieri, 93–110. Manchester: Manchester University Press.

Sheringham, Michael. 2006. *Everyday Life: Theories and Practices from Surrealism to the Present.* Oxford: Oxford University Press.

Shklar, Judith. 1989. "The Liberalism of Fear." In *Liberalism and the Moral Life,* edited by Nancy L. Rosenblum, 21–38. Cambridge, MA: Harvard University Press.

Shoshan, Nitzan. 2016. *The Management of Hate: Nation, Affect, and the Governance of Right-Wing Extremism in Germany.* Princeton, NJ: Princeton University Press.

Shweder, Richard. 2007. "The Resolute Irresolution of Clifford Geertz." *Common Knowledge* 13:191–205.

Sidnell, Jack, Marie Meudec, and Michael Lambek. 2019. "Ethical Immanence." *Anthropological Theory* 19:303–322.

Smith, Neil. 1992. "Contours of a Spatialized Politics: Homeless Vehicles and the Production of Geographical Scale." *Social Text* 33:54–81.

Sorel, Georges. [1906] 1999. *Reflections on Violence.* Cambridge: Cambridge University Press.

Springs, Jason. 2008. "What Cultural Theorists of Religion Have to Learn from Wittgenstein; or, How to Read Geertz as a Practice Theorist." *Journal of the American Academy of Religion* 76:934–969.

Sternhell, Zeev, Mario Sznajder, and Maia Asheri. 1989. *The Birth of Fascist Ideology.* Princeton, NJ: Princeton University Press.

Stewart, William. K. 1928. "The Mentors of Mussolini." *American Political Science Review* 22:843–869.

Storchi, Simona. 2013a. "Margherita Sarfatti and the Invention of the Duce." In *The Cult of the Duce: Mussolini and the Italians,* edited by S. Gundle, C. Duggan, and G. Pieri, 41–57. Manchester: Manchester University Press.

Storchi, Simona. 2013b. "Mussolini as Monument: The Equestrian Statue of the Duce at the Littorial Stadium in Bologna." In *The Cult of the Duce: Mussolini and the Italians,* edited by S. Gundle, C. Duggan, and G. Pieri, 193–208. Manchester: Manchester University Press.

Storchi, Simona. 2019. "The Ex-Casa del Fascio in Predappio and the Question of the 'Difficult Heritage' of Fascism in Contemporary Italy." *Modern Italy* 24:139–157.

Strathern, Marilyn. 1995. "The Nice Thing about Culture Is That Everyone Has It." In *Shifting Contexts,* edited by Marilyn Strathern, 153–176. London: Routledge.

Strathern, Marilyn. 2004. *Partial Connections.* Walnut Creek, CA: Alta Mira Press.

Summerson Carr, E., and Michael Lempert. 2016. *Scale: Discourse and Dimensions of Social Life.* Berkeley: University of California Press.

Taylor, Charles. 1989. *Sources of the Self: The Making of the Modern Identity.* Cambridge, MA: Harvard University Press.

Tramonti, Ulisse. 2014. *Progetto di recupero, rifunzionalizzazione e valorizzazione dell'architettura razionalista a Predappio: Ex Casa del Fascio e dell'Ospitalità.* Predappio, Italy: Comune di Predappio.

Trotsky, Leon. [1944] 1993. *Fascism: What It Is and How to Fight It.* https://www.marxists.org/archive/trotsky/works/1944/1944-fas.htm.

Tsing, Anna. 2000. "The Global Situation." *Cultural Anthropology* 15:327–360.

Tsing, Anna. 2005. *Friction: An Ethnography of Global Connection.* Princeton, NJ: Princeton University Press.

Tsing, Anna. 2012. "On Nonscaleability: The Living World Is Not Amenable to Precision-Nested Scales." *Common Knowledge* 18:505–524.

Williams, Raymond. [1958] 2001. "Culture Is Ordinary." In *The Raymond Williams Reader*, edited by J. Higgins, 1–18. Oxford: Blackwell.

Wittgenstein, Ludwig. 2018. *The Mythology in Our Language: Remarks on Frazer's Golden Bough*, translated by Stephan Palmié and edited by G. Da Col and S. Palmié. Chicago: Hau Books.

Wolf, Eric. 1999. *Envisioning Power: Ideologies of Dominance and Crisis.* Berkeley: University of California Press.

Wolin, Richard. 2006. *The Seduction of Unreason: The Intellectual Romance with Fascism from Nietzsche to Postmodernism.* Princeton, NJ: Princeton University Press.

Wu Ming. 2017. "Predappio: Toxic Waste Blues." *Giap*, October 27. https://www.wumingfoundation.com/giap/2017/10/predappio-toxic-waste-blues-1-di-3/.

Yanagisako, Sylvia. 2002. *Producing Culture and Capital: Family Firms in Italy.* Princeton, NJ: Princeton University Press.

Yurchak, Alexei. 2015. "Bodies of Lenin: The Hidden Science of Communist Sovereignty." *Representations* 129:116–157.

Zigon, Jarett. 2014. "An Ethics of Dwelling and a Politics of World-Building: A Critical Response to Ordinary Ethics." *Journal of the Royal Anthropological Institute* 20:407–425.

Zoli, Renato, and Paolo Moressa. 2007. *Caro Mussolini.* Cesena, Italy: Raffaelli.

Index

Page references in *italics* refer to illustrative material.

Milton Keynes UK
Ingram Content Group UK Ltd.
UKHW031155071124
450868UK00001B/53